A PRACTICAL GUIDE TO EARLY CHILDHOOD INCLUSION
EFFECTIVE REFLECTION

Ann M. Gruenberg
Eastern Connecticut University

Regina Miller
University of Hartford, Emerita

Boston   Columbus   Indianapolis   New York   San Francisco   Upper Saddle River
Amsterdam   Cape Town   Dubai   London   Madrid   Milan   Munich   Paris   Montreal   Toronto
Delhi   Mexico City   Sao Paulo   Sydney   Hong Kong   Seoul   Singapore   Taipei   Tokyo

Vice President and Editor in Chief: Jeffery W. Johnston
Executive Editor: Ann Castel Davis
Editorial Assistant: Penny Burleson
Vice President, Director of Marketing: Quinn Perkson
Senior Marketing Manager: Christopher Barry
Senior Managing Editor: Pamela D. Bennett
Senior Production Editor: Sheryl Langner
Project Manager: Susan Hannahs
Senior Art Director: Jayne Conte

Cover Designer: Jayne Conte
Photo Coordinator: Sandy Schaefer
Cover Art: Getty Images, Inc.
Full-Service Project Manager: Aparna Yellai, GGS Higher Education Resources/PMG
Composition: GGS Higher Education Resources/PMG
Printer/Binder: RR Donnelley
Cover Printer: RR Donnelley
Text Font: Palatino

Credits and acknowledgments borrowed from other sources and reproduced, with permission, in this textbook appear on appropriate page within text.

Every effort has been made to provide accurate and current Internet information in this book. However, the Internet and information posted on it are constantly changing, so it is inevitable that some of the Internet addresses listed in this textbook will change.

Photo Credits:
Scott Cunningham/Merrill, p. 1; Lori Whitley/Merrill, p. 10; Bold Stock/Unlisted Images, Inc., p. 21. Anne Vega/Merrill, p. 33; Scott Cunningham/Merrill, p. 40; Krista Greco/Merrill, p. 46; Frank Siteman, p. 56; Laura Bolesta/Merrill, p. 61; Bold Stock/Unlisted Images, Inc., p. 70; Frank Siteman, p. 80; Laura Bolesta/Merrill, p. 88; Frank Siteman, p. 99; T. Lindfors/Lindfors Photography, p. 107; Bold Stock/Unlisted Images, Inc., p. 115; Laura Bolesta/Merrill, p. 121; Krista Greco/Merrill, p. 128; Krista Greco/Merrill, p. 136; Scott Cunningham/Merrill, p. 145; T. Lindfors/Lindfors Photography, p. 163; Barbara Schwartz/Merrill, p. 169; T. Lindfors/ Lindfors Photography, p. 177; Nancy Sheehan Photography, p. 187; Shirley Zeiberg/PH College, p. 195; Index Open, p. 205; Todd Yarrington/Merrill, p. 214; Frank Siteman, p. 222; Laura Bolesta/Merrill, p. 231; Krista Greco/Merrill, p. 242; Getty Images–Digital Vision, p. 250; Photodisc/Getty Images, p. 256

Library of Congress Cataloging-in-Publication Data

Gruenberg, Ann M.
   A practical guide to early childhood inclusion: effective reflection/Ann M. Gruenberg.—1st ed.
      p. cm.
   Includes bibliographical references and index.
   ISBN-13: 978-0-13-240279-8
   ISBN-10: 0-13-240279-3
1. Inclusive education—United States.   2. Early childhood education—United States.   3. Children with disabilities—Education (Early childhood)—United States.   I. Title.
   LC1201.G78 2011
   371.9'046—dc22
                                                                                         2009053889

10 9 8 7 6 5 4 3 2 1

www.pearsonhighered.com

ISBN 10:   0-13-240279-3
ISBN 13: 978-0-13-240279-8

PREFACE

During the past twenty-five years there have been dramatic, often exciting, changes in the fields of early childhood education and special education. This text focuses on enduring and innovative practices regarding diversity, especially inclusive programs and adaptations for children who are at risk or who have disabilities. A combination of factors, such as changing laws, practices, and standards for both the National Association for the Education of Young Children and the Division for Early Childhood, Council for Exceptional Children have affected the ways in which early childhood personnel need to be prepared.

RATIONALE

With many outstanding texts and resources available on the subject of early childhood special education, the intent of this book is to focus on the integration of reflection into personnel preparation; it is meant to enhance rather than supplant existing materials. The qualitative interactive dynamics of intervention are typically included in personnel preparation programs for social workers but are less often included in personnel preparation for teachers. This book focuses on support for the ongoing consideration of multiple factors regarding intervention and how practitioners can play active roles in translating the research on evidence-based practices to effective application in everyday practices. With its focus on intentionality and accountability, it is expected that this text will provide practical support to those who are using a variety of strategies to enhance the quality of inclusive programs for young children with challenges as well as their families.

STRUCTURE OF THE BOOK

This book is organized so readers representing a wide range of prior experience and knowledge will be able to select their preferred areas of focus. That is, if a reader has significant preparation regarding foundations and history, he or she can quickly scan some sections in the book and focus more extensively on other sections regarding intervention. In contrast, when readers have extensive background in early childhood education but not special education, they may choose to focus in more detail on information regarding the foundations and background information addressing the needs of children with exceptional development. The primary focus of this text is on the process of creating and implementing curricular adaptations for the individual needs of children with developmental challenges. We have included a broad array of perspectives to support readers as they address areas that are especially relevant to their own professional development.

ACKNOWLEDGMENTS

There are many who must be acknowledged regarding the conception, writing, and production of this book. The inspiration came from many sources, including young children and their families over time, students, colleagues in early childhood classrooms and universities, and leaders involved with national initiatives. The editors at Pearson, along with their staff, have made this text possible. Without their efforts and skill, it would not exist.

Drs. Jeffrey Trawick-Smith, Sudha Swaminathan, and Theresa Bouley continue to be wonderful colleagues at Eastern Connecticut State University. We have worked together as faculty in a teacher-preparation program engaged in the transformation to become increasingly integrated. This has been an opportunity for me to better understand the dynamics and complexity of the changing profession. Others involved with the Early Childhood Unit and Center for Early Childhood Education, along with the entire Education Department, have been extraordinarily supportive. University colleagues, the Sabbatic Leave Committee, and President Elsa Nunez have been unwavering in their support of this project.

We are very appreciative of the team at Pearson: Ann Davis, who guided this project to fruition with her keen editorial skill and sensibility, Allyson Sharp, who encouraged the concept of this initiative; Penny Burleson, editorial assistant, who kept us focused and organized; Sheryl Langner, project manager, who demonstrated an infinite capacity to balance details with the big picture; as well as Carol Sykes and Sandra Schaefer, who researched and organized the photographs. Lastly, we thank the production team at GGS led by Aparna Yellai. The reviewers provided constructive, detailed feedback and increased the relevance and quality of this text. They are Karen Applequist, Northern Arizona State University; Lynn Arnault, Mississippi State University; Nancy Cupolo, Hudson Valley Community College; Blanche Glimps, Tennessee State University; Gay Goodman, University of Houston; Colleen Klein-Ezell, University of Central Florida; Barbara Fiechtl, Utah State University; Rebecca Ingram, Auburn University; Barbara Lowenthal, Northeastern Illinois University; Jo Ellyn Peterson, Bluffton University; Cathi Draper Rodriguez, California State University–Monterey; Carmel Collum Yarger, Utah State University; and Nancy Yost, Indiana University of Pennsylvania.

Dr. Regina Miller, Professor Emeritus from the University of Hartford, has been an extraordinary collaborator. Shared perspectives, along with the insight borne of many years of experience have greatly enhanced this book. Dr. Miller has significantly contributed to this project in countless ways, including her good humor and faith that it was possible. As one who has always believed in and practiced blending, it was her pleasure to collaborate with Ann and see this project to completion.

Finally, family members and friends provided immeasurable support, understanding, and good counsel while this book was being written.

BRIEF CONTENTS

CONTENTS

Chapter 1

Introduction

Effectiveness in a Changing World

OBJECTIVES

After reading this chapter, students will demonstrate:

- A concept of the structure, content, and goals for this book;
- An understanding of how early childhood and special education have been changing, becoming more inclusive;
- A concept of the changing laws and trends affecting children with disabilities in the United States as well as global perspectives;
- An awareness of the importance of maintaining professionalism during changing times and
- An understanding of how reflective practice can be used to enhance the "match" between individual children's needs and the strategies that are employed.

OVERVIEW

This book was inspired by the dynamic and rapidly changing field of inclusive early childhood education. It was prompted by a need to provide support through a "sea change" in the field, during which practitioners and team members on all levels are now expected to have expertise in the **inclusion** of children with disabilities within early childhood programs. This is an exciting time and also one fraught with challenges. We hope, as you read this book, you will increase your capacity to use your own "internal compass" to make responsible decisions regarding young children with developmental challenges within inclusive classrooms.

Goals of the Book

The primary purpose of this book is to provide support to practitioners as they develop skills and strategies to adapt curriculum for effective inclusion of children with disabilities within inclusive classrooms using reflective practices to match each child's developmental needs with effective, appropriate interventions. This book provides a working model that enhances the process of problem solving to address each child and family's unique needs. The book is designed to be useful along an entire continuum of placement options. It is understood that some practitioners will be working in fully inclusive settings, while others will be working in contexts providing more comprehensive supports. Given the ongoing variation of interpretations regarding inclusion initiatives, it is important for the authors to state explicitly that this book is not intended to provide guarantees or magic solutions when children are placed in fully inclusive settings. It is, however, intended to provide a framework for the support of a dynamic process of problem solving among caregivers, so they may exercise positive professional judgment to the best of their abilities, given relevant information to help guide them in their daily practices with children and families. We identify this process as reflective rather than reflexive. That is, we all have certain habits that may allow us to perform certain actions without giving them much thought, on "automatic pilot." While reading this book, however, you will be invited to consider why you do what you do and whether there might be other options. Certainly, there are many times when we all do what we do without overthinking it, and in many situations that may be fine as well as efficient. When children need accommodations, we must be able to shift our focus and be prepared to adjust as appropriate.

We hope readers will be supported in deeply considering many factors and variables, both external and internal, to enhance their ability to address the unique needs of each child and his or her family. Inclusion provides children with natural opportunities to learn from each other and actively participate in high-quality early childhood settings. We view preparation for inclusion as an ongoing process, with programs being customized for each individual child. This process is transformative rather than additive. That is, the solutions may be found in the *way* we provide intervention rather than just *how much* intervention is offered (Jung, 2003). This book is designed to support the process of adjusting how we think about unique circumstances.

The paradigm shift toward increased inclusion has resulted in many changes among teacher preparation programs, with new teachers usually having more exposure to issues and topics regarding exceptional development within their programs. There are, however, many highly skilled teachers who have decades of experience as competent professionals who now need to change their approaches toward working with young children. For some, this can be daunting. While seasoned teachers may not feel comfortable acknowledging their reactions, some may be anxious, overwhelmed, and frustrated. It is not uncommon for teachers to feel inadequate or "out of their league." The myth that special education teachers have to be "special" has set a tone that may inadvertently perpetuate the notion that not everyone can be effective working with children who have developmental challenges. This book presents a working model that acknowledges those feelings and assumptions, while providing support to readers to clear those potential misconceptions that, if unaddressed, may interfere with the application of evidence-based practices.

Age Levels Addressed in This Text

The main focus of this book is on preschool- and kindergarten-age children who are often served by programs within school systems or local education agencies. We will, to an extent, address issues affecting children from birth to age 3 as well as those who are primary age. This will be done primarily by extending discussion of the scenarios regarding children who are presented as preschool or kindergarten age, to consider the developmental needs prior to age 3 and after age 5 or 6.

Distinctiveness: How This Book Is Different from Others

While many books focus on characteristics of conditions, theoretical perspectives, and/or curriculum, this book is distinctive in its focus on the reflective process through which decisions are made to adapt curriculum. Scenarios, guiding questions, and opportunities for reflection provide scaffolding that will support your engagement in active problem solving. The development of optimal matches between the unique needs of children and strategies to provide intervention within your own contexts is the heart of this book.

The Importance of Reflection

This book is based on the fundamental premise that effective inclusion involves an ongoing process of considering how to overcome obstacles and resolve issues as they emerge. It is based on the belief that if we stay attuned to positive factors while we are considering challenges, we will be able to maintain perspective and to believe in possibility (Anderson, Chitwood, Hayden, & Takemoto, 2008). While a reflective process may involve the transformation of intuition to a more explicit understanding of what works, it may also include gaining perspective on and articulating the multitude of elements and factors in the physical and social environments that potentially affect the development of young children. Through the process of reflection, external variables such as organizational structure and schedule may be considered, along with intrapersonal variables such as tone of voice, volume, and proximity to each child. Sometimes children are especially sensitive to certain factors or signals, and through careful observation and communication among team members, we may gain perspectives that enhance our ability to effectively work with each child.

A necessary prerequisite to effective reflection is a willingness to be fully honest with oneself and others regarding one's areas of strength and need. While honesty about feelings and dispositions is important and there is a need to validate feelings without judging or being judged, it is also important to be able to consider factors in nonreactive ways. To acknowledge that one is afraid or overwhelmed often makes it possible to expand one's sense of a situation, so it becomes less frightening or overwhelming. Creating and maintaining a zone in which people can be mutually supportive and willing to address challenges makes a substantial difference in their reflection on complex issues regarding young children and their families. Reducing defensiveness and increasing trust is very helpful. Honest reflection involves feeling as well as thinking about multiple variables. It involves consideration of various possibilities and hypotheses, especially as we work together to find out what is effective for each child. The operational definition for reflection used in this book includes all of those factors.

Ultimately, this book is grounded in a deep optimism about the abilities of families and teams to work together to enhance the educational experiences of young children with disabilities in a variety of inclusive educational settings. Our optimism is not based on a denial of the degree to which there are difficulties and challenges. Instead, it is based on a strong consolidation of experience and evidence that excellent examples of inclusion exist: They are possible (Diener, 2005; Grisham-Brown, Hemmeter, & Pretti-Frontczak, 2005; Pretti-Frontczak & Bricker, 2005).

Structure of the Book

Throughout the text you, the reader, will be given opportunities to use a variety of reflective processes that can contribute to your increased effectiveness. Reference will be made to relevant theorists, but this book is not intended primarily as an introduction to conceptual frameworks and characteristics of conditions. It is, instead, intended as a structure to guide your reflective practice, as you work with young children and their families. We hope you will use this as a resource that will be both practical and inspirational as you create classrooms for young children that are wonderful examples of high-quality inclusive practices.

Because readers may have a broad range of background knowledge and experience, this book is structured for easy access to information, such as chronology regarding the laws. If you are already very familiar with this information, a review may be sufficient. If this is new information for you, the resources included in each section can guide you toward more comprehensive understanding. You will find background information presented in boxes with questions such as "Did you know . . . ?" If you have already taken a course on the foundations of special education or assessment in special education, you probably will not need to spend much time relearning that information. If, however, you are unfamiliar with that information, it may be very helpful to have easy access. Thus, you as a reader will approach this book based on your own entry level.

CHAPTER TOPICS

Developmentally and Individually Appropriate Practices

Reflective practice supports a dynamic of problem solving that enhances the ability of practitioners to create and sustain a match between each child's developmental needs and the strategies that are used to support him or her. We present many examples of approaches to interacting with young children through the use of reflection regarding a range of variables. The use of constructivist methods, long recognized as recommended practice for young children who are developing typically is an integral aspect of increasing inclusive services for children with exceptionalities (Copple & Bredekamp, 2009; Hyson, 2003, 2008; Sandall, Hemmeter, Smith, & McLean, 2005). Theoretical perspectives ranging from those of Lev Vygotsky (1978) to Howard Gardner (2000) and Urie Bronfenbrenner (1979) are applicable to children receiving special services within inclusive contexts. Familiarity with concepts such as the zone of proximal development, scaffolding, multiple intelligences, and ecological systems theory provide a framework for the reflective process through which practitioners can consider ways to adapt and adjust approaches to working with young children. Sometimes, for example, it helps to sit near a child who needs extra support. At other times, it helps to step back and provide opportunities for more independent interaction with a peer who may model communication and social development in natural contexts.

The "dance," or spontaneous interaction, is often full of surprises, even with children who are developing typically. For many, this interaction occurs intuitively in natural settings with "incidental learning" that occurs without direction. Teachers may adjust what they are doing without having a conscious awareness of exactly how they are making adaptations. Such intuitive sensibility is wonderful. It helps, however, to have some explicit awareness of what is effective, so it can be replicated and done intentionally (Copple & Bredekamp, 2009; Epstein, 2007). We currently refer to full accessibility as **universal design for learning** (McGuire-Schwartz & Arndt, 2007). Changes have included embedding strategies within curricular activities to meet the needs of children with developmental differences (Grisham-Brown, Pretti-Frontczak, & Hemmeter, 2005). Strategies such as allowing more time, providing different or adapted materials, and providing supportive feedback are all options in terms of adjusting the learning environment for people with disabilities (Grisham-Brown, Pretti-Frontczak, & Hemmeter, 2005). The concept of **least restrictive environment (LRE)** refers to options that are well suited to individual children. Figure 1.1 presents an explanation of LRE.

Families and Teams: Shared Responsibility

A key feature of effective inclusion is shared responsibility among and between team members. Success is not just determined by skilled and competent special educators. It is contingent upon the active involvement of parents and also those who consider themselves "general" educators. When children with exceptionalities are included in early childhood programs, all involved in many different roles must share a sense of

> The least restrictive environment (LRE) is a relative concept combining each individual child's needs with environmental factors. For many children the least restrictive environment is a fully inclusive, general classroom with related services provided in that context.
>
> For other children, however, there may be a need for a more specialized environment with more comprehensive services. If children need more direction, structure, and support with fewer children in the group, they may be placed in a more specialized classroom and that would be considered the least restrictive environment.
>
> If, for instance, children have significant behavioral challenges and do not perform well consistently in a general classroom, they might be placed in a smaller group. This would be considered, for them, the least restrictive environment.
>
> A fully inclusive general classroom is not the least restrictive environment for every child.

FIGURE 1.1   The Concept of Least Restrictive Environment

responsibility for all children. This is a profoundly important paradigm shift from previous models of special services (Anderson, Chitwood, Hayden, & Takemoto, 2008).

There is no question that individual competence is necessary to be an effective teacher of young children. Competence on one's own, however, in the absence of healthy communication and teamwork, is not enough. By definition, inclusion involves more than one child and more than one adult. There are many configurations and models for positive inclusion, but they all have in common that this is a team process, not a solo endeavor.

The process of implementing high-quality inclusion, then, depends on mutuality, communication, and willingness to process/solve problems in the context of a team (Allred, Brien, & Black, 2003; Kaczmarek, 2007). Interpersonal interaction is certainly central to the collaborative process necessary for effective inclusion. Sports usually have mutually understood rules of the game in question. In a similar way, the democratic process of governance follows certain systems, rules of problem solving, communication, and systems change. These rule systems and mutually understood protocols for governance provide structures for maintenance and change within certain parameters (Wischnowski, 2008). High-quality programs are characterized by excellent communication and mutually supportive teams, so there is a context of safety. This enhances the ability of team members to support each other as they develop new skills. Creating a safe zone in which team members can communicate and be mutually supportive is an essential aspect of high-quality inclusion. Members of the team must be able to trust each other as they move beyond levels of doubt and fear into more confidence about their competence in working with young children who have developmental challenges. Having a mutual commitment to problem solving makes it possible to move past levels of defensiveness that can otherwise interfere with effective intervention.

Assessment: Use of Information About Children's Development for Planning

Educational planning for children with developmental challenges involves knowing each child's individual pattern of strengths and needs beyond just a diagnosis. It also involves being able to anticipate to an extent how each child will respond in different contexts during varied activities. It involves preparing through active problem solving with plans A, B, and even C. Even with the best-laid plans, teachers must be prepared to engage in ongoing, formative assessment and ongoing adjustment of strategies, based on children's responses to the intervention being used. Response to intervention and recognition and response can be used systematically to guide both assessment and strategies (Buysse, Wesley, Snyder, & Winton, 2006). Ultimately, assessment supports accountability, as well, and data-driven decision making can be used to ensure appropriate intervention. Data-driven decision making involves using formative assessment to adjust the interventions used with children, ensuring relevance and effectiveness.

Curricular Adaptations: Strategies for Success

Several chapters in this book specifically address curricular adaptations, with a focus on how we can effectively match the needs of children with the strategies and modifications we use. While certain somewhat predictable patterns exist among young children who are developing typically, those with exceptionalities have unique needs and responses to intervention. In each of the chapters on curricular adaptations, you will be guided through a process of considering how to identify effective practices for individual children. Topics include social experience, language, and literacy; music and movement; and math/science problem solving. The chapters will share specific examples illustrating the use of reflection to make decisions about how to select and implement strategies based on individual needs. The intent of the book is to present a transparent process through which you can also begin to hear yourself think about options and possibilities using differentiated instruction. This book uses the tiered model of intervention in which the lower level of the triangle represents general practices available to all, the top of the triangle represents highly specialized intervention, and the middle of the triangle represents some amount of individual intervention used throughout.

Professionalism

The topic of professionalism is addressed throughout the book and is the focus of the culmination in Chapter 10. The standards developed by the National Association for the Education of Young Children (NAEYC) and the Division of Early Childhood, Council for Exceptional Children (DEC/CEC) provide the foundation for our work (Hyson, 2003; Sandall, Hemmeter, Smith, & McLean, 2005). Both organizations contribute some basic premises to our approach in this book. Paramount in our motivation is the need for reflection and dynamic problem solving to determine what is effective. It is necessary for professionals to be confident enough to distinguish between what is and what is not working as they use differentiated methods. Some approaches do not result in immediate evidence of effectiveness, so we may need to try an intervention and systematically document outcomes for children over time (LaRocque & Darling, 2008). Professionals must demonstrate commitment and resourcefulness, along with high ethical standards. It is important from the start to acknowledge that proficiency in special education is a relatively new requirement for general early childhood educators. Professionalism is essential in the process of using evidence-based practices while creating healthy inclusive environments (Chandler & Loncola, 2008).

REFLECTION IN ACTION

MS. LIGHTBORNE

Ms. Lightborne is a naturally gifted early childhood teacher who has been working in the field for nearly 20 years. She is a college graduate. When she went through a personnel preparation program, inclusion was not fully established within programs. She did not have any special education courses as an undergraduate but took one course in special education as a graduate student. In her many years of teaching, she has worked with a vast variety of children and families, and for the most part she has enjoyed the feeling of competence that comes with experience.

Last September, a 3-year-old child, Jordan, was enrolled in her program, and Ms. Lightborne found herself questioning her abilities and her choice of profession. As much as she adored this child every day brought new challenges. Jordan could be very affectionate but also very aggressive and disruptive. His lack of self-control affected the dynamics of the entire group. With many team members, it was very difficult to guide Jordan through the process of learning how to adjust to this new setting. Ms. Lightborne found herself experiencing a surprising level of anxiety regarding these challenges.

Initial Reflections

While Ms. Lightborne grappled for solutions, one of the dynamics that emerged was how difficult it was for her to ask for help. As one of the most seasoned teachers, she was used to being a leader to whom others looked for guidance and support. She realized, as she reflected, that it was difficult for her to need support and guidance from others. Eventually, it became evident to her that asking for and receiving support was healthy and not a sign of weakness.

Another element that emerged as she reflected was the need for healthy communication. She had always been aware of this, but the situation with Jordan and his mother highlighted the need to be willing to work through misunderstandings toward shared trust and a mutual sense of positive outcomes.

Finally, it became evident that having an up-to-date awareness of the laws affecting special education, including those impacting private programs, was absolutely necessary. She reflected on the gaps in her own knowledge, and identified reliable sources for accurate information. Ms. Lightborne's willingness to be honest with herself about what she needed to learn was very helpful in reaching positive outcomes. Figure 1.2 provides an overview of the process of reflection.

Focus on Positive Outcomes

During Ms. Lightborne's initial reflection, it was very helpful that she focused on positive resolution and outcomes rather than becoming increasingly reactive, defensive, and discouraged. Honestly acknowledging her anxiety, her need for support, and her need for accurate information made it possible to continue to progress, leading the way toward implementation of effective strategies and appropriate program planning.

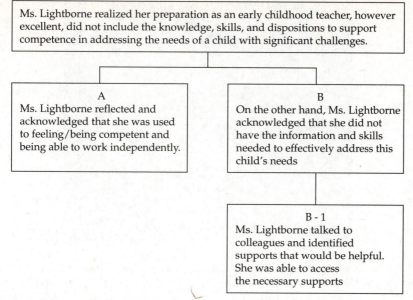

FIGURE 1.2   Decision Tree

INCLUSION

Inclusion: Here to Stay, or Just a Trend?

The term *inclusion* evokes different responses from different people. Some assert that it is merely a trend and that before long, the pendulum will swing back toward previously established practices and separate services for children with and without disabilities (Shanker, 1994). So how can we determine what the future will bring? This book was inspired by the practical realities faced by teams working on a daily basis with young children who have exceptionalities. We do not presume to be able to predict future trends. We do, however, believe there is ample evidence that the degree to which inclusion is already occurring warrants support for a process through which it can be done well (Buysse & Wesley, 2006; McWilliam, Wolery & Odom, 2001). Leaders from the DEC and the NAEYC have been working together to develop and disseminate the joint statement on inclusion (2009), which is presented in Figure 1.3.

We believe it is possible to have inclusive programs that provide optimal opportunities for young children across a range of developmental levels and needs. Such a program provides a wonderful and exciting opportunity for children to learn from peers as well as learn from established curriculum. The benefits of such opportunities have been well documented over time (Kaczmarek, 2007).

We are not naïve regarding some of the obstacles to positive inclusion. Research has indicated that some patterns of difficulty have occurred enough to be substantiated. Some of the reported challenges are lack of time, lack of administrative support, and difficulties in establishing cohesive teams that are mutually supportive (Lieber et al., 2000). In early childhood programs, staff turnover may also be a factor, making it difficult to

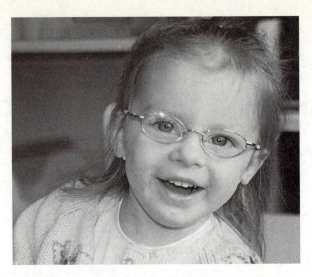

We focus on children first, while also considering their individual challenges.

establish continuity. Conversely, factors such as administrative support, shared planning time, and high-functioning teams with healthy communication support inclusion (Lieber et al., 2000).

Funding issues may also be significant in the planning and implementation phases. Inclusion is often cost-effective, but there are times, particularly during initial phases when professional development opportunities are essential for general education teachers, when long-term financial savings may not be immediately evident. That is, an initial investment may be necessary to support long-term gains (Lieber et al., 2000).

Importance of Shared Commitment and Responsibility

On multiple levels, it is important to have a shared commitment to inclusion. This cannot be overstated. Given the changes in early childhood and special education, it is necessary for all staff to see themselves as responsible for all children rather than assuming that only "special" educators will be able to address the needs of children with disabilities. To share responsibility, one must also learn to believe in the possibility of high-quality inclusion. It is unlikely that inclusion will be successful if individuals and communities attempt to implement such models yet do not believe in their efficacy and/or value. It is vital to understand and believe in the benefits of early childhood inclusion, not just for children with identified challenges but also for children who are "normal." Believing, however, is unlikely in itself to solve all the challenges. If it were, Tinkerbell and her colleagues could just clap their hands, as they did in the J. M. Barrie classic novel *Peter Pan*, and everything would be taken care of. Belief and commitment are necessary prerequisites but are not in themselves sufficient to establish and maintain high-quality inclusive early childhood environments. The quality and quantity of people's changing experiences may contribute to the degree to which their own transformation results in increased acceptance.

Today an ever-increasing number of infants and young children with and without disabilities play, develop, and learn together in a variety of places—homes, early childhood programs, neighborhoods, and other community-based settings. The notion that young children with disabilities and their families are full members of the community reflects societal values about promoting opportunities for development and learning, and a sense of belonging for every child. It also reflects a reaction against previous educational practices of separating and isolating children with disabilities. Over time, in combination with certain regulations and protections under the law, these values and societal views regarding children birth to 8 with disabilities and their families have come to be known as early childhood inclusion. The most far-reaching effect of federal legislation on inclusion enacted over the past three decades has been to fundamentally change the way in which early childhood services ideally can be organized and delivered. However, because inclusion takes many different forms and implementation is influenced by a wide variety of factors, questions persist about the precise meaning of inclusion and its implications for policy, practice, and potential outcomes for children and families.

The lack of a shared national definition has contributed to misunderstandings about inclusion. DEC and NAEYC recognize that having a common understanding of what inclusion means is fundamentally important for determining what types of practices and supports are necessary to achieve high-quality inclusion. This DEC/NAEYC joint position statement offers a definition of early childhood inclusion. The definition was designed not as a litmus test for determining whether a program can be considered inclusive, but rather, as a blueprint for identifying the key components of high-quality inclusive programs. In addition, this document offers recommendations for how the position statement should be used by families, practitioners, administrators, policy makers, and others to improve early childhood services.

April 2009

A Joint Position Statement of the Division for Early Childhood (DEC) and the National Association for the Education of Young Children (NAEYC)

Definition of Early Childhood Inclusion

Early childhood inclusion embodies the values, policies, and practices that support the right of every infant and young child and his or her family, regardless of ability, to participate in a broad range of activities and contexts as full members of families, communities, and society. The desired results of inclusive experiences for children with and without disabilities and their families include a sense of belonging and membership, positive social relationships and friendships, and development and learning to reach their full potential. The defining features of inclusion that can be used to identify high-quality early childhood programs and services are access, participation, and supports.

What Is Meant by Access, Participation, and Supports?

Access. Providing access to a wide range of learning opportunities, activities, settings, and environments is a defining feature of high-quality early childhood inclusion. Inclusion can take many different forms and can occur in various organizational and community contexts, such as homes, Head Start, child care, faith-based programs, recreational programs, preschool, public and private pre-kindergarten through early elementary education, and blended early childhood education/early childhood special education programs. In many cases, simple modifications can facilitate access for individual children. Universal design is a

FIGURE 1.3   DEC/NAEYC Joint Position Statement on Inclusion

concept that can be used to support access to environments in many different types of settings through the removal of physical and structural barriers. Universal Design for Learning (UDL) reflects practices that provide multiple and varied formats for instruction and learning. UDL principles and practices help to ensure that *every* young child has access to learning environments, to typical home or educational routines and activities, and to the general education curriculum. Technology can enable children with a range of functional abilities to participate in activities and experiences in inclusive settings.

Participation. Even if environments and programs are designed to facilitate access, some children will need additional individualized accommodations and supports to participate fully in play and learning activities with peers and adults. Adults promote belonging, participation, and engagement of children with and without disabilities in inclusive settings in a variety of intentional ways. Tiered models in early childhood hold promise for helping adults organize assessments and interventions by level of intensity. Depending on the individual needs and priorities of young children and families, implementing inclusion involves a range of approaches—from embedded, routines based teaching to more explicit interventions—to scaffold learning and participation for all children. Social-emotional development and behaviors that facilitate participation are critical goals of high-quality early childhood inclusion, along with learning and development in all other domains.

Supports. In addition to provisions addressing access and participation, an infrastructure of systems-level supports must be in place to undergird the efforts of individuals and organizations providing inclusive services to children and families. For example, family members, practitioners, specialists, and administrators should have access to ongoing professional development and support to acquire the knowledge, skills, and dispositions required to implement effective inclusive practices. Because collaboration among key stakeholders (e.g., families, practitioners, specialists, and administrators) is a cornerstone for implementing high-quality early childhood inclusion, resources and program policies are needed to promote multiple opportunities for communication and collaboration among these groups. Specialized services and therapies must be implemented in a coordinated fashion and integrated with general early care and education services. Blended early childhood education/early childhood special education programs offer one example of how this might be achieved. Funding policies should promote the pooling of resources and the use of incentives to increase access to high-quality inclusive opportunities. Quality frameworks (e.g., program quality standards, early learning standards and guidelines, and professional competencies and standards) should reflect and guide inclusive practices to ensure that all early childhood practitioners and programs are prepared to address the needs and priorities of infants and young children with disabilities and their families.

APPROVED BY DEC EXECUTIVE BOARD: April 2009

APPROVED BY NAEYC GOVERNING BOARD: April 2009

Suggested citation

DEC/NAEYC. (2009). *promote the pooling: A joint position statement of the Division for Early Childhood (DEC) and the National Association for the Education of Young Children (NAEYC).* Chapel Hill: The University of North Carolina, FPG Child Development Institute.

Permission to copy not required—distribution encouraged.

http://community.fpg.unc.edu/resources/articles/Early_Childhood_Inclusion

FIGURE 1.3 (*continued*)

Knowledge, Skills, and Dispositions

In addition to belief and commitment, there is a need for knowledge, skills, and dispositions related to exceptional development (Hyson, 2003; Sandall et al., 2005). Because there are conditions and syndromes that are extremely rare as well as those that are complex, it is imperative that practitioners learn how to acquire information and know how to keep up with changing laws, regulations, and policies. Using web-based resources is an excellent way to successfully stay current with accurate information (Bennett, 2007; Catlett, 2009; Catlett, Winton, & , 2008).

Is early childhood inclusion just a trend, or is it here to stay? While we do not have an answer that is 100% certain, it is clear that much progress has already occurred on all levels. There have been transformations of systems nationally, along with international initiatives. Part of the current challenge is that this transformation is ongoing. It is a work in progress.

Evidence-Based Practices: What Works?

In many ways this process of change can be viewed as a manifestation of a paradigm shift parallel to the ongoing struggle for increased equity regarding civil rights. As a social initiative, this change requires a deep level of commitment. Sustained, coordinated effort on the part of early childhood and special education leaders is necessary to provide structure as well as accountability regarding the transformation of services. Major multi-state research has been conducted over a number of years to generate evidence-based recommended practices (Catlett & Winton, 2008 Dunst & Trivette 2009; Guralnick, 2001; Lieber et al., 2000; Odom, 2009). The substantiation of these methods and practices through research has increased the likelihood that strategies implemented in classrooms reflect well-established research-based methodology.

National Initiatives: Coordinated Standards

In the United States, changes have been manifested through integration of early childhood and special education standards, as evidenced in the most recent standards for the NAEYC and the DEC/CEC. Leaders in the fields of early childhood and early childhood special education have worked together to structure changes and establish a shared vision as well as recommended practices (Bruder, 1993; Dunst, Bruder, Trivette, Raab, & McLean, 2001; Hyson, 2003; Lieber et al., 2000). A highly participatory process has yielded the position statement on inclusion from the DEC/CEC and the NAEYC (DEC & NAEYC, 2009).

These coordinated efforts have involved full collaboration in the process of setting standards for both early childhood and early childhood special education. The creation of new and/or revised standards reflecting NAEYC and DEC priorities was a tremendously significant step in the direction of more effective inclusion (Hyson, 2003; Sandall, Hemmeter, Smith, & McLean, 2005). Such increased coordination of standards has also made it much more possible for programs to be accountable for their practices. That is, with increased clarity about expectations, there has been increased ability to meet those expectations and engage in practices that would be considered appropriate from developmental as well as exceptional perspectives (Buysse et al., 2006; Pretti-Frontczak & Bricker,

NAEYC	CEC/DEC
Child Development	Foundations
Families and Community Assessment	Development and Characteristics
Learning and Teaching	Individual Learning Differences
Professionalism	Instructional Strategies
	Learning Environments and Social Interactions
	Language
	Instructional Planning
	Assessment
	Professional and Ethical Practice
	Collaboration

FIGURE 1.4 NAEYC/CEC Standards

2003) As the construct of developmentally appropriate practices continues to be reconsidered, the implications for changing standards continue to emerge (Copple & Bredekamp, 2009). Figure 1.4 provides an overview of standards from the NAEYC and the DEC/CEC.

Transformation of Services

There has been transformation of services in local communities in all regions of the United States, as well as other parts of the world. While variation still exists regarding the specific details of systems change and service provision, there is ample evidence that key elements of high-quality inclusion take many forms. A number of states have instituted "blended" certification, through which all early childhood practitioners receive some preparation to work with children with disabilities within inclusive settings (Stayton, Miller, & Dinnebeil, 2003). Recent research has carefully studied the degree to which personnel preparation has met the needs for expertise regarding exceptionalities in the early childhood field, and there is documentation that more professional development opportunities are necessary (Bruder, 2009). That is, research has indicated that many professionals have been insufficiently prepared to work in inclusive settings with young children who have disabilities (Bruder, 2009). This evidence of insufficiency could be interpreted as support for the notion that we should reverse inclusive initiatives. It can also, however, be powerful evidence that we need to acknowledge and address the necessity of increased pre-service and in-service opportunities for professionals. The question, however, is not just how much preparation professionals have. It is also a matter of what sorts of preparation they have (Jung, 2003).

Considerable debate has focused on how much preparation is "enough." It is clear that simply adding more coursework is not the solution. Restructuring teacher preparation during this paradigm shift is an important part of positive outcomes. Integrating topics regarding special education in all early childhood education courses appears to help.

Blended, or Unified, Certification

In some instances, initiatives have corresponded with changing teacher certification, with more "unified" or "blended" teacher credentials and certification programs using inclusive models (Stayton, Miller, & Dinnebeil, 2003). A shared vision of recommended practices can provide a guiding star and direction to help us navigate our course during our journey.

Range of Options

Many changes have continued the momentum toward inclusion in early childhood special education, but there is still a considerable range of ways in which initiatives are being implemented. Some would advocate for what has been termed "responsible inclusion" (Turnbull, Turnbull, & Wehmeyer, 2007), with the LRE being determined individually, based on the unique characteristics of each child and his or her needs.

Others have advocated for "full inclusion," in which there is a perceived priority of placements that are the same for children with and without disabilities, with adaptations within the general classrooms. There is evidence that a continuum still exists, providing a range of options (Turnbull, Turnbull, & Wehmeyer, 2007).

HISTORICAL PERSPECTIVES ON SPECIAL EDUCATION

The initiative to increase social inclusion of people with disabilities has been gaining momentum internationally since the 1980s. It is worth noting that there are many sources of momentum for these changes. A significant thrust came from the shift, initiated in Canada, toward social inclusion of people with developmental differences of all ages

REFLECTION IN ACTION
MR. FRESHETTE

Mr. Freshette recently graduated from a teacher preparation program in a state with a blended general and special education certification for prekindergarten and kindergarten. In this state, the option of attaining general certification without the special education component is no longer available. That is, all teachers are now prepared to address the varied needs of all young children. When he first began teaching in a program serving a highly diverse population, Mr. Freshette admitted that he was unsure about whether he had the ability and skill necessary to address a wide range of developmental levels. He acknowledged that he lacked confidence and was not sure he was prepared to meet such a broad range of needs. Once he began working with other teachers, however, he realized that he was beginning his teaching career with much more background and preparation in special education than did most of his colleagues, some of them with many years of experience.

(Pearpoint, Forest, & Snow 1992). This initiative has had an effect on social systems internationally (Guralnick, 2005). We are including information on historical perspectives for those who may be less familiar with these initiatives. If you are already very familiar with this topic, you may choose to scan this section.

For almost 30 years, individuals, families, and groups have advocated for inclusion (Pearpoint & Forest, 1992). Initially this was a controversial topic, eliciting opposition from many, including some educational leaders (Shanker, 1994).

Many of the strongest advocates in the inclusion movement initially approached it from a civil rights perspective, interpreting lack of full inclusion as a form of exclusion or a denial of civil rights (Guralnick, 2001). Others attempted to evaluate the effectiveness of inclusion based on children's success or perceived lack thereof, basing placement options and decisions on evidence of benefits to children (Wolery & Sainato, 1996).

As this initiative continued, various perspectives contributed to the course of change. It is currently clear that whatever professionals and families might have predicted 25 years ago, inclusion in early childhood education appears to be here to stay, with ample documentation of the benefits associated with opportunities for interaction among and between peers as well as participation in communities.

Research: Identification and Integration of Evidence-Based Practices

Teachers who perhaps courageously pioneered efforts 25 years ago often admitted that they did not have all the answers but were willing to solve problems in teams to figure out what was effective for individual children. It was found that some strategies might work well for more than one child. In fact, many strategies might frequently be effective. Some examples of effective strategies include provision of more structure, more time, clearer directions, visual cues, consistency, routines, predictability, and guidance. Actual implementation of effective inclusion, however, has always involved tailoring strategies to individual children and their needs. If a child is capable of participating in independent activity, we must be prepared to reposition and support his or her autonomy.

The Changing Nature of the General Classroom

We have witnessed major changes since 1980, when children were expected to meet certain criteria of the "general classroom" before they were permitted to be "mainstreamed" (Guralnick, 2001). It is now understood that it is the responsibility of the general inclusive classroom to adjust to meet each child's needs. All personnel need to be prepared to address a continuum of developmental diversity. Table 1.1 provides a general overview of historical trends affecting special education.

Sources of Change: Families

Over time, advocacy efforts have become more coordinated, with a growing effectiveness in promoting the restructuring of systems to be more inclusive (Anderson, Chitwood, Hayden, & Takemoto, 2008; Winton, McCollum, & Catlett, 2008). The intense debates regarding the efficacy of inclusion have gradually subsided, with an increasing acceptance of more integrated models of service provision. This has corresponded with

TABLE 1.1   Did You Know? Historical Trends and Events Affecting Special Education

1800s—Some pioneering initiatives, especially regarding the blind and deaf

1930s—The movement to build institutions for people with developmental disabilities is perceived as innovative.

1950s—Epidemics of measles, mumps, rubella, and polio

1960s—War on poverty; civil rights; new information about brain development

1970s—Federal legislation is passed regarding special education for school-age children

1980s—Federal legislation extended to younger children; Epidemic of babies prenatally exposed to drugs

2000s—Several re-authorizations of legislation providing support

changing laws and practices. It is important to note that an increasing trend toward inclusion unfortunately does not mean it has universal support or is always implemented well.

There is considerable evidence that the initiatives for changes in the laws and policies have been the direct result of concerted advocacy efforts, often by families and individuals with disabilities (Turnbull, Turnbull, & Wehmeyer, 2007). Several nationally and internationally recognized legal cases have set precedent in terms of inclusion.

One such case is the P. J. settlement, which involved five families, all of whom had children with intellectual disabilities. The families coordinated their efforts in a class action suit after each had been denied inclusion through due process. Each of the separate local education agencies cited reasons why the children's characteristics warranted separate services for some portion of the day. The families disagreed. After 10 years of legal proceedings, those involved reached a settlement, and the state involved is making demonstrable efforts to increase and document the quantity of inclusive services available to children with intellectual disabilities (Guralnick, 2001). This has set a precedent recognized by other states. The settlement resulted, in part, in the establishment of a clear system of accountability for towns and cities to ensure that inclusive options had been considered, and to aim for an inclusion rate of at least 80% of the time spent in general classrooms.

Sources of Change: Theoretical Perspectives

The model used in this book is firmly grounded in constructivist theory and practice, based on the beliefs that children in general learn well through sensory experience and engagement through which they can develop their own concepts in ways that are meaningful. We recognize that children's learning styles vary, as do their patterns of strengths and needs (Bruder, 1993). This is true among children who are "typical" as well as those who have exceptional development.

Sources of Change: Changing Laws

During the past 30 years, there has been remarkable change in the field of early childhood special education laws and regulations. Prior to the passage of Education for All Handicapped Act (P.L. 94-142) in 1975, services for children with disabilities were inconsistent. In the early 1970s, Head Start was a leader in addressing the needs of young

TABLE 1.2   Did You Know? Changing Laws

1950—Some specialized hospitals and institutions, viewed as innovative at the time

1960s—Head Start added services for young children with disabilities

1968—Handicapped Children's Early Education Program (HCEEP)

1973—Section 504 of the Rehabilitation Act

1975—P.L. 94-142 Education of All Handicapped Act

Mandated services within public schools/local education agencies

1980—Some states voluntarily added preschool services in public schools before the federal mandate. Many programs were in separate self-contained classrooms rather than inclusive settings.

1986—P.L. 99-457 lowered the age of federal mandate to younger children, preschool age and birth to 3.

1990—Individuals with Disabilities Education Act (IDEA)

Americans with Disabilities Act (ADA)

Significant pressure to increase the provision of inclusive options.

"Presumption of Inclusion"

2001—No Child Left Behind (NCLB). Inclusion of children with mild to moderate challenges in standardized testing.

2004—Amendments to IDEA (Individuals with Disabilities Education Improvement Act)

2008—Reauthorization of Americans with Disabilities Act

children with disabilities by offering individualized services (Rab & Wood, 1995; Wood & Youcha, 2009; Zigler & Styfo, 2004). No Child Left Behind (NCLB), in its original as well as changing versions, has also had an impact on services. Table 1.2 provides an overview of significant changes in policy and legislation.

While Head Start was a federal program, it did not create a general mandate for services. It established a quota and stipulated that 10% of enrollment would be for children with developmental challenges. This was accompanied by resources and comprehensive services for children and families that focused on prevention as well as intervention. The mandates created by P.L. 94-142, well recognized as landmark legislation, did not specifically address very young children. The main elements of the mandate, a **"free, appropriate public education** in the least restrictive environment" (Rab & Wood, 1995,; Wood & Youcha, 2009), initially focused on school-age children. Not until P.L. 99-457 was passed in 1986, which required states to lower the age level of children served, did the federal government demonstrate responsibility for addressing the needs of young children with disabilities. Prior to that time, some states had voluntarily elected to serve preschool children. After the passage of P.L. 99-457, those states were expected to further lower the age level to provide services to infants and toddlers, if they had not already done so (Guralnick, 2001). Figure 1.5 presents a situation to consider.

INDIVIDUALS WITH DISABILITIES EDUCATION ACT In 1990, the Individuals with Disabilities Education Act (IDEA) was passed, incorporating key features from both P.L. 94-142 and 99-457 and renaming the new law using **"people first" language** and updated terminology. IDEA provided a federal mandate for young children with disabilities.

Jessica is a 4-year-old girl with multiple health concerns. She was born at 26 weeks gestation, and in many ways is thriving developmentally, but she does have a number of conditions that potentially interfere with her daily activities. Of these, currently the most significant are allergies and asthma. She has many allergies, some of which are present year-round, with environmental "triggers," and others that are seasonal, becoming much worse at times when, for instance, the pollen count is high. The primary way in which her allergies manifest is through asthma. She takes medication on a daily basis, and uses an additional inhaler, as needed. She is becoming very good at monitoring her own condition, taking a break when she starts to lose her breath. She is also very good about communicating her needs and her feelings.

- Which laws might provide supports for Jessica?
- If you are unsure of the answer, where might you find more information?
- Who might be helpful as a resource?

FIGURE 1.5   What Do You Think?

It further addressed issues of transition and made it clear that planning and placement teams (PPTs) needed to start with the **"presumption of inclusion."** After careful consideration of placement options, children might receive services in classrooms that were not inclusive, as long as that decision could be justified educationally (Guralnick, 2001; Turnbull, Turnbull, & Wehmeyer, 2007).

There have been several reauthorizations of IDEA since 1991, each bringing some changes but also sustaining the basic mandates. These changes have co-occurred with other initiatives, notably the Americans with Disabilities Act (ADA) and NCLB. The ADA has had an enormous impact on early childhood programs, even though it is a sweeping piece of legislation that affects agencies of all sorts, from movie theaters to hotels, as well as schools. While it has at times been criticized for being an unfunded mandate, it nonetheless has been effective in removing some of the barriers to inclusion (Rab & Wood, 1995; Wood & Youcha, 2009). Legislative changes are not the primary focus of this book; they are, however, central to understanding the imperative of inclusion currently experienced in early childhood. Figure 1.6 presents a situation for you to consider regarding legal ramifications.

Other Sources of Change: The Process of Systems Change

During the extended period of changing paradigms, it has been important to note that some systems and agencies have been methodical in planning and orchestrating a concerted effort to shift toward inclusive practices. In many instances, the efforts are less

Jordan is almost 4. He received early intervention for language delays. Now that he is in a preschool that is not administered by the local education agency, his mother is reluctant to have him identified as eligible for special services. The staff of the preschool includes well-prepared professionals but none with special education certification. Jordan is not toilet trained. The director of the program is aware that according to the Americans with Disabilities Act (ADA) programs are legally not allowed to exclude children with disabilities based on lack of toileting skills. The team has discussed its legal requirements regarding this child.

- Is this program obligated to continue services for Jordan?

FIGURE 1.6   What Do You Think?

systematic. They may be the result of pressures from some, but not all, constituents. In some cases they are the result of legal action, either as individual or class action suits (Guralnick, 2001).

Laws may change based on pressure, advocacy, and/or initiative from constituent groups such as families and coalitions. Ultimately, the sequence of changes as related to the driving forces of transformation is relevant to this text. That is, if all the implementation of inclusive practices were planned so that all personnel were prepared before entering a classroom or before a child with exceptionalities was included in a general class, the current situation with early childhood special education would be considerably different. Personnel would already have the necessary prerequisite knowledge, skills, and dispositions.

In fact, what has been occurring has involved change generated from several potential sources, sometimes in combination. These changes also have followed varied courses, depending on community support, administrative support, and the population served. We have discussed how the federal laws have changed over time. They do not, however, currently mandate full inclusion. They do mandate the consideration of inclusion as an option for every child. When a child's unique needs appear not to be addressed in an inclusive setting, the federal government permits other placement options.

From a civil rights perspective, the compelling argument is that inclusion within a general classroom is somehow more equitable than another type of placement. This would, for some, be an issue of equity and fairness as a principle that might override the educational justifications for more specialized programs. It is important for practitioners to have perspectives on the sources of inclusion initiatives.

Marsha Forest and Jack Pearpoint played leadership roles in the international inclusion initiatives.

"A child or adult with a disability is a symbolic personal crucible where we face our feelings about differences head on. Inclusion is about how we tolerate people who look, act or think differently than so called 'ordinary' people. . . . The questions become very personal. How would I feel if I were unable to walk, talk or more? How would I feel if I had a child who was labeled?(sic) How do I feel about myself?. . . . Inclusion instigates this kind of reflection. No wonder people react! /reflection is vital to everyone. Life must be examined to be lived fully. It may be painful, but the inquiry can be the beginning of building new personal futures."

From: http://www.inclusion.com/artbiggerpicture.html retrieved on 11/2/2009

PHYSICAL ACCESSIBILITY   Over time, many types of programs within communities have been changing to become more physically as well as developmentally accessible to people with a range of challenging conditions. Such changes were implemented in the 1960s, with Head Start (Zigler & Styfco, 2004), and continued in the 1970s, with Section 504 of the Rehabilitation Act, P.L. 99-456. The ADA and IDEA supported such changes (Rab & Wood, 1995; Wood & Youcha, 2009; Turnbull, Turnbull, & Wehmeyer, 2007; Walsh, Smith & Taylor, 2001).

To an extent, these changes in policies and laws have reflected changing theories, as well as a paradigm shift toward more integration and inclusion of people with disabilities. They have, for instance, been indicative of a broader concept of normalcy and a greater acceptance of those with disabilities. It was not uncommon, for instance, to have "the norm" challenged by individuals with disabilities, such as members of the deaf community who assert their rights over an extended period of time, changing previously established patterns of exclusion (Reagan, Case & Brubacker, 2000).

Sources of Change: Educational Reform Movements

Educational reform movements have further supported trends toward inclusion in the United States. Notable among those advocating for quality education for all children has been John Goodlad (Goodlad, Mantle-Bromley, & Goodlad, 2004). The steady assertion that all children can learn has been the bedrock of the movement that has been sustained over decades. Philosophically, this has been central to initiatives that have grown and flourished through a variety of institutions and scholars, such as Larry Cuban (1993) and Deborah Meier (2002). While these scholars have not primarily focused on inclusion, as have Marcia Forest and Jack Pearpoint (1992), the effect of their initiatives should not be minimized or overlooked. Their efforts have increased the quantity and quality of inclusion. Cuban (1993), Goodlad and Lovitt (1993), Goodlad, Mantle-Bromley, & Goodlad, (2004), Tyack (2004), and other educational reformers have focused on general education while broadening the definition of inclusion. That is, educational reform has not systematically incorporated methods historically used by

Decisions regarding placement are based on individual patterns of strength and need.

special educators but has instead applied fundamentally sound constructivist theory to children representing the full continuum of developmental abilities as well as cultural diversity.

EFFECTIVENESS IN A CHANGING WORLD

This book was motivated by enormous changes in early childhood and early childhood special education professions during the past 25 years. We are living in a time of exciting new opportunities. It is also a time of unprecedented challenges for professionals working with young children. Many resources exist that provide valuable perspectives related to effectively developing intervention strategies for young children with disabilities and their families.

Methods Used to Determine Directions

Some of the methods used for navigating the sea change that has been occurring in early childhood and special education have involved focus groups, surveys, and structured interviews through which participant involvement has contributed to outcomes and collective decision making (Rous & Hallam, 2007). The DEC/CEC coordinated focus groups charged with developing a set of recommended practices (Sandall, Hemmeter, Smith, & McLean, 2005). DEC leaders also participated in the revision of NAEYC standards, to ensure that issues of exceptional development were fully included (Hyson, 2003).

Our Roles in Contributing to Future Directions

Ultimately, the extent to which early childhood inclusion continues to positively develop may depend on each person working with young children Our commitment to ongoing professional development on all levels, along with our belief in possibilities, will make a positive difference. Practitioners need to be lifelong learners (Larrivee, 2008). Not only do professionals need experience, they also need to learn from experience through careful consideration and reflection (Reagan et al., 2000; Yost, Forlenza-Bailey, & Shaw, 1999). In addition, systems need to be able to work in a coordinated way, which is especially difficult during times of change. This book is designed to support an active process of problem solving during the implementation of strategies for adaptation within inclusive programs through universal design for learning (McGuire-Schwartz & Arndt, 2007).

Bridge Between Theory and Practice

While it is clear that background knowledge is an essential element in personnel preparation, it is not enough. The ability to apply knowledge in meaningful, appropriate, and responsible ways is ultimately what will make a difference. The purpose of this text is to address the crucial need for a bridge between theory and practice. This book focuses on enduring and innovative practices regarding diversity (Filler & Xu, 2007), especially the acceptance of and adaptations for young children with disabilities within inclusive programs. A combination of factors such as changing laws, practices, and NAEYC and DEC/CEC standards have impacted the ways in which early childhood education personnel need to be prepared (Hyson, 2003; Stayton et al., 2003).

When William was a toddler, he was enrolled in a birth-to-three program. He has Down syndrome. His family was exceptionally supportive and involved. He made significant progress in the birth to 3 program, demonstrating healthy interactions with others. His parents put him on a waiting list for the local preschool program his older brother had attended almost a year before William's transition from birth to 3. When June arrived, however, the family was notified that William would not be able to attend the preschool program because another child with Down syndrome in the program was going to repeat a year in the 3-year-old group rather than move on to the 4-year-old group. According to the administrators, therefore, William would not be able to attend the program because there was already a child with Down syndrome enrolled in that class. The year was 1986.

Questions for Reflection:

- How might William's parents respond to this situation?
- How have the laws changed to ensure that the scenario would not occur today?

FIGURE 1.7 William

Continuum of Program Options

Over time, a continuum of options based on the extent of the challenges for people with disabilities shifted somewhat, paralleling the changing laws in the United States to focus on the "presumption of inclusion." It did not mean that all children with disabilities would be fully included. It did mean that consideration of inclusion is part of planning and placement.

The ADA made it illegal for agencies, including private child care programs, to exclude those with disabilities. One example of the ways in which the ADA required inclusion affected children with spina bifida, a neural tube defect. People living with spina bifida may have symptoms ranging from very mild to very significant. Children may be able to walk, or they may have quadriplegia, with paralysis in arms as well as legs. One very common characteristic of spina bifida is lack of sphincter muscle control, rendering many individuals with this condition incontinent.

As long as private child care programs could exclude children if they were not toilet trained, children with spina bifida were usually not included. This was very common, even if there were no other characteristics among the children that would interfere with their learning or functioning in early childhood settings. Passage of the ADA made that practice illegal. Programs had to amend their policies on toilet training (French & Cain, 2006). Figure 1.7 presents an anecdote for your consideration.

With gradual changes in philosophical and pedagogical frameworks, there has been far more incorporation of individual differences in basic educational structures (Yost, Forlenza-Bailey, & Shaw, 1999).

CURRENT PERSPECTIVES: MAINTAINING PROFESSIONALISM DURING CHANGING TIMES

Learning styles, multiple intelligences (Gardner, 2000), cultural variables, and developmental status have become well established in the educational profession. Given the increased focus on diversity, the work of infusing methods and practices related to children with developmental differences is perhaps now more of a natural process than when it began.

Implications for Early Childhood Educators

The implications of the many initiatives in professional development for practitioners, teachers, and other team members continue to be profound. Spurred by necessity, changes in early childhood and special education have involved some deep reconsiderations of recommended practices. Willingness of professionals to adjust based on the needs of young children has facilitated the creation of opportunities to enhance the match between children and adaptations.

Some states, such as Connecticut, have had precedent-setting class action suits, with resulting changes in protocol expected on a statewide level. That is, there have been increased expectations of accountability to document the amount of time children are in general inclusive classrooms. Optimally, these changing expectations are also accompanied by appropriate administrative support and professional development experiences to ensure quality opportunities for children.

The many different ways in which systems are changing to become more inclusive, as well as the range of models being implemented, have highlighted the importance of having a clear set of shared priorities and desirable outcomes, as well as a shared commitment to high-quality inclusive experiences. This involves the active engagement of team members in a wide variety of roles. It involves initiatives and processes that provide plentiful opportunities for those with varying perspectives to share their unique points of view and priorities.

Alignment of Systems During Change

Sometimes systems change occurs through deliberate, intentional, strategically orchestrated dynamics. Agreed upon outcomes as well as procedures for change can be mutually developed. Such a process can be a very positive experience, with increased understanding and commitment regarding collective responsibility at every phase of change.

When initiatives for change are less organized and less rooted in consensus, creating mutuality is possible, but doing so involves a willingness among all team members to consider alternatives and adjust roles as needed. The shared accountability can be significantly expedited when a system is created for coordinating efforts. Such systems, including accurate record keeping, can greatly enhance the effectiveness of the outcomes. When states have embraced restructuring of systems, methods to ensure accountability are generally established as required by statute.

AVOIDANCE OF ALPHABET SOUP   Alignment of systems may at times be difficult because people do not have a shared set of terms. Explaining the complexity of conditions is often accompanied by terminology that is not part of most people's vocabulary. The team should avoid jargon that may result in obstacles to healthy communication. Given the amount of terminology, it is not uncommon for those discussing special education to use many acronyms, sometimes referred to as "alphabet soup."

When abbreviations are routinely used, it is very important that team members, including families and professionals, all have shared understanding. Using

FAPE—Free, appropriate public education

IEP—Individualized Education Program

IFSP—Individualized Family Service Plan

LEA—Local education agency

LRE—Least restrictive environment

PPT—Planning and placement team

FIGURE 1.8 "Alphabet Soup" Related to Inclusion

abbreviations without explaining meanings can inadvertently contribute to a lack of engagement of team members. Figure 1.8 provides an overview of frequently abbreviated terms.

OVERCOMING A HISTORY OF DISCRIMINATION

Given the history of discrimination against and misunderstanding of those with disabilities, a major aspect of professionalism involves dispositions. It is, quite simply, unacceptable for professionals to demonstrate bias against those with disabilities. Less obvious, but nonetheless insidious, is an approach to those with disabilities that perhaps inadvertently conveys condescension, pity, or treatment such as "rescuing," which implies a lack of competence on the part of those with challenging conditions. The quotation presented in Figure 1.9 provides a sense of historical perspective regarding people with disabilities.

Experience with people who have disabilities often makes it more possible to develop confidence and understanding. Exposure without support and resources,

"For years hospitals remained the only institution caring for crippled children. But with the founding of the Home of the Merciful Saviour in Philadelphia, in 1884, began the recognition—long before accorded to the blind and deaf—of the public obligation of caring for cripples as a class. This home, and others that followed, still treated the cripple as an unfortunate best taken apart from the world altogether, and consequently educated him only for his own mental health and that he might be happy and useful within the little artificial charity-given world of the institution where he must live and die because the world outside had no place for him. The first institution with a purely educational purpose was the Industrial School for Crippled and Deformed Children established in Boston in 1893. This was the first fruit of the perception that if cripples could be educated as a matter of charity, they could also be educated for the purpose of taking them out of the charity class, in which, except for the utterly maimed few, they emphatically do not belong."

Louise Eberle, "The Maimed, the Halt and the Race," *Hospital Social Service,* VI (August 1922), 59–63.

This article was written in 1914.

Source: From Bremner, R.H. (Ed.) (1971). *Children and youth in America: A documentary history.* Vol. II: 1866–1932. Cambridge, MA: Harvard University Press.

Reprinted with permission from Harvard University Press.

FIGURE 1.9 Historical Perspectives on Special Education

however, may exacerbate biases and feelings of inadequacy about program planning and implementation. That is, practitioners may be well intentioned but immobilized by a lack of confidence in their abilities to adapt appropriately for young children with disabilities.

Understanding the many ways in which systems and programs have changed over time has provided a more meaningful context in which to increase effective inclusion. Understanding that the increase in inclusion in early childhood is a relatively recent change makes it more possible for professionals to play active, constructive roles in this process, with a shared sense of positive outcomes. This is essential, especially as we work together (Epstein, 2007).

Advocacy

Advocacy is an integral aspect of the collaborative process, because there are many who may not have information, skills, or confidence to play leadership roles (LaRocco & Bruns, 2005). It is also crucial because the momentum toward effective inclusion is a work in progress. It is not a process that has a defined date of completion. Shared accountability, responsibility, and participation will greatly increase the potential for inclusion to be a positive experience for all (Robinson & Stark, 2002).

Reflection

While there have been many valuable new resources that address the changing needs of early childhood educators, this book is intended to approach the topics from a somewhat different perspective. Specifically, this book is designed to be used to support an active problem-solving and reflective practice (Reagan, Case, & Brubacker, 2002; Yost, Forlenza-Bailey, & Shaw, 1999).

Throughout this book, you will read about real-life children and situations that will help you consider the various factors contributing to the development and implementation of effective strategies for intervention in the context of inclusive classrooms. We believe it is important to have a basic understanding of characteristics of challenging conditions as well as a repertoire of possible strategies for adapting curriculum within inclusive settings. The actual effectiveness of practitioners who are working with young children with developmental challenges is determined by their ability to match the intervention with the unique needs of each child rather than mechanically use a script or prescribed methodology.

This book supports a reflective process designed to help you, the practitioner, better understand the dynamics of what you do in the classroom and how you might adjust your interactions to enhance the outcomes of young children. A solid foundation in developmental theory and practice is especially helpful because optimally practitioners can become very good at monitoring themselves, reflecting on situations and adjusting, as needed. A strong and flexible concept of child growth and development, encompassing the myriad variations and surprises that occur along with more predictable patterns, makes it far easier to consider the many ways in which those with exceptional needs may respond to appropriate strategies for intervention.

The reflective model used in this text is intended to be very user-friendly and accessible to you, the practitioner. Beginning with variables that have been identified

"In order to understand the nature of reflection one must first know that it makes use of perception, which is the act by which the perceptive creature becomes conscious of that which is outside of him. Of all creatures the animals are the only ones that enjoy this faculty: they perceive external objects by means of the senses with which God has endowed them. There are 5: hearing, seeing, smelling, tasting, and touching. The faculty of reflection. . . . uses . . . certain powers which, situated in the ventricles of the brain, seize the forms of things, turn them into comprehension, and give them new forms by means of abstraction. Reflection . . . together with the faculty of comprehension, sorts and combines the sense impressions . . .

The faculty of reflection has different degrees of intensity: in the first place it gives us an understanding of the order of things as we find them in nature and human society so that, by the use of his own power, man can achieve the results he wants. This sort of reflection is composed, to a large degree, of concepts or simple ideas and is called "*discerning intelligence.*"

Ibn Khaldoun (1332–1406). Excerpt from *Universal History*.

Source: From: *Three thousand years of educational wisdom: Selections from great documents* (2nd ed.). R. Ulich (Ed.) (1971). Cambridge, MA: Harvard University Press.

Reprinted with permission from Harvard University Press.

FIGURE 1.10   Historical Perspectives on Reflection

through research as being significant, we provide a structure to guide you in reflection on what is actually occurring in your classroom. In addition, this structure provides support and guidance in considering what might happen and what might be possible, given some adjusted circumstances over which you may have control.

Intrapersonal, interpersonal, and instructional factors are considered with the reflective model being used in this text. It is expected that readers will gather and be guided by data about children's performance, as well as more qualitative factors, such as children's interactive styles. This combination of data-driven decision making and responses to qualitative factors provides a fertile opportunity for professional growth. The quotation in Figure 1.10 provides some historical perspectives on the process of reflection.

Reframing Beliefs

Sometimes what is effective involves making adjustments that hadn't previously been considered. The process of identifying and adjusting key factors or variables is an essential first step toward positive inclusive practices.

Another essential first step is reframing one's own beliefs about inclusion. A deeply ingrained belief that inclusion is not likely going to work will undermine any techniques and methods that are tried, no matter how effective they might be under other conditions. Rather than being self-deprecating about doubt, it may help to put skepticism in a historical context. Such perspective makes it possible to create options and adjust as needed.

In addition to consideration of the methods used with children, other variables related to high-quality inclusion have been investigated (Lieber, 2000). One of the obstacles identified was lack of time, especially for joint planning and communication among and between team members. Administrative support has also been identified as

Strengths:

Please identify areas of strength in your background knowledge, experience, and motivation regarding the education of young children with disabilities in inclusive settings.

Areas to work on:

Please identify areas that you believe you need to work on.

Examples might include classroom management; specific strategies; responding to cultural diversity; addressing needs of children with special needs while also working with children who are developing typically; working with families; adjusting your own responses.

Guide for Reflection:

Are you: Responsive to children's initiative?

Available to children?

Sensitive to family concerns/culture?

Aware of cultural values and priorities?

Comfortable asking for and accepting support?

Willing to accept constructive feedback?

Willing to keep learning about the many conditions?

Confident in your knowledge of typical and exceptional development?

Do you: Provide clear directions, structure?

Have realistic expectations?

Demonstrate confidence in your interactions with children?

Use a repertoire of strategies to adjust to the developmental needs of each child?

Provide appropriate activities to meet the individual needs of children?

Adjust your volume and tone of voice, as needed? As appropriate?

Monitor the volume and tone of children, as appropriate?

"Scan" the room, switching between focus on whole group and individual children and/or small groups?

Engage children in interaction/activities, and support their engagement with each other?

Reflect on your own teaching, and revise as necessary/appropriate?

Tune in to the communicative intent of children?

"Read" and respond to nonverbal cues?

FIGURE 1.11   Personal Inventory

a priority (Smith & Rous, 2008). Figure 1.11 invites you to participate in an initial personal inventory, to help you focus on your own professional development.

Reflective Supervision

Significant recent initiatives focusing on reflective supervision have supported the ongoing practice of reflection on the part of practitioners (Eggbeer, Mann, & Steibel, 2007; Caruso & Fawcett, 1999). Administrators and supervisors are encouraged to use methods that support ongoing reflection on the part of practitioners. When obstacles to high-quality inclusion are identified and addressed, the potential for implementing the best possible programs increases. It is also more possible to advocate for specific elements of effective intervention if one recognizes their importance (LaRocco & Bruns, 2005).

We believe it is possible to have high-quality opportunities for children that exemplify recommended practices in general and special education. There is potential for every program serving young children to be appropriate for children with disabilities and those who are developing typically. The movement toward effective inclusion is one that has firmly established itself, and we believe it is worth our concerted effort to work strategically toward ensuring that this is done well.

Questions for Reflection

1. From your perspective, what changes in special services have been especially significant?
2. Do you have family members with disabilities? If so, please elaborate.
3. What experiences have you had with people with disabilities?
4. Are you aware of your own beliefs about disabilities?
5. Please describe your own confidence level regarding working with people who have disabilities.

Summary

In this chapter, we have presented an overview of topics that will be covered in the book. We have provided an overview of the changing field of early childhood special education. Finally, we have focused on the dynamic of reflection as it contributes to the application phase of intervention, when practice is informed by theory, and theory is informed by constant consideration of practice. This is an opportunity for you to develop an internal compass to help you navigate the changing field of early childhood special education. We encourage you to keep a reflective journal as you work with children and read this book.

You will find certain consistent elements in each chapter. In the beginning of each chapter is a list of objectives. The end of each chapter lists some key terms, as well as resources that may be helpful.

Key Terms

Free, appropriate public
    education
Inclusion

Individualized Education
    Program (IEP)
Least restrictive
    environment (LRE)

People first language
Presumption of inclusion
Universal Design for
    Learning

Websites

Division for Early Childhood; Council for Exceptional Children
http://www.dec-sped.org

The National Association for the Education of Young Children
http://www.naeyc.org

The National Dissemination Center for Children and Youth with Disabilities
http://www.nichcy.org

Center for Culturally and Linguistically Appropriate Services
http://CLAS@uiuc.edu/

References

Allred, K., Breim, R., & Black, S. (2003). Collaboratively addressing the needs of young children with disabilities. In C. Copple (Ed.), *A world of difference* (pp. 131–134). Washington, DC: NAEYC.

Anderson, W., Chitwood, S., Hayden, D., & Takemoto, C. (2008). *Negotiating the special education maze* (4th ed.). Bethesda, MD: Woodbine House.

Bronfenbrenner, U. (1979). *The ecology of human development.* Cambridge, MA: Harvard University Press.

Bremner, R. H. (1971). *Children and youth in America: A documentary history*, Vol. II. Cambridge, MA: Harvard University Press.

Bricker, D. (2000). Inclusion: How the scene has changed. *Topics in Early Childhood Special Education, 20*(1), 14–19.

Bruder, M. (1993). The provisions of early intervention and early childhood special education within community early childhood programs: Characteristics of effective service delivery. *Topics in Early Childhood Special Education, 13,* 19–37.

Bruder, M. (2009). The national status of in-service professional development systems for early intervention and early childhood special education. *Infants and Young Children, 22*(1), 13–20.

Buysse, V., Wesley, P., Snyder, P., & Winton, P. (2006). Evidence-based practice: What does it really mean for the early childhood field? *Young Exceptional Children, 9*(4), 2–11.

Caruso, J. & Fawcett, T. (1999). *Supervision in early childhood: A developmental perspective.* New York: Teacher's College Press.

Catlett, C. (2009). Resources within reason. *Young Exceptional Children, 12*(4), 40–41.

Catlett, C., & Winton, P., (2008). Resources within reason. *Young Exceptional Children, 12*(1), 42–43.

Chandler, L., & Loncola, (2008). In M. LaRocque & S. Darling (Eds.), *Blended curriculum* (pp. 1–26). Boston: Allyn & Bacon.

Copple, C. & Bredekamp, S. (2009). *Developmentally appropriate practice, (3rd ed.).* Washington, DC: NAEYC.

Cuban, L. (1993). *How teachers taught.* New York: Teachers College Press.

DEC & NAEYC. (2009). *Early childhood inclusion: A joint position statement of the Division for Early Childhood (DEC) and the National Association for the Education of Young Children (NAEYC).* Chapel Hill: The University of North Carolina, FPG Child Development Institute.

Diener, P. (2005). *Resources for educating children with diverse abilities, (4th ed.).* Clifton Park, NY: Thomson/Delmar.

Dewey, J. (1919/1933). *How we think: A restatement of the relation of reflective thinking to the educative process.* Lexington, MA: Heath.

Dunst, C., Bruder, M. B., Trivette, C., Raab, M., & McLean, M. (2001). Natural learning opportunities for infants, toddlers, and preschoolers. *Young Exceptional Children, 4*(3), 18–22.

Dunst, C., & Trivette, C. (2009). Using research evidence to inform and evaluate early childhood intervention practices. *Topics in Early Childhood Special Education, 29*(1), 40–52.

Eberle, L. (1922). The maimed, the halt and the race, *Hospital social service, VI,* 59–63. In R. H. Bremner (Ed.), *Children and youth in America: A documentary history,* Vol. II: 1866–1932 (p. 1026). Cambridge, MA: Harvard University Press.

Eggbeer, L., Mann, T., & Seibel, N. (2007). Reflective supervision: Past, present, and future. *Zero to Three, 28*(2), 5–9.

Epstein, A. (2007). *The intentional teacher.* Washington, DC: National Association for the Education of Young Children.

Filler, J., & Xu, Y. (2007). Including children with disabilities in early childhood education programs; individualizing appropriate practice. *Childhood Education: Association of Early Childhood International, 83*(2).

Forest, M., & Pearpoint, J. (1992). *Inclusion! The bigger picture.* http://www.inclusion.com/artbigger-picture.html. retrieved on 11/2/2009.

French, K., & Cain, H. (2006). Including a child with spina bifida. *Young Children, 61*(3), 78–84.

Gardner, H. (2000). *The disciplined mind: Beyond facts and standardized tests, the K-12 education that every child deserves.* New York: Penguin Putnam.

Goodlad, J. I., & Lovitt, T. (Eds.) (1993). *Integrated general and special education.* Upper Saddle River, NJ: Pearson.

Goodlad, J. I., Mantle-Bromley, C., & Goodland, S. J. (2004). *Education for everyone.* San Francisco: Jossey-Bass/John Wiley.

Grisham-Brown, J., Hemmeter, M. L., & Pretti-Frontczak, K. (2005), *Blended practices.* Baltimore: Paul H. Brookes.

Guralnick, M. (Ed.). (2001). *Preschool inclusion.* Baltimore: Paul H. Brookes.

Guralnick, M. (Ed.). (2005). *Developmental systems theory.* Baltimore: Paul H. Brookes.

Harbin, G., & Rous, B. (2006). *Transitions in early childhood education.* Baltimore: Paul H. Brookes.

Hemmeter, M. L. (2000). Self-assessment: Child-focused interventions. In S. Sandall, M. McLean, & B. Smith (Eds.), *DEC recommended practices* (pp. 121-124). Longmont, CO: Sopris West.

Hyson, M. (Ed.). (2003). *Preparing early childhood professionals: NAEYC's Standards for Programs.* Washington, DC: National Association for the Education of Young Children.

Wood, K. & Youcha, V. (2009). *The abc's of the ADA.* Baltimore: Paul H. Brookes.

Jung, L. (2003). More is better: Maximizing natural learning opportunities *Young Exceptional Children, 6*(3), 21–26

Kaczmarek, L. (2007). A team approach: Supporting families of children with disabilities in inclusive programs. In D. Koralek (Ed.), *Spotlight on young children and families* (pp. 28–36). Washington, DC: NAEYC.

Khaldoun, I.1. Excerpt from *Universal history.* In R. Ulich (Ed.) (1971), *Three thousand years of educational wisdom: Selections from great documents* (2nd ed., p. 199). Cambridge, MA: Harvard University Press.

Kochhar, C. A., West, L., & Taymans, J. M. (2000). *Successful inclusion.* Upper Saddle River, NJ: Merrill/Pearson Education.

LaRocco, D., & Bruns, D. (2005). Advocacy is only a phone call away. *Young Exceptional Children, 8*(4), 11–18.

LaRocque, M., & Darling, S. (2008). *Blended curriculum.* Boston: Allyn & Bacon.

Larrivee, B. (2006). *Authentic classroom management.* Boston: Pearson Education.

Leiber, J., Hanson, M., Beckman, P., Odom, S. Sandall, S., Schwartz, I., Horn, E, & Wolery, R. (2000). Key influences on the initiation and implementation of inclusive preschool programs. *Exceptional Children, 67*(1), 83–98.

McGuire-Schwartz, M., & Arndt, J. (2007). Transforming universal design for learning in early childhood teacher education from college classroom to early childhood classroom. *Journal of Early Childhood Teacher Education, 28,* 127–139.

McWilliam, R., Wolery, M. & Odom, S. (2001). Instructional perspectives in inclusive preschool classrooms. In Guralnick, M. (Ed.). (2001). *Preschool inclusion.* (pp. 503–527). Baltimore: Paul H. Brookes.

Meier, D. (2002). *In schools we trust.* Boston: Beacon Press.

Miller, P., Ostrosky, M., Laumann, B., Thorpe, E., Sanchez, S., & Fader-Dunne, L. (2003). Quality field experience underlying performance mastery. In V. Stayton, P. Miller, & L. Dinnebeil (Eds.), *Personnel preparation in early childhood special education; Implementing the DEC recommended practices* (pp. 113–138). Longmont, CO: Sopris West.

Odom, S. (2009). The tie that binds: Evidence-based practice, implementation science, and outcomes for children. *Topics in Early Childhood Special Education, 29*(1), 53–61.

Ostrosky, M., & Cheatham, G. (2005). Teaching the use of a problem-solving process to early childhood educators. *Young Exceptional Children, 9*(1), 11–19.

Pearpoint, J., Forest, M., & Snow, J. (1992). *The inclusion papers.* Toronto, Ontario, Canada: The Inclusion Press.

Pretti-Frontczak, K., & Bricker, D. (2004). *An activity-based approach to early intervention* (3rd ed.). Baltimore: Paul H. Brookes.

Pruitt, P. L. (1997). Inclusive practices for preschoolers with disabilities. In P. Zionis (Ed.), *Inclusion strategies* (pp. 369–390). Austin, TX: Pro-Ed.

Rab, V., & Wood, K. (1995). *Child care and the ADA.* Baltimore: Paul H. Brookes.

Reagan, T. G., Case, C. W., & Brubacker, J. W. (2000). *Becoming a reflective educator: How to build a culture of inquiry in the schools.* Thousand Oaks, CA: Corwin Press.

Robinson, A., & Stark, D. (2002). *Advocates in action.* Washington, DC: NAEYC.

Rous, B., & Hallam, R. (2007). *Tools for transitions in early childhood.* Baltimore: Paul H. Brookes.

Sandall, S., Hemmeter, M. L., Smith, B., & McLean, M. (2005). *Recommended practices: A comprehensive guide.* Longmont, CO: Sopris West.

Shanker, A. (1994). Full inclusion is neither free nor appropriate. *Educational Leadership, 52,* 18–21.

Smith, B. J. & Rous, B. (2008). Policy in early childhood education and early intervention: What every early childhood educator needs to know. In P .J. Winton, J. McCollum, & Catlett, C. (Ed.), *Practical approaches to early childhood professional development* (pp. 247–263). Washington, DC: Zero to Three.

Stayton, V. (2009). State certification requirements for early childhood special educators. *Infants and Young Children, 22*(1), 4–12.

Stayton, V., Miller, P., & Dinnebeil, L. (2003). *Personnel preparation in early childhood special education: Implementing the DEC recommended practices.* Longmont, CO: Sopris West.

Turnbull, R., Turnbull, A., & Wehmeyer, M. (2007). *Exceptional lives* (5th ed.). Upper Saddle River, NJ: Merrill/Pearson Education.

Tyack, D. (2004). *Seeking common ground.* Cambridge, MA: Harvard University Press.

Ulich, R. (Ed.). (1971). *Three thousand years of educational wisdom.* Cambridge, MA: Harvard University Press.

Villa, J., & Colker, L. (2006). Making inclusion work. *Young Children, 61*(1), 96–100.

Vygotsky, L. (1978). *Mind in society* (M. Cole, Trans.). Cambridge, MA: Harvard University Press.

Walsh, S., Smith, B., & Taylor, R. C. (2001). *IDEA requirements for preschooler with disabilities.* Reston, VA: Council for Exceptional Children.

Winton, P., McCollum, J. A., Catlett, C. (Eds.). (2008). *Practical approaches to early childhood professional development.* Washington, DC: Zero to Three.

Wischnowski, M. (2008). Getting the board on board: Helping board members understand early childhood programs. *Young Exceptional Children, 12*(1), 21–30.

Wolery, M., & Sainato, D. M. (1996). General curriculum and intervention strategies. In S. L. Odom & M. E. McLean (Eds.), *Early intervention/early childhood special education: Recommended practices* (pp. 125–158). Austin, TX: Pro-Ed.

Yost, D. S., Forlenza-Bailey, A., & Shaw, S. F. (1999). The teachers who embrace diversity: The role of reflection, discourse, and field experience in education. *The Professional Educator, 21*(2), 1–14.

Zigler, E., & Styfco, S. (2004). *The Head Start debates.* Baltimore: Paul H. Brookes.

Chapter 2

Developmentally and Individually Appropriate Practices

OBJECTIVES

After reading this chapter, students will:

■ Demonstrate an understanding of significant changes in services for children with disabilities, as they relate to program models;

■ Identify evidence-based practices;

■ Demonstrate a concept of dynamic perspectives on development;

■ Identify key features of developmentally and individually appropriate practices with a bridge between theory and practice;

■ Recognize ways in which reflection may support the process of using evidence-based practices to match children's needs;

■ Identify priorities and strategies for working with children.

INTRODUCTION

Overview of Significant Changes in Services, With Implications for Practice

Sung Bin is a young man with athetoid cerebral palsy (CP) that significantly affects his mobility and causes involuntary movement patterns and significant spasticity. "Athetoid cerebral palsy can affect movements of the entire body. Typically, this form of CP involves slow, uncontrolled body movement that make it hard for the person to sit straight and walk" (http://www.nichcy.org. Retrieved June 27, 2009). Sung Bin was adopted when he was 5 years old, after spending his early years in Korea, where he was born. In 1980, he attended a preschool special education class. This was the first year such programs were mandated in a state in the northeastern United States and several years before the federal mandate of P.L. 94-142 had been expanded to include preschoolers. This program had a "reverse mainstream" component, integrating children who were developing typically into the classroom for some portion of each day. The curriculum was **developmentally appropriate**, with the necessary adaptations for children with developmental challenges. Sung Bin received comprehensive services, including speech and language therapy, physical therapy, and occupational therapy.

Sung Bin is an engaging young man who enjoys socializing with others. He is currently employed at a state university, working in auxiliary services. In his job, he has regular contact with students, and the interaction is mutually enjoyable. He has an apartment in a renovated stone mill next to a river, where artists and community members live affordably. He has a room dedicated to computers, where he is actively involved with a variety of projects. He is also engaged to his long-term girlfriend who also has an apartment in the building.

Thanks to the passage of Individuals with Disabilities Education Act (IDEA) and the Americans with Disabilities Act (ADA), this young man has been able to pursue education and put his skills to use in constructive ways through employment. He is quite independent, living in his own apartment, though he does need personal assistance due to his physical challenges. Sung Bin is an example of a person whose life has been affected dramatically by the changing laws and social structures. In turn, he has touched many others with his warm personality and inspiring determination. When he began school as a young child, decisions about a child's placement were based upon each child's developmental level. In order to be integrated into general classrooms, children had to attain certain knowledge and skills comparable to typically developing classmates. Adapting the expectations within a general inclusive classroom had not yet emerged.

Legal Changes in Perspective

As we consider circumstances over time, it helps to put legal changes into perspective by thinking about and getting to know real people. Some of you reading this book may have been born before 1975, when the first special education law, P.L. 94-142, was passed. Some of you may have been born after 1986, when P.L. 99-457 was passed; this law reauthorized the original law and added a mandate for early childhood services. In the United States, anyone born since these major federal legislative decisions were made has been exposed to the blending of early childhood and special education. Contact with diverse peers has become far more common in the lives of young children. Inclusion, rather than mainstreaming or reverse mainstreaming, is currently considered best practice. The term *inclusion* is used here in its broader sense, referring to culture and gender. It is, however, more specifically defined in terms of children who are "differently abled."

Technological Transformations

To further understand the magnitude of these changes and how they are occurring, it may help to contextualize the changes within a world transformed by Internet access (Catlett, 2009). At a time when rapid dissemination of information contributes to the successful transformation of systems, there are now a plethora of resources about disabilities available on the Internet. A challenge for many is to distinguish between information that is reliable and that which is not. Many highly credible materials are now available to those with computer access and computer literacy skills. Being able to access disability information has made it possible for many to enhance their levels of expertise, thus supporting the ease with which federal mandates are implemented. The speed with which information is transmitted through technology appears to significantly contribute to the degree to which systems can actualize their potential for change.

Presumption of Inclusion

A major shift from the original early childhood special education classes occurred with the 1997 reauthorization of IDEA. IDEA shifted the focus on least restrictive environment (LRE) within a continuum of services to a "presumption of inclusion" (Guralnick, 2001; Turnbull, Turnbull, Shank, & Smith, 2004; Turnbull, Turnbull, & Wehmeyer, 2007). The law did not assume or mandate that each child would be placed in a fully inclusive (general education) setting, but it was both assumed and mandated that the planning and placement team (PPT) would consider the option of full inclusion. Justification needed to be provided if another choice was made. Fully inclusive options had to be considered and, if appropriate, attempted. In essence, the option of full inclusion could not be ruled out until it was determined based on documented evidence that this placement was not benefiting the student.

Blended Programs

The impact of this paradigm shift has been enormous, especially in personnel preparation and the need for in-service opportunities for professionals who are expected to learn new skills and strategies. The importance of supporting early childhood professionals through professional development has been highlighted in the position statement on inclusion published by the National Association for the Education of Young Children (NAEYC) and the Division for Early Childhood, Council for Exceptional Children (DEC/CEC). Many states have adjusted their teacher certification to reflect an increased focus on inclusion, sometimes eliminating the "general education" option and replacing it with dual or blended certification in both general and special early childhood education. Conceptually, this certainly makes sense as an important step toward full inclusion (Chandler & Loncola, 2008; Sandall, Hemmeter, Smith, & McLean, 2005). However, when there are blended or unified programs, it is essential that quality not be compromised (Leatherman, 2007).

Early childhood educators are expected to have some expertise in special education, and anyone providing special services is expected to have an understanding of typical developmental theory and practice. Even if full inclusion was initially a challenge to professionals, it is clear this trend of inclusion is not likely to reverse itself. There is ample documentation regarding the efficacy of full inclusion; the current challenge is to ensure that it is done well. Practitioners both from general and special education need to demonstrate a full commitment to inclusion, along with the knowledge, skills, and dispositions necessary to do it well (Hyson, 2003; 2008; Stayton, Miller, & Dinnebeil, 2003). Generally, this results in positive developmental outcomes for children.

EVIDENCE-BASED PRACTICES

Some of the research-based evidence includes an evolution of initiatives that have been studied over time and validated extensively (Buysse & Wesley, 2006; Dunst & Trivette, 2009; McWilliam, & Casey, 2007 Odom, 2009; Winton, McCollum, & Catlett, 2008).

Dynamic Perspectives on Development

RISK FACTORS AND PROTECTIVE FACTORS During the 1960s there was a strong surge of research regarding **central nervous system** (CNS) or brain development. Emerging technologies showed that the brains of young children continue to develop after birth (Bailey, Bruer, Symons, & Lichtman, 2001). This ongoing development was found to be significantly affected by experience and the environment. The "malleability," or "plasticity," of the CNS has the potential of increasing vulnerability over time. It also has the potential of making it possible for children who are significantly at risk to increase **resilience** and improve dramatically (Farran, 2001; Fraser, Kirby, & Smokowsky, 2004; Shonkoff & Phillips, 2001).

This basic principle of malleability of the CNS contributes to the degree to which our *practices* are significant with young children. What we do and how we do it has the potential to have considerable effects on development. Table 2.1 provides an overview of major **risk and protective factors,** as well as potential outcomes.

The significance of the dynamic view of development and our potential roles in contributing to positive outcomes cannot be overstated. When children are born with or

TABLE 2.1 Risk Factors and Protective Factors		
Protective Factor	**Risk Factor**	**Potential Outcomes**
Adequate resources	Poverty associated multiple risk factors	Lack of access to services
Good nutrition	Malnutrition (eg lack of folic acid)	Problems with brain development; physical development; attention Spina bifida
High parental education level	Low parental education level	Behavioral challenges related to lack of information about child development
Adequate medical care	Lack of medical care	Developmental challenges secondary to untreated conditions
Healthy prenatal development	Prenatal exposure to toxic substances	Neurological challenges secondary to toxic exposure (alcohol-related birth defects)
Healthy environments		
Healthy birth process	Neonatal risk	Prematurity; Anoxia; Cerebral palsy
Strong social support	Lack of social support	Isolation; lack of resources
Minimal genetic risk	Genetic risk	Genetic conditions such as Down syndrome
Safe environments	Physical trauma	Traumatic brain injury
Healthy relationships	Abuse and maltreatment	Difficulty with relationships Posttraumatic stress disorder Reactive attachment disorder
Maternal age, within range	Maternal age—very young or older	Increased risk for certain developmental disabilities
Strong family support	Lack of family supports; healthy relationships	Difficulty with relationships Compounded issues

develop challenges when they are very young, it is often possible to affect positive change with appropriate intervention because of the malleability and ongoing growth of the CNS. If, for instance, a child has been exposed to neurotoxins such as lead or drugs, the child may have neurological risk such as hyper-reactivity and difficulty with impulse control. A "busy" general classroom might be pleasantly stimulating for most children but for this child might be significantly overstimulating, potentially contributing to impulsive or even aggressive behavior. This difficulty with self-regulation and calming, along with difficulty filtering out extraneous stimulation, could quite easily be addressed by adjusting the amount and quality of environmental stimulation. When we are aware of the triggers as well as the specific vulnerabilities of children, we can strategically adjust the environment and our intentional interactions, thus contributing to positive outcomes for children. Table 2.2 provides an overview of some significant positive developmental outcomes in different domains for young children.

The shift toward the presumption of inclusion has passed a stage during which debates may have occurred about the efficacy of inclusion. This is no longer a philosophical or pedagogical issue. With the laws shifting toward full inclusion, or "responsible inclusion" (Turnbull, Turnbull, & Wehmeyer, 2007), it is now necessary for all practitioners to know how to meet the needs of all children, regardless of developmental status. Realistically, this involves an entirely new repertoire of skills, as well as the belief that inclusion is indeed possible. It involves a shared commitment to

TABLE 2.2 Positive Developmental Outcomes for Children	
Domain Area	**Postive Outcomes**
Social emotional	Trust
	Healthy attachment
	Autonomy
	Self-regulation
Language and communication	Intent to communicate
	Association of sounds with meaning
	Use of gestures and other signals to communicate
Cognition	Concept development
	Problem solving
	Memory; retrieval
Motor development	Mobility
Gross	Independence
Fine	Coordination
	Self-help skills
	Activities of daily living

solving problems and working through obstacles together. It involves administrative and financial support, as well as a new accountability. It also involves a commitment to reflecting honestly on stigmas and their association with developmental disability.

DEFINITIONS OF DEVELOPMENTALLY APPROPRIATE PRACTICES

Significant research has helped to change views on **developmentally appropriate practices**. Early discussions on the topic addressed theoretical perspectives (Mallory & New, 1995), specifically integrating constructivist methodology, which is well established in the early childhood field. With time, developmentally appropriate practices have evolved toward perspectives and standards that incorporate much clearer indicators and consider a broader range of factors (Copple & Bredekamp, 2008/2009). Many forms of diversity—developmental as well as multicultural—are understood to be integral elements.

Theoretical Perspectives

In addition to the evolving definitions of developmentally appropriate practices, we need to consider a range of theoretical perspectives that provide different conceptual frameworks about human development. Various theories, such as constructivist theories compared with behavioral theories, have different operating principles, priorities, and assumptions. Table 2.3 provides a concise overview of some of the major theories currently used in early childhood education.

At times, practitioners may have allegiance to one theoretical framework over others. Programs may align themselves and their curricula with particular conceptual frameworks. Most early childhood programs identify themselves as primarily constructivist, based on the belief that children can construct their concepts through engagement

TABLE 2.3   Did You Know? Major Theories in Early Childhood Education

Theory	Key Features	Relevance for Children with Disabilities
Multiple intelligence theory, Howard Gardner	Nine different kinds of intelligence	Demonstration of competence in different ways
Socio-cultural, Lev Vygotsky	Zone of proximal development; Scaffolding	Problem-solving strategies; Verbalization
Constructivist, Jean Piaget	Importance of "hands-on" experiences Concepts	Concepts; Generalization
Maria Montessori	Sensory experiences Structured experiences Carefully designed materials	Functional use of skills
Reggio Emilio	Use of constructivist theories Importance of social experience and social problem solving	Social problem solving
Behavioral theory Applied behavior analysis	Stimulus, response, reinforcement	Systematic use of feedback to increase "appropriate" behavior Discrete trial interventions

in appropriate activities (Copple & Bredekamp, 2009). When such approaches do not work with individual children, other options may be considered.

Practical Implications

As with the enormous shift away from discrimination based on race or ethnicity, a first step in change is often to acknowledge current perspectives. When team members have had little or no experience working with children who have significant developmental challenges, and they grew up in a world in which there were discriminatory attitudes, they must reframe concepts regarding disability. Sometimes that means honestly acknowledging the spoken or unspoken values and beliefs about those with developmental differences. In short, it does not work to be superficially positive when there are negative undercurrents. Denial of those undercurrents can further perpetuate discrimination; acknowledgment of misunderstanding and judgment can make it possible to move ahead positively (Trawick-Smith, 2008; Wah, 2004).

It is necessary to understand the historical context to make it clear why negative stereotypes and exclusive practice have been the norm. Given the current momentum, we do not want to assume that changing these patterns will necessarily take a very long time, but we do believe a consistent level of social support and constructive policies will contribute to more productive transformation. It is completely possible that through your participation in this process, some beliefs, attitudes, and ways of thinking will change.

Inclusive Mandates and Imperatives

During this time of change in providing services for young children with disabilities, there have been additional federal mandates, such as the No Child Left Behind (NCLB) Act of 2001. A major way in which this impacted schools and children with disabilities was by mandating the inclusion of children identified as being eligible for special services in standardized assessment. Unless there is a demonstrated delay of 3 standard deviations from the mean, school-age children have been expected to participate in the standardized assessment process through which schools are subsequently assessed (Walsh & Taylor, 2006). Concerted advocacy efforts, however, may have the potential to change certain provisions of laws.

In ways, the politicization of education has contributed to a new level of ethical imperative. Most basically, if the decision to implement full inclusion has become a political mandate, there needs to be an accompanying moral imperative and shared commitment to do it well. In one precedent-setting case, five families who had children with intellectual disabilities filed a class action suit against the state where they lived, resulting in significant changes toward fuller inclusion (Guralnick, 2001).

Organizations Working Together

Collaboration between organizations, groups, and people is necessary for effective inclusion. Inherent in inclusion's success is a solid foundation of developmentally appropriate practices and the conceptual framework of constructivism. This is central to best practices for children who are developing typically (Allred, Briem, & Black, 2003; Zigler, & Styfo, 2004) and to the effective inclusion of children with exceptionalities.

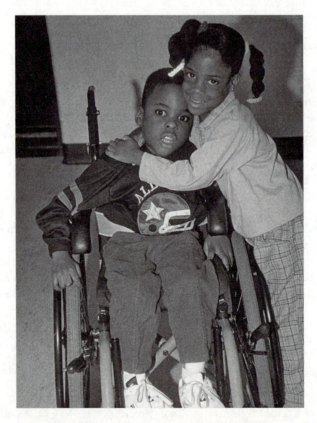

Peer support is very meaningful for children.

It may help team members to tune into their own sense of inclusion as a natural state and to be willing to be creative about the positive possibilities of inclusion. Staying centered in one's own values and positive outlook decreases the likelihood that mandates will stifle the momentum toward positive change. In short, we aren't just doing it because we have to; we're doing it because it has the potential to enhance the overall quality of education for young children.

Research and Practice

Many research studies have looked at methods of interacting with and teaching young children with and without identified disabilities (Smith, Mclean, Sandall, Snyder, & Broudy-Ramsey, 2005). Increasingly, there is a collective repertoire of methods that are generally considered recommended practices, because they are evidence based (Buysse & Wesley, 2006). Some examples include the provision of increased structure, promotion of children's engagement, and the use of a continuum of intervention (LaRocque & Darling, 2008; Winton, McCollum, & Catlett, 2008).

Blending of Early Childhood and Special Education

Over the past 25 years, there has been a blending, "unification," or integration of early childhood and special education that has involved changes in theory, standards, and practice. This blending has had major implications for practitioners and personnel preparation. It is now expected that practitioners will have some expertise in adapting curriculum to meet the needs of *all* children, including those with developmental challenges (Copple & Bredekamp, 2009; Hyson, 2003; 2008; Mallory & New, 1995; Sandall, McLean, & Smith, 2000; Stayton, Miller, Dinnebeil, 2003). This is well articulated in the DEC/NAEYC joint position statement on inclusion (2009). In addition to having a repertoire of possible strategies to use with children who have developmental differences, it is necessary to work in teams to develop individualized plans to address diverse needs (Allred, Briem, & Black, 2003).

When the Education of All Handicapped Act (P.L. 94-142) was passed in 1975, it did not include early childhood services. Some initiatives, such as Head Start, did integrate structure to include children with disabilities, but the federal special education laws were not changed to include preschool children until 1986, with the passage of P.L. 99-457, the reauthorization of P.L. 94-142. Some states had already voluntarily initiated early childhood services before 1986, but most had not. In practical terms, the impact of those changes involved the beginning of a major paradigm shift in both early childhood and special education. This was further supported by the passage of the ADA (Rab & Wood, 1995; Wood & Youcha, 2009), which had significant impact on private child care programs by making it illegal for community-based programs to exclude children with disabilities under most circumstances.

In the late 1990s there were significant adjustments to P.L. 94-142 and P.L. 99-457, resulting in the IDEA and its subsequent reauthorizations (1997, 2001, & 2004). Some updates of the law have impacted early childhood services more than others and have brought the need for adjustments in everyday practice (Walsh & Taylor, 2006).

In a sense, blending early childhood and special education has the potential to be informed by the best of both professions. The coherent, conceptual framework of early childhood, through which children are understood holistically, brings the rich heritage of respect for the developmental process and a shared commitment to the facilitation or scaffolding of development. Appropriate interventions are informed by what we know about recommended practices.

When children have exceptionalities, it is understood that their developmental progression is going to vary from that which is considered "typical." At the same time, with blended professions there is an understanding and acceptance of the nature of children, even when they have exceptionalities. Their needs may be unique and require specialized care, but they are still children for whom a developmental framework has some relevance (Ostrosky & Sandall, 2001; Pretti-Frontczak, Barr, Macy, & Carter, 2003). This understanding is clear in the use of "people first" language as well as the focus on healthy aspects of development.

Even when we use very specialized methods such as task analysis, we can do so in the context of developmentally appropriate programs that offer sensory experiences, language opportunities, and meaningful concept development.

BRIDGING THEORY AND PRACTICE: EVIDENCE-BASED PRACTICES AND GROUNDING IN RESEARCH

When we consider evidence-based practices, we are looking at research in both early childhood and special education methods that have been assessed as effective (Buysse & Wesley, 2006; Winton, McCollum, & Catlett, 2008). Research has focused on the importance of social interaction, support for culturally diverse experiences, and guided inquiry (Goodwin, 1997; Trawick-Smith, 2008). In "typical" early childhood, all of these are valued and validated by substantial research, including research conducted by NAEYC. This is evident in the joint position statement on inclusion published by the NAEYC and DEC/CEC.

Early Childhood Education

In early childhood education, well-established pedagogy supports constructivism because it is understood that "hands-on" and "minds-on" active learning is developmentally appropriate. It is established practice to provide environments that are rich with sensory opportunities. It is understood that what is "typical" for a child at one age is often not at another age. A classic example of this is when children are 2 years old, it is considered "normal" for them to have tantrums. When they are older, it is not. It is accepted that young children enjoy autonomy, and the roles of adults are often responsive, guided by initiations of children. When children are developing typically, they may need support in certain ways, but they also demonstrate the ability to learn and grow through engaging experiences that provide opportunities for concept development, social interaction, and sensory activity. When children have challenges, they need extra support beyond what would typically be available. Explicit clarification of need for enhanced support is vital to accessing that support. Figure 2.1 provides basic information about NAEYC.

While there are certain, often predictable, patterns of development within a "normal" range, there are also many individual differences. Each child is valued as a unique

The National Association for the Education of Young Children (NAEYC) has developed a mission and focus. It is a "high-performing, inclusive" organization (Hyson, 2003) with a wide range of services and materials. It provides networking opportunities, support, and professional development activities to hundreds of thousands of early childhood educators around the world, in a variety of roles. Many resources are available through NAEYC. Leaders in this organization have worked closely with those focusing on exceptionalities during the past 15 years, to increase the extent to which NAEYC reflects the needs of children with disabilities.

Some of the specific ways in which NAEYC has adapted to the changing field are:

Topics at conferences

Topics of articles

Online communities

Standards

For more information: http://www.naeyc.org

FIGURE 2.1 National Association for the Education of Young Children

person, with a distinct blend of temperament, interests, motivation, and personality, as well as strengths and areas of need.

Special Education

Evidence-based practices in special education have been based on systematic research regarding the effectiveness of certain methods. These methods include, but are not limited to, the intentional use of various prompts, the use of reinforcement, and the use of time-delay or wait time. Other methods include task analysis, through which a complex task is "chunked" down into smaller, more manageable units; increased structure; predictable routines; opportunities for peer interaction; and individualized pacing. Methods such as peer modeling are especially relevant.

Response to Intervention

In addition to general strategies that are evidence based, another level of systematically determining which strategies are most effective for individual children involves focusing on specific behavior, using a strategy, and collecting data over time to determine the effectiveness of the strategy (Dunst, Bruder, Trivette, Raab, & McLean, 2001). Thus, evidence-based practices may be more general, or they may be more specific to individual children. Identification of individual areas of concern is an integral part of the process, as is addressing those needs. Response to intervention or recognition and response (Buysse & Wesley, 2006) is a tiered, hierarchical approach to addressing the difficulties children might be having. The hierarchy is represented by a triangle symbolizing a continuum of services, with the bottom tier denoting most children who would have the benefit of a developmentally appropriate environment supportive of their optimal development. Tier 2, in the middle, would be offered to children who need more support, and could include more focused intervention. Tier 3, at the very top of the triangle, involves a much smaller group of children with more significant developmental challenges, who need more focused instructional strategies.

Early Childhood Special Education

Some of the differences between evidence-based practices in early childhood and evidence-based special education are relatively easily reconcilable. Constructivist methodology, which supports children's development of concepts, is relatively uncontestable, provided that one believes that children with developmental differences are capable of concept development on some level, even if their comprehension is not comparable to their chronological peers. Increasingly, there has been an infusion of methods related to positive behavioral supports (Sugai & Horner, 2002) as well as some highly specialized interventions, such as discrete trial intervention. With early childhood special education, a combination of approaches is more commonly being used based on children's unique needs. Figure 2.2 provides an overview of the DEC/CEC.

In theory, using sensory activities to support this process of concept development is also broadly accepted. (Jalongo & Isenberg, 2008; Trawick-Smith, 2008). It is important for practitioners to understand that difficulty with sensory processing in some children result at times in tactile defensiveness. If a child has sensory integration dysfunction, he or she may still benefit from sensory experiences, and we need to take this into consideration when planning activities. Options might include using alternative textures, of gloves, or other adaptations. Figure 2.3 provides an example.

The Division for Early Childhood (DEC) is an official group within the Council for Exceptional Children (CEC). The DEC has played an integral role in the changing paradigms of service delivery for young children with exceptionalities during the past 15 to 20 years. Always committed to excellence, leaders within DEC have been devoted to identifying and disseminating best practices, over the years. These have consistently included research and evidence-based practices. DEC has been thoroughly involved with the evolving models of practice, working closely with leaders from NAEYC during this transition from separate services to inclusive practices (Sandall, Hemmeter, Smith, & McLean, 2005).

This journey has been well documented through numerous publications, now established as "classic" in the profession (Mallory & New, 1995; Miller, 1996; Wolery & Sainata, 1996). DEC has also provided leadership in revisiting standards to reflect a more inclusive model, along with leaders within NAEYC (DEC & NAEYC 2009; Hyson, 2003).

The Personnel Preparation Committee, an established group within the DEC, has worked consistently over years to craft recommendations for practitioners in the field. Several publications have supported these efforts (Stayton, Miller, & Dinnebeil, 2003). Outreach has been an identified priority, and much cooperative work has been done to ensure the ongoing collaboration with NAEYC and other organizations serving young children.

For more information, see http://www.dec-sped.org.

FIGURE 2.2 Division for Early Childhood, Council for Exceptional Children

Karly is a 5-year-old girl who has received special services since she was 18 months old. When she was 15 months old, her parents noticed she had some language delays. Her receptive language was age appropriate, as demonstrated by how she followed directions and responded non-verbally to the requests and comments of others. She is creative, showing her attributes in a variety of ways from a young age. While she enjoys sensory experiences, she does have some tactile defensiveness regarding certain textures. Karly is an affectionate and expressive child, who demonstrates a strong, healthy attachment to her parents and friends. She has one friend with whom she has been especially close for several years. She was recently diagnosed as having a significant learning disability. Karly's parents are very involved, and she has many opportunities for a wide range of experiences outside the classroom. She has been in an inclusive setting since preschool. Both of her parents are college graduates.

FIGURE 2.3   Karly—Sensory Processing Difficulties

IMPLEMENTATION OF EVIDENCE-BASED PRACTICES: UNCONDITIONAL ACCEPTANCE AND CONDITIONAL LEARNING

While some practices that are evidence based have been identified through reliable research processes, others are determined to be effective based on individual responses (Buysse & Wesley, 2006; Cheatham, & Ostrosky, 2005). Through identification of goals and objectives, along with systematic data collection, practitioners can determine whether an intervention is working with individual children over time. Efficacy of practice has the potential to increase team member confidence. Such methods also make it evident that effective strategies do not need to be implemented by only one professional; they can be used by all team members.

While healthy child and family-centered communities have embraced unconditional acceptance, evidence-based practices require effective adaptations or the creation of effective conditions for the unique needs of children with developmental differences. Creating the conditions that support optimal development for children with disabilities naturally enhances measurable positive outcomes. Some of the environmental conditions or factors that appear to be helpful are predictability, routines, structure, effective use of small groups, design and accessibility of room layout. Environmental factors such as noise level, organization, and procedures for transition can also contribute to the healthy development of children (Watson & McCathren, 2009). An approach's effectiveness depends on the match between what is needed and what is offered. Table 2.4 provides an overview of how theory and practice can be matched.

The Developmental Match

In the education profession, it has long been acknowledged that a key to effectiveness is finding and supporting the match between what a child needs developmentally and what is offered in the curriculum. Many professionals have described this over time. It is fully relevant to effective teaching within inclusive classrooms because adaptations are always individualized. Rather than assuming that a child must be "ready" for a certain grade-level curriculum, there is momentum toward adapting curriculum and routines to meet the unique needs of each child. Acknowledging the importance of the match is at the heart of this dynamic.

TABLE 2.4 Matching Theory and Practice Relevant Theory

Situation	Relevant Theory	Developmental Element
Child was born prematurely and spent first months in neonatal intensive care unit of hospital	Attachment theory Erik Erikson's psychodynamic theory	Need to develop trust, healthy relationships
Child with autism has exceptional abilities in certain areas, such as music	Multiple intelligences theory, Howard Gardner	Individual patterns of intelligence acknowledged and supported
Child with Down syndrome	Piaget's theory of cognitive development	Focus on concepts and sensory experience
Child with behavioral challenges	Positive behavior supports	Focus on positive outcomes rather than reacting to negative behavior
Child with learning disabilities	Information processing theory	Specific areas of processing difficulty addressed (e.g., word retrieval)

Reflective Practice

The process of reflection is an integral aspect of the effective application of methods in early childhood special education. How do we know what will work best for each child? For our purposes, reflection is a consideration of multiple factors, including intrapersonal, interpersonal, and environmental. These factors can have a potential impact on the outcomes of children. Reflection is the process that team members engage in to determine the effect of what is being done in the classroom. This can include consideration of how a child responds when someone initiates contact or responds to him or

Participation in engaging activities supports healthy development.

her. In some situations, it may include soul-searching, but it is not assumed that it is a necessary part of the process. At times, children may have profound effects on others. When this happens, it is often helpful if a team member is able to discuss the issues with others, respecting confidentiality, and reflect on the dynamic.

Ultimately, data collection and ongoing observation of individual children provides necessary information about each child's current levels of functioning, as they change over time. Decisions, however, about when and how to implement intervention strategies are usually made by teams. Using both reflection and communication between team members about the effectiveness of intervention makes it possible to monitor intervention strategies over time. This process has the potential to change the developmental "trajectory" or progress of children, especially those who might have developmental challenges.

Dispositions

Positive dispositions, including empathy and acceptance of differences, are integral to effective implementation of strategies and methods. For that reason, guided reflections in this book include consideration of dispositions. Professional dispositions have become well recognized as an important aspect of the practical application of theory and methods (Jalongo & Isenberg, 2008), yet it is still sometimes difficult to explicitly define dispositions because they inherently involve qualitative factors. Dispositions refer to the "how" as well as to the "what" someone does. To be effective professionals, it is important that practitioners demonstrate positive affect, mutual respect, and healthy communication skills. It is also important that professionals demonstrate responsibility and recognize that at times there are cultural variations in what is considered the norm. Some cultures, for instance, view eye contact as a sign of respect, while others view it as a sign of confrontation (Hanson & Lynch, 2007; Trawick-Smith, 2008).

The ability to read social cues can also manifest in positive dispositions. Even with outstanding coping skills, however, there may be times when there are "disconnects," making it necessary to identify the source of misunderstanding. If someone proceeds without acknowledging or demonstrating respect for what others are doing or saying, the effect can be negative and would not represent positive dispositions. Through honest reflection and receptivity to constructive feedback from others, there is an opportunity to adjust one's way of interacting with children, families, and teams (Ostrosky & Sandall, 2001). One essential feature of positive dispositions for professionals who work with children with special needs and their families is being nonjudgmental. It is not uncommon for families to feel vulnerable, especially while they are adjusting to the reality that their child has developmental differences (Erwin, Soodak, Winton, & Turnbull, 2001). With time, families' concerns about the potential for judgment may significantly diminish. During this process of social transition and transformation of systems, however, there may be residual resistance because of dispositions, so reflection on one's own dispositions and willingness to accept constructive feedback are important parts of preparation and ongoing professional development (Division of Early Childhood, 2006; Hanft, Rush, & Sheldon, 2004).

Positive Child Outcomes

When teams come together to support children and families, they work to identify individual strengths and needs; to identify positive, attainable child outcomes; and to develop strategies that will increase the likelihood that these outcomes will occur

(Hanft, Rush, & Shelden, 2004). Objectives may be identified based on knowledge of healthy patterns of child development. Having reasonable expectations is a fundamental component of success. While we do not want to "lower the bar" and assume that children will not be able to accomplish performance outcomes, we do not want to set the bar too high and increase the likelihood a child will fail. Identification of positive developmental outcomes that can become objectives for the focus of intervention is key to success. When a professional has an informed perspective on a child's capability, he or she needs to consider strategies to support the child's optimal development. We consider more than *what* we would like to see the child accomplish, but also *how* that is likely to occur, based on evidence-based strategies, adaptations, and interventions. Thus, we are working in the child's "zone of proximal development," or the range just beyond the child's current level of functioning (Vygotsky, 1978). We base our plans on what we observe and assess regarding each child's current level of performance, as well as learning styles and pace. We continue with ongoing formative assessment and use that to adjust our strategies as needed (Grisham-Brown Hemmeter, & Pretti-Frontczak, 2005).

New Standards Reflecting Blending of Two Fields/Professions

While major organizations such as DEC and NAEYC have not merged, there is increasing alignment of their priorities, standards, and goals in the form of optimal performance outcomes for children and families. All share values such as family-centered practice and appreciation for cultural diversity. As systems, they currently maintain their own structures, but increasingly there is evidence among all that working together is optimal. Some programs have integrated priorities and requirements from different organizations relatively seamlessly, reducing the potential isolation of each.

Working Through the Systems

In addition to developing and maintaining a basic understanding of how organizations such as NAEYC, DEC/CEC, and National Head Start Association operate and set standards, there is a pressing need for practitioners to understand how the special education systems work within school systems. A broad range of policies and procedures provide guidelines on a variety of topics, including the use of pre-referral strategies. Pre-referral strategies are sometimes followed by a referral, especially when there are concerns about a child's developmental progress. The referral is used to develop an Individualized Family Service Plan (IFSP) or Individualized Education Program (IEP). Generally, a professional with more extensive preparation in special education would be in charge of this, but team members, even those with less comprehensive backgrounds in special education, are expected to participate. It is important that team members, including families and professionals, have a clear understanding of policies and procedures related to identification, program planning, and adaptations (Anderson, Chitwood, Hayden, & Takemoto, 2008).

Whether in private or public early childhood programs, practitioners are expected to be familiar with "normal" development in ways that also provide insight into that which is outside the range of typical skill development. Practitioners are expected to be able to identify red flags if a child's development seems compromised. Without jumping to conclusions, practitioners must document their concerns, try a variety of strategies, and document the child's progress, or lack thereof, over time. These pre-referral strategies are mandated by the IDEA.

Understanding Systems

It is very important for team members to know when some aspect of a child's development warrants concern. Understanding appropriate protocol for making a referral for special services increases the likelihood of positive outcomes for the child. If a private program does not have special education staff but has recognized that a child's development is behind that of his or her peers, it is important for the staff to know who might help in the local education agency (LEA), which is the public school system and the responsible agent. Staff members need to be aware of families' legal rights, especially regarding confidentiality and informed consent. A PPT cannot be convened to discuss the child's needs without permission from the legal guardian. Likewise, assessment to determine eligibility for services cannot be conducted without permission.

It is helpful when teachers understand that birth-to-3 and preschool services, though both mandated by the federal government, may have different administrative structures in various states. In some states, there is more continuity from birth to age 5; in other states, the birth-to-3 system may be administered by an agency providing human services, and the preschool programs may be administered by the LEA. Furthermore, these administrative functions and designations are subject to change through legislation, such as IDEA 2004, which offered families more flexibility in continuing with the same administrative structure (Guralnick, 2005; Walsh & Taylor, 2006). Support for children and families during transitions is a crucial factor in sustaining developmental progress of children as they change programs.

When providing support to families who have children with developmental differences, it is important that teachers and those providing related services have some ability to negotiate the systems and gather information for individual children, as necessary (Turnbull, Turnbull, Shank, & Smith, 2004). Practitioners must, for instance, know that there is a legal timeframe of 45 working days after a referral is made for some resolution. With young children, in some instances, more time may be needed to fully determine the developmental status of a child, in which case a PPT meeting would be held to make a decision about placement based on current available information.

Identifying Roles and Responsibilities

If a practitioner has questions about protocol, it is important that he or she has a support network and administrative resources to provide information. This is true whether a teacher is working in a public or private early childhood program. Generally, a professional within the LEA is designated as someone responsible for early childhood services. It would be this person's responsibility to address issues within public as well as private programs. Personnel in private programs, however, together with families, may need to make the initial contact with the LEAs if the required screening procedures have not already identified a child who may be at risk.

As we identify important priorities, we are also compelled to acknowledge the well-documented fact that when systems are in the process of changing, the potential exists for imbalance. We are currently at a crucial juncture to align systems as they have not been aligned before. There is an increasing need to use our resources efficiently (Catlett, 2009). Coordinated systems increase the effectiveness of programs, which results in more positive outcomes for children while minimizing excess cost. As we advocate for effective inclusion, however, we must understand and be prepared to clarify that it is not always less costly than separate classrooms. Appropriate supports need to be provided to ensure that programs enhance positive outcomes for children. Just eliminating separate self-contained classrooms does not, by itself, ensure that inclusion will have positive results.

Discussion of Implications for Intervention

Given the paradigm shift toward more blended programs in which children with exceptionalities are included in general education programs, there are major implications for intervention. Central among these is the ability to think differently about strategies in the process of adapting curriculum (Hanft, Rush, & Shelden, 2004). It is necessary, but not sufficient, to have a repertoire of strategies from which to draw when planning interventions. It is necessary for practitioners, whether they are primarily general educators, special educators, or both, to be able to work in teams while planning and implementing adaptations. Using differentiated instruction to effectively address the unique needs of children is a function of coordinated teamwork.

Using Problem Solving to Enhance Positive Outcomes

The basic structure and procedure for problem solving is organized in a relatively predictable pattern. First, patterns of strength and need are explicitly identified, based on each child's characteristics. Second, objectives are identified based on the areas of need, working within Vygotsky's zone of proximal development, which is the range that appears attainable for each child beyond what he or she is currently doing (Vygotsky, 1978). Third, those objectives are addressed through the application of adaptation strategies, drawn from a repertoire and selected to match the child's characteristics rather than simply a diagnosis. Next, the strategies are embedded within daily activities and routines, providing extensive opportunities to address the unique needs and objectives of each child (Grisham-Brown, Hemmeter, & Pretti-Frontczak, 2005). Finally, the developmental progress of the child and the child's response to the intervention strategies are assessed, with the results contributing to the course of the ongoing intervention.

GETTING STARTED WITH REFLECTION

Central to effectiveness in strategy implementation is the ability to "think on one's feet," to respond to situations as they arise. In early childhood education, it is fully understood that spontaneity is a natural and valued aspect of child development (Jalongo & Isenberg, 2008). A caregiver's responsiveness creates mutuality for social interactions, communication, shared problem solving, and physical synchrony. Attunement and being psychologically available are essential in the relationships that provide the context for healthy development.

Range of Modifications

When children need interventions, the methods used may range from adjustments of the environment to adapted equipment. In some instances, the adaptations may include more adult-directed interventions, with child-centered activities as the starting point. Within an inclusive context, we start with methods that are developmentally appropriate recommended practices and adjust based on children's individual needs. When children need increased amounts of structure, explicit clarity regarding limits and boundaries, and more direct guidance during interactions, those interventions are integrated throughout daily activities (LaRocque & Darling, 2008).

The practitioner provides the perspective to adjust the curriculum as needed. This is similar to applying the principles of navigation while sailing. Sometimes, but not always, a straight line is the best route between two points. Sometimes the course is adjusted based on various factors. In sailing, the wind and currents are crucial to navigation. In early childhood special education, the sometimes shifting characteristics of children guide us in our interventions. Being an excellent sailor and adjusting your course while reading children's and team member's cues is essential to effective intervention. At the same time, being familiar and proficient with methods that support positive outcomes is necessary.

Getting to Know the Children With Whom You will Work

There are several ways we learn the unique patterns of strengths and needs of the children we teach. Sometimes we meet the children through the paper files that arrive prior to their attendance at school. We may be the recipients of volumes of information on an individual child, or we may have some very basic written information about an individual child. Some children will have much assessment data that presents a picture about them, and some children will have little to no assessment data about them.

There are other times when we meet the child prior to receiving any paperwork. The child is brought to the classroom and becomes a member of the class. When a child has not yet been identified as being eligible for services, you meet him or her in person, and use observation as well as interaction to more fully understand the child. In any event, you will begin to form concepts about the child and follow those initial impressions with your own forms of assessment and fact-finding. What you determine about a child's developmental level will become the basis for how you teach the child as well as what adjustments and interventions might be needed. When children have not yet been identified, working closely with families on pre-referral strategies and initial screenings helps to build trust and ease the transition to attaining consent for full-scale assessment.

In the beginning of this chapter, you met Sung Bin, who was born in Korea. Here is some more information about him. At 5 years, he was adopted by a family in the United States. Given the circumstances of his birth, it is probable he would not have survived had he not been adopted. He has athetoid cerebral palsy that resulted in involuntary movement patterns and significant spasticity. He has extremely high muscle tone. As a preschooler, he was not able to bear weight, so his primary form of mobility was rolling, which he could do independently. For this reason, the physical therapist created adaptations that included moving from one area to another independently. This involved rearranging the physical space of the classroom. Sung Bin participated in daily activities, including play and group games, and received physical support and guidance. Sometimes adaptive seating was used, and sometimes assistive technology was used. He received speech and language therapy, with a special focus on breath control and concentration on the content of what he was saying. Sung Bin had the ability to make strong, positive connections with his peers and many adults. He made excellent progress in all areas of development but continued to have long-term physical challenges. As he became more communicative, his comprehension and intelligence became more evident. If Sung Bin were a preschooler today, he would be using a great deal of assistive technology.

Questions for Reflection:

1. What features of developmentally appropriate practices do you believe are especially important? Why?
2. Consider your own practices of adjusting, as needed. What are some of factors you consider as you adjust your practice?
3. We have discussed the dynamic of development and the ongoing development of the central nervous system in young children. In your own words, state the significance of this scientific finding for early childhood education and what you do in your classroom.

Summary

This chapter presents the concept of central nervous system plasticity in the context of considering the potential for children's development to be significantly influenced by the environment and by appropriate intervention. Evidence-based practices have been identified regarding "typical" as well as "exceptional" development in young children. Creating a match between the unique needs of individual children and the methods we used can be enhanced through reflective practices.

Key Terms

Central nervous system plasticity
Developmentally appropriate practices

Resilience
Risk factors and protective factors

Websites

Center for Culturally and Linguistically Appropriate Services
http://clas.uiuc.edu/

Center on the Developing Child, Harvard University
http://www.developingchild.harvard.edu/content/publications.html

Division for Early Childhood, Council for Exceptional Children
http://www.DEC-SPED.org

Frank Porter Graham Child Development Center
http://fpg.unc.edu/~scpp/pdfs/rguide.pdf

National Association for the Education of Young Children
http://www.NAEYC.org

National Dissemination Center for Children and Youth with Disabilities
http://www.Nichcy.org

Video that accompanies the DEC/NAEYC joint position statement on inclusion
http://community.fpg.unc.edu/connect

References

Allred, K., Briem, R., & Black, S. (2003). Collaboratively addressing the needs of young children with disabilities. In C. Copple (Ed.), *A world of difference* (pp. 131–134). Washington, DC: NAEYC.

Anderson, W., Chitwood, S., Hayden, D., & Takemoto, C. (2008). *Negotiating the special education maze* (4th ed.). Bethesda: Woodbine House.

Bailey, D., Bruer, J., Symons, F., & Lichtman, J. (2001). *Critical thinking about critical periods.* Baltimore: Paul H. Brookes.

Beatty, J. (2008). *Skills for preschool teachers* (8th ed.). Upper Saddle River, NJ: Merrill/ Pearson Education.

Bricker, D. (2000). Inclusion: How the scene has changed. *Topics in Early Childhood Special Education, 20*(1), 14–19.

Buysse, V. & Wesley, P. (Eds.). (2006). *Evidence-based practices in the early childhood field.* Washington, DC: Zero-to-Three.

Catlett, C. (2001). Resources within reason: Teaching strategies. In M. Ostrosky & S. Sandall, *Teaching strategies: What to do to support young children's development, Monograph Series # 3, Young Exceptional Children.* The Division of Early Childhood, Council for Exceptional Children. Longmont, CO: Sopris West.

Catlett, C. (2009). Resources within reason: *Young Exceptional Children, 12*(4), 40–41.

Chaille, C. (2008). *Constructivism across the curriculum in early childhood classrooms.* Boston: Allyn & Bacon/Pearson Education.

Chandler, L., & Loncola, J. (2008). Rationale for a blended education. In M. LaRocque & S. Darling (Eds.), *Blended curriculum in the inclusive classroom* (pp. 32–60). Boston: Allyn & Bacon/Pearson Education.

Cheatham, G., & Ostrosky, M. (2005). Teaching the use of problem-solving process to early childhood educators. *Young Exceptional Children, 9*(1), 11–20.

Copple, C., & Bredekamp, S. (2008). Getting clear about developmentally appropriate practice. *Young Children, 63*(1), 54–55.

Copple, C., & Bredekamp, S. (2009). *Developmentally appropriate practices* (3rd ed.). Washington, DC: National Association for the Education of Young Children.

Corso, R., Santos, R., & Roof, V. (2002). Honoring diversity in early childhood education materials. *Teaching Exceptional Children, 34*(3), 30–36.

DEC & NAEYC. (2009). *Early childhood inclusion: A joint position statement of the Division for Early Childhood (DEC) and the National Association for the Education of Young Children (NAEYC).* Chapel Hill: The University of North Carolina, FPG Child Development Institute.

Dunst, C., Bruder, M. B., Trivette, C., Raab, M., & McLean, M. (2001). Natural learning opportunities for infants, toddlers, and preschoolers. *Young Exceptional Children, 4*(3), 18–22.

Dunst, C., & Trivette, C. (2009). Using research evidence to inform and evaluate early childhood intervention practices. *Topics in Early Childhood Special Education, 29*(1), 40–52.

Eliason, C., & Jenkins, L. (2008). *A practical guide to early childhood curriculum* (8th ed.). Upper Saddle River, NJ: Merrill/Pearson Education.

Erwin, E. J., Soodack, L. C., Winton, P. J., & Turnbull, A. (2001). "I wish it wouldn't all depend on me:" Research on families and early childhood inclusion. In M. Guralnick (Ed.), *Early childhood inclusion* (pp. 127–158). Baltimore: Paul H. Brookes.

Farran, D. (2001). Critical periods and early intervention. In D. Bailey, J. Breuer, F. Symons, & J. W. Lichtman (Eds.), *Critical thinking about critical periods.* Baltimore: Paul H. Brookes.

Fraser, M. (Ed.). (2004). *Risk and resilience in childhood.* Washington, DC: National Association of Social Workers.

Goodwin, A. Lin (Ed.). (1997). *Assessment for equity and inclusion.* London: Routledge.

Grisham-Brown, J., Hemmeter, M. L., & Pretti-Frontczak, K. (2005). *Blended practices.* Baltimore: Paul H. Brookes.

Guralnick, M. (Ed.). (2001). *Early childhood inclusion.* Baltimore: Paul H. Brookes.

Guralnick, M. (Ed.). (2005). *Developmental systems theory.* Baltimore: Paul H. Brookes.

Hanft, B. E., Rush, D. D., & Shelden, M. (2004). *Coaching families and colleagues in early childhood.* Baltimore: Paul H. Brookes.

Hanson, M., & Lynch, E. (2004). *Developing cross-cultural competence* (3rd ed.). Baltimore: Paul H. Brookes.

Hemmeter, M. L. (2000). Classroom-based interventions: Evaluating the past and looking to the future. *Topics in Early Childhood Special Education, 20*(1), 56–60.

Hyson, M. (Ed.). (2003). *Preparing early childhood professionals: NAEYC's standards for programs.* Washington, DC: National Association for the Education of Young Children.

Hyson, M. (2008). *Enthusiastic and engaged learners.* New York: Teachers College Press.

Wood, K., & Youcha, V. (2009). *The ABC's of the ADA.* Baltimore: Paul H. Brookes.

Jalongo, M. R., & Isenberg, J. P. (2008). *Exploring your role as a reflective practitioner.* Upper Saddle River, NJ: Merrill/Pearson Education.

LaRocque, M., & Darling, S. (Eds.). (2008). *Blended curriculum in the inclusive classroom.* Boston: Allyn & Bacon/Pearson Education.

Leatherman, J. (2007). "I just see all children as children": Teachers' perceptions about inclusion. *The Qualitative Report, 12,* 594–611.

Mallory, B., & New, R. (1995). *Individually and developmentally appropriate practices.* New York: Teacher's College Press.

McWilliam, R., & Casey, A. (2007). *Engagement of every child in the preschool classroom.* Baltimore: Paul H. Brookes.

McWilliam, R., Wolery, M., & Odom, S. (2001). Instructional perspectives in inclusive preschool classrooms. In M. Guralnick (Ed.), *Early childhood inclusion: Focus on change* (pp. 503–530). Baltimore: Paul H. Brookes.

Miller, R. (1996). *The developmentally appropriate inclusive classroom.* New York: Delmar.

Odom, S. (2000). Preschool inclusion: What we know and where we go from here. *Topics in Early Childhood Special Education, 20*(1), 20–27.

Odom, S. (2009). The tie that binds: Evidence-based practice, implementation science, and outcomes for children. *Topics in Early Childhood Special Education, 29*(1), 53–61.

Ostrosky, M., & Sandall, S. (2001). *Teaching strategies: What to do to support young children's development.* DEC Monograph #3. Longmont, CO: Sopris West.

Pianta, R., LaParo, K., & Hamre, B. (2008). *Classroom assessment scoring system.* Baltimore: Paul H. Brookes.

Pretti-Frontczak, K., & Bricker, D. (2004). *An activity-based approach to early intervention* (3rd ed.). Baltimore: Paul H. Brookes.

Rab, V., & Wood, K. (1995). *Child care and the ADA.* Baltimore: Paul H. Brookes.

Sandall, S., Hemmeter, M. L., Smith, B., & McLean, M. (2005). *Recommended practices: A comprehensive guide.* Longmont, CO: Sopris West.

Sandall, S., & Ostrosky, M. (Eds.). (2000). *Natural environment and inclusion.* DEC Monograph No. 2. Longmont, CO: Sopris West.

Sandall, S., & Schwartz, S. (2008). *Building blocks, (3rd ed.).* Baltimore: Paul H. Brookes.

Shonkoff, J. P. (2004). *Science, policy, and the young developing child; Closing the gap between what we know and what we do.* Waltham, MA: National Scientific Council on the Developing Child.

Shonkoff, J. P., & Phillips, D. (Eds.). (2000). *From neurons to neighborhoods.* Washington, DC: National Academy Press.

Smith, B. J., McLean, M. E., Sandall, S., Snyder, P., & Broudy-Ramsey, A. (2005). Recommended practices: The procedures and evidence base used to establish them. In S. Sandall, M. L. Hemmeter, B. J. Smith, & M. E. McLean (Eds.), *DEC recommended practices* (pp. 27–44). Longmont, CO: Sopris West.

Stayton, V., Miller, P., & Dinnebeil, L. (2003). *Personnel preparation in early childhood special education: Implementing the DEC recommended practices.* Longmont, CO: Sopris West.

Stormont, M. (2008). *Fostering resilience in young children at risk for failure.* Upper Saddle River, NJ: Merrill/Pearson Education.

Sugai, G. & Horner, R.H. (2002). The evolution of discipline practices: School-wide positive behavior supports. *Child and Family Behavior Therapy, 24,* 23–50.

Tertell, E., Klein, S., & Jewett, J. (Eds.). (1998). *When teachers reflect: Journeys toward effective, inclusive practice.* Washington, DC: National Association for the Education of Young Children.

Trawick-Smith, J. (2008). *Child development: A multicultural perspective.* Upper Saddle River, NJ: Merrill/Pearson Education.

Turnbull, R., Turnbull, A., Shank, M., & Smith, S. (2004). *Exceptional lives* (4th ed.). Upper Saddle River, NJ: Merrill/Pearson Education.

Turnbull, R., Turnbull, A., & Wehmeyer, M. (2007). *Exceptional lives* (5th ed.). Upper Saddle River, NJ: Merrill/Pearson Education.

Vygotsky, L. (1978). *Mind in society* (Trans. M. Cole). Cambridge, MA: Harvard University Press.

Wah, L. M. (2004). *The art of mindful facilitation.* Oakland, CA: Stir Fry Seminars and Consulting.

Walsh, S., Smith, B., & Taylor, R. (2000). *IDEA requirements for preschoolers with disabilities.* Reston, VA: Council for Exceptional Children.

Walsh, S., & Taylor, R. (2006). *Understanding IDEA: What it means for preschool children with disabilities and their families.* Reston, VA: Council for Exceptional Children.

Watson, A., & McCathren, R. (2009). Including children with special needs: Are you and your early childhood program ready? *Young Children, 64*(2) 20–26.

Winton, P., McCollum, J., & Catlett, C. (2008). *Practical approaches to early childhood professional development.* Washington, DC: Zero-to-Three.

Wolery, M., & Sainato, D. M. (1996). General curriculum and intervention strategies. In S. L. Odom & M. E. McLean (Eds.), *Early intervention/early childhood special education: Recommended practices* (pp. 125–158). Austin, TX: Pro-Ed.

Zigler, E., & Styfco, S. (2004). *The Head Start debates.* Baltimore: Paul H. Brookes.

Zipper, I. N., & Simeonsson, R. (2004). Developmental vulnerability in young children with disabilities. In M. Fraser (Ed.), *Risk and resilience in childhood* (pp. 161–181). Washington, DC: National Association of Social Workers.

Chapter 3

Families, Teams, and Communication

OBJECTIVES

After reading this chapter, students will demonstrate:

- An understanding of the importance of dynamic teams and families working
- together;
- Clarity about roles and responsibilities;
- Consideration of cultural differences;
- An understanding of how professionals can work in teams to help families negotiate special education systems;
- An understanding of ways in which reflection may be used to enhance the quality of intervention in teams.

INTRODUCTION

The Importance of Working Together

Teams are at the heart of effective intervention. Team members include families and professionals such as physical, occupational, and speech and language therapists, as well as teachers. **Family-centered practices** are well established (Turnbull, Turnbull, Erwin, & Soodak, 2007; Turnbull, Turnbull, & Wehmeyer, 2007). This is refreshing progress after years of compounded discrimination against families that included the historic misconception that parents were to blame for their children's disabilities. An extreme example of such blame was the term "refrigerator mothers," which some professionals used to refer to mothers of children with autism. Fortunately, such misconceptions are not currently prevalent. In fact, there has been a recent upsurge in momentum from families, sometimes individually and sometimes collectively, regarding children with disabilities. Parents in the U.S. who have young children may have grown up after 1975, when P.L. 94-142 was passed, so they may have never known a world in which established discrimination against those with disabilities was "normal." It is also important, however, to keep in mind that children who grew up in other countries may not have experienced the same level of classroom integration as children with disabilities in the United States. We are living in an era of dramatic change. Unfortunately, this does not mean that all the issues have been addressed. Overall, we are in the process of major transformations (Buysse & Wesley, 2006; Guralnick, 2001/2005). The main focus of this chapter is on those factors that directly affect interaction among teams, including families and professionals. These factors include communication, rapport, development of trust, and support for resourcefulness. Integral to understanding how teams work and how professionals may participate is understanding the concept of families and teams from a developmental systems perspective. This has been carefully articulated by Guralnick (2005) and others and has been widely recognized as providing crucial perspectives.

A basic premise of this book is that resilience makes it possible for children and families to overcome obstacles. This chapter addresses dynamics that may be adjusted or affirmed, depending on the situation. It provides some structure for you to reflect about some of your own patterns and helps you develop the ability to put your own personal perspectives aside, so you can be clear and present for other team members.

Paradoxically, this often requires intrapersonal honesty. Denying one's own perspectives or value systems does not ensure being able to transcend those beliefs.

Roles and Responsibilities

In addition to understanding the need to work together, this chapter also addresses the need for shared understandings of roles and responsibilities, along with the ability to work effectively in existing systems of care or service coordination (Dunst & Bruder, 2006; Guralnick, 2005; McWilliam, 2005). When there are clear, mutually agreed upon goals and directions, it is easier to maintain a shared momentum. It is also easier to maintain a shared sense of direction and outcome. The Developmental Systems Model provides a useful framework (Guralnick, 2005).

The Reflective Process with Teams: Creating Common Ground

A reflective process can be sustained with structures and a fundamental belief that each of us has options regarding how we interact with one another. Carefully but not rigidly defining roles and goals creates a sense of shared vision and direction (Hanft, Rush, & Sheldon, 2004). Indeed, we are working together for the benefit of children. Defining goals provides a certain orientation and sense of parameters or boundaries. While families may at first be unfamiliar with the nature of inclusive services, working together can provide some shared sense of common ground.

FAMILIES

Most parents do not make a deliberate choice to conceive a child with disabilities. It is a life circumstance that may have been totally unanticipated. For some, this experience may be perceived as a tragedy. For others, it may be considered a test or a sign that they have been deemed strong enough to handle such a challenge. Because opportunities for individuals with disabilities have dramatically improved, families may not perceive the birth of a child with developmental differences as a major challenge. When professionals work with families to create an Individualized Education Program (IEP), they must appreciate the emotional realm. Professionals in early childhood education are often involved with a family before a child has been officially identified as eligible for services. This phase requires deep sensitivity as parents come to terms with the reality of their child's developmental functioning, and especially as they consider what the future may hold for their children and families. Professionals should also have strong support networks to help them cope with their own emotions, so they can be psychologically available to families who are in the midst of major adjustments.

Impact of Social Inclusion Movement on Families

During the past few decades, social inclusion has experienced a number of global changes. These changes may have significant impact on the options available for a child with disabilities and his or her family. Self-determination of individuals with disabilities and family-centered practices are now firmly established (Turnbull, Turnbull, Erwin, & Soodak, 2007; Turnbull, Turnbull, & Wehmeyer, 2007). Both of these major paradigm shifts have significant implications for children, families, and the teams that

Family-centered practice is based on a core set of values, beliefs, and principles that recognize that families can contribute to all aspects of services through their active participation. Family-centered practice involves getting to know the family, discovering their strengths, and ensuring all family members are safe. This is followed by identifying outcomes and unmet needs of the family. A family team is formed that develops a plan that addresses unmet needs to achieve defined outcomes in ways that use the strengths of the family. Family-centered practice is a strength-based approach to working with children, youth and families. It is an approach that allows the family to drive the planning process and focuses on the priorities defined by the family. As a result, family-centered practice is individualized and aimed at helping people meet their needs while they remain in their homes and their neighborhoods whenever possible. Families receive support in facilitating the process and identifying individuals, both within and outside of formal human services systems, who might serve as helpful resources. Family-centered practice builds on people's strengths to achieve outcomes that are important to them in ways that reflect their values, culture, and preferences.

FIGURE 3.1   Did You Know? Family-Centered Processes

serve them. Figure 3.1 provides an overview of key elements of family-centered practices.

 After a young child is identified as having a disability or developmental delay, having the opportunity to adjust to this information can increase the likelihood that families and children will be able to focus on positive aspects of their lives together (Hanft, Rush, & Shelden, 2004). Some parents elect to intentionally adopt children with challenges, knowing they have the resources to provide for them.

Children and Families: A Package

It is imperative that anyone planning to work with young children with disabilities be prepared to work closely with families and other team members (Batshaw, 2001; Batshaw, Pellegrino, & Roizen, 2007). On a practical level, there are major implications regarding the need for quality communication. Given the uniqueness of each family, professionals must be prepared to "think on their feet" and respond to a wide range of dynamics (Lee & Ostrosky, 2004; McWilliam, 2005). In some areas of expertise, mastery means being able to generalize certain specific skills. In the inclusion of children with special needs in general classrooms, skill application, whether with children or families, should always be individualized to address unique patterns of strength and need. The interests, priorities, and daily activities are relevant to the development of a plan that fully addresses the child in the most meaningful context of family.

 Just as each child is unique and has an individualized program, so, too, are families. The Individualized Family Service Plan (IFSP) or IEP should reflect the unique patterns and priorities within each family (Turnbull, Turnbull, Shank, & Smith, 2004; Turnbull, Turnbull, & Wehmeyer, 2007). Figure 3.2 highlights some of the key features of IFSPs and IEPs.

 The Individuals with Disabilities Education Act (IDEA), a federal law, requires that certain information be included in the IEP but does not specify how the IEP should look. The required information includes the child's current level of performance as well as goals and objectives. Because states and local school systems may require additional information, forms differ from state to state and may even vary among school systems

The Individualized Family Service Plan (IFSP)

An IFSP is a vehicle through which effective early intervention is implemented in accordance with Part C of the Individuals with Disabilities Education Act (IDEA). It contains information about the services necessary to facilitate a child's development and enhance the family's capacity to facilitate the child's development. Through the IFSP process, family members and service providers work as a team to plan, implement, and evaluate services tailored to the family's unique concerns, priorities, and resources.

The Individualized Education Program (IEP)

An IEP is a written document that is developed for each public school child who is eligible for special education. A team creates the IEP and reviews it at least once a year. Before an IEP can be written, a child must be identified as eligible for special education. By federal law, a multidisciplinary team must determine that the child has both a disability and a requirement for special education and related services to benefit from the general education program.

http://www.schwablearning.org/articles.aspx?r=31&d=5

FIGURE 3.2   Did You Know? Individualized Programs

within a state. It is important to find out about state laws and regulations through local resources.

Confidentiality

Clearly, confidentiality is always a consideration. Professionals should understand that families have different thresholds regarding what they consider private or privileged information. Professionals need to abide by legally required protocol for obtaining consent to share information. It is helpful when a team can be mutually supportive on behalf of a child. When developing a way of working as a team it is critical that no one individual feels as though he/she needs to be the "star" of the team but that all work together for the benefit of the children. When there is a true sense of collaboration within a team, respecting confidentiality is a shared understanding. Figure 3.3 provides a sample consent form for sharing information about a child.

I, _____,
(print name of parent/guardian)

give consent to _____,

to read educational and medical reports on my child, _____,
as they relate to   (name of child)

his/her educational program at Goodkind Early Childhood Center.

_____
Signature of parent/guardian- Date

FIGURE 3.3   Goodkind Early Childhood Center Consent Form

Collaboration and quality communication are essential.

Capacity Building

While professionals must be aware of families' emotions and feelings of vulnerability during their time of adjustment to having a child with a developmental difference, professionals must also be appreciative of the great strength many families demonstrate. Professionals and parents can both help create a context for quality communication. Capacity building is an integral part of healthy team functions. Rather than expect families to be dependent on professionals, teams can work together to increase everyone's resourcefulness (Erwin, Soodak, Winton, & Turnbull, 2001). Optimally, professionals can be supportive during this process, as needed. Capacity building includes becoming knowledgeable about how systems work and what resources are available.

Range of Challenges

It is important to keep in mind that children identified as being eligible for special services may have conditions that range from developmental delays to rare syndromes. The degree of challenge may range from mild to complex, often with proportional differences in the impact on families and the intensity of services needed. When conditions/syndromes are relatively rare, it becomes especially important that families and professionals be able to learn together. Families rarely seek pity from others. Compassion, understanding, support, and empathy can all be shared without the message of shame. Professionals and families should focus on what is positive and what is strong to help provide perspective for that which is more difficult or challenging. Families need to think and act positively.

Cultural Differences in Perception of Social Services and Disability

Disability is not perceived the same in all cultures. In some cultures there is no word for disability. In other cultures, having a child with a disability is perceived as being a special test or message. Some ethnic groups might perceive that the extended family can and should support the child and the family. In other families, the parents know they will have to do everything themselves if their child has a disability. Professionals should understand the culture of the family they are serving; it is critical to the success of inclusion and intervention (Banks, Santos, & Roof, 2003; Barrera, Corso, & Macpherson, 2003; Lopez, Salas, & Flores, 2005; Maschinot, 2008). Knowing how a culture generally perceives accepting support from social services is basic to the design of an intervention (Kayanpur & Harry, 1999). Being sensitive to the way in which services need to be delivered will make all the difference in the world in the success of the service provided (Banks, Santos, & Roof, 2003; Cheatham, & Milagros Santos, 2005).

COMMUNICATION

The Interpersonal Aspect of Intervention

Preparing for social interaction is an integral part of learning to be a psychotherapist. Learning to have healthy boundaries is considered basic preparation for many human services. This is not typically the primary focus, however, in early childhood special education personnel preparation, which focuses more on curricular issues and program planning. Learning healthy boundary setting is valuable for personnel preparation for birth-to-3 programs, probably because of the intimate often home-based nature of the programs (McWilliam, P.J., 2000; McWilliam, R. 2005; Pawl, 2000; Thomas, Cooke, & Scott, 2005). Healthy boundary setting needs to be a central and vital element for team members working with preschool-aged children who have disabilities as well. This is certainly supported by major organizations, such as the National Association for the Education of Young Children (NAEYC) (Hyson, 2003) and the Division for Early Childhood (DEC) (Sandall, Hemmeter, Smith, & McLean, 2005). NAEYC Standards 2 and 5 are especially relevant. DEC/CEC Standards 9 and 10, on professionalism and collaboration, are central to these themes.

Dispositions

On a practical level, personal and professional dispositions are often important as people begin to work together. These include qualitative factors, such as a tone of mutual respect. Dispositions play a special role in relationships with families. Team members are all people whether they are professionals, family members, or both. The oath taken by doctors is fitting: "First, do no harm."

Boundaries and Interactive Style

Another crucial aspect of dispositions relates to boundaries and interactive style. Families have varying styles and preferences regarding social interaction. Sometimes these differences relate to personalities, sometimes to cultural variation, and sometimes to both. What is a professional to do in order to interact effectively with families? Figure 3.4 provides some factors to consider as you reflect on your interactive style.

Are you aware of your own customs regarding interactive styles? Are there ways of communicating that are outside your comfort zone?

Are you aware of supports you might need to help you move beyond a realm that is more familiar to you?

Do you have strategies for working through your own uncertainty and/or anxiety regarding sensitive situations?

FIGURE 3.4 Sensitive Interactions

The Importance of Communication

An important part of communication is to listen well and fully. Rather than assume that families want abundant information, it helps to observe, pick up on cues, and allow ample room for expression of a whole range of feelings and communication about the details of an individual child's needs. Active listening and a supportive tone are important in establishing rapport and trust with families. Once begun, this process will hopefully continue to develop and will continue to provide a context for solving problems and developing programs. Listening well and offering supportive feedback are valuable in clarifying central issues and putting them in perspective (Meanden, Ostrosky, & Halle, 2006). Sometimes family members and professionals get along exceptionally well. This does not always happen, however, and it is just as important for professionals to know how to communicate effectively with family members with whom they may not have much in common as it is for them to communicate effectively with those who have similar perspectives and worldviews. Demonstrating respect for others regardless of agreement is a good starting place. Team members should treat others as they wish to be treated and attempt to understand the perspectives of others.

Building Trust

When professionals and family members interact, trust is the basis of their relationship building. As Erik Erikson (1962) so wisely noted, trust is at the heart of the connections people have with one another. It is integral to attachments and associations. A discussion of the importance of teams would be incomplete without the recognition of the central need for trust. We can play active roles in the creation of classroom and program atmospheres that contribute to high levels of trust through the ways in which we interact with each other. Professionals can nurture a climate of trust by demonstrating reliability, honest, respect, mutuality, and shared commitment to the provision of high-quality inclusive services.

Clarification of Misunderstandings

Misunderstanding is easy; clarification of a misunderstanding takes concerted effort. Even professionals in the same field often experience misunderstandings. Everyone does not always have the same information, but there may be an assumption that if professionals share the same title and credentials, they will know the same things and share the same perspective. Of course, this is not true, and it is from this assumption that many misunderstandings develop. If two people from the same field can have a misunderstanding, then certainly diverse team members such as family members and professionals from different fields can easily develop misunderstandings. One way to clarify misunderstandings is to review plans often and review the details of the plans using everyday language, not professional jargon. Another technique that will help to remedy or even prevent misunderstandings is to put everything in writing and not assume that everyone will remember important information. We all have different learning styles and can use all the help available to totally understand a situation.

Conflict Resolution

Conflicts from many possible sources occur among groups of people. Sometimes personality differences contribute to people rubbing each other the wrong way. Sometimes there are genuine disagreements regarding programmatic issues. Sometimes one team member has a stronger connection with a child and/or parent than does another. These and other factors may be challenging for the team; they can often be resolved, especially in a climate of mutual respect where it is understood that people do not have to agree with each other in order to get along and work together. Being willing to communicate openly about issues is vital. This is not, however, always easy, especially with very sensitive subjects. It is helpful when team members are supportive and willing to work together to resolve differences. Sometimes this means "agreeing to disagree" or refocusing the situation on shared priorities.

Humor

When misunderstandings occur, it is very helpful to maintain perspective, to avoid taking things personally, and to sustain good humor. It is also important to remember that misunderstanding is part of the human condition, in part due to the infinite complexity of personalities, motivations, and experiences and in part because different people process similar experiences differently. Clearly, good humor requires a highly attuned sense of respect and appreciation for others' boundaries and values. Making fun of another's sacred beliefs is not an appropriate use of humor in a professional context. Being willing to consider the potential for something to be misconstrued or to have unintended consequences is integral to reflective practice, as is receptivity to constructive feedback from other team members.

Use of Active Listening and Reading Cues

Imagine a person with arms folded across the chest, eyes focused out the window or toward the ceiling. These behaviors are cues that a person is feeling uncomfortable about something. We must read the cues individuals exhibit as well as our own cues so that we do not unintentionally offend someone. Often while working as part of a team, parents are greatly outnumbered by professionals. It is very easy for a parent to become intimidated and withdraw, thus removing himself or herself as an active participant in a meeting or a process.

Engaging in active listening can be beneficial for all involved. Active listening is a way of listening and responding to another person that improves mutual understanding. In active listening, one listens for meaning. Often when people talk to each other, they do not listen attentively. They are frequently distracted, half listening and half thinking about something else. When people are engaged in a conflict, they are often busy formulating their response to what is currently being said. They may assume that they have heard what the other person is saying many times before, so rather than pay attention, they focus on how they can respond to win the argument. Active listening is a structured form of listening and responding that focuses attention on the speaker. The listener must take care to attend to the speaker fully and then repeats, in the listener's own words, what he or she thinks the speaker has said. The listener does not have to agree with the speaker but must simply state what he or she thinks the speaker said. This enables the speaker to find out whether the listener has really understood and, if not, explain further.

Mutual Respect

Mutual respect is another aspect of interaction between professionals and families. Mutual respect is conveyed in many ways. It is important for professionals to check in with themselves and make sure they are effectively communicating their regard for those with whom they work. It sets the tone for family-centered interaction with mutual decision making. Consequently, with mutual decision making as a central feature of team building, families have the opportunity to lead and direct the course of their children's futures. Such leadership has certainly been evident in the international initiative to increase inclusive practices. Families have become powerful advocates for their children and have worked effectively within systems to enforce changes in programs and laws. The paradigm shift from asking *whether* children with disabilities will be included to asking *how* children with disabilities will be included is most likely a result of persistent advocacy on the part of families, internationally, in a concerted effort, over several decades.

Perspective Taking and the Need for Shared Goals

It would be quite challenging for team members to share perspectives and mutually agreed on outcomes if each did not participate in the development of goals or at least agree with the goals as stated. Divergent opinions and practices come from the variety of professionals who serve as team members for a specific child and family. All parties will not design the same goals. It is critical that the family, classroom teacher, and specialists who work with a child all provide perspectives to be considered, so the team can develop common goals that will enhance the child's development. Team members who are involved in providing services to young children with special needs and their families are not always in the same physical place at the same time, and this makes having shared goals especially important. Harris and Klein (2002) describe the challenges of itinerant consultation in early childhood special education as related to the movement toward full inclusion. Working with professionals in a variety of contexts, with varying levels of support for teamwork and varying levels of training for inclusion, requires a great deal of emphasis on shared goals.

Communication Between Home and School

Communication in school settings is often one way. Notes home often just go home. Notes from home to school are often just as one way and only serve the purpose of information delivery. Effective communication must be two way. For communication to enhance and support perspective taking, all individuals involved need to develop and agree to ground rules regarding how and when communication will take place. Consent must be obtained in order to engage in the kind of ongoing, detailed communication between professionals that can really enhance the potential for success for a child. Assumptions of understanding are risky. Professionals must be willing to check in for understanding with other team members on a regular basis. Even professionals and parents who have had years of experience with inclusion and service to children can still easily make erroneous assumptions. Checking in for understanding maintains relationships and supports the flow of information (Anderson, Chitwood, Hayden, & Takemoto, 2008; Hanson & Lynch, 2004).

One effective strategy for increasing efficiency in communication with families is to use simple picture schedules that can be tailored for each student as he or she reviews what occurred during the day. Specific activities can be easily identified from a menu of choices to leave more time for specific communication regarding notable experiences or anecdotes.

TEAMS

Roles and Responsibilities: Functions

Generally, a team needs to clarify roles, responsibilities, and identified functions. Sometimes roles and functions come with the territory of a specific job title or description. Other times roles and responsibilities are well established and accepted, as with certain family dynamics. Sometimes, they are flexible, and other times roles and functions may need to be revisited to determine alternative possibilities. Sometimes roles and responsibilities are maintained as habits, without having been questioned. Whatever the case, when teams, including families, get together to address the unique needs of children, it helps tremendously if the team can discuss individual roles and functions to decide together about positive options (Hanson & Lynch, 2004). It helps when options are explored together and joint decisions can be made regarding program planning, which includes setting priorities and adapting curricula. When teams have a full sense of family priorities and children's interests, it is much more feasible to effectively plan and implement differentiated instruction. Universal design implies mutuality and shared decision making.

Collaborative Decision Making

To fully engage in a collaborative process for decision making, it is useful to have an awareness of interaction patterns, some of which may be related to established roles within a team. For instance, if, a father is accustomed to making financial decisions and a mother is more involved with the day-to-day care of children, these patterns are likely to continue in team dynamics. On the other hand, it is possible to acknowledge the dynamics that exist and intentionally work together to change some of the patterns. This is certainly true for professionals as well. Some team members may be more inclined to assume leadership, while others may be quieter, especially in the context of a group. When this sort of dynamic is acknowledged, it may be possible to adjust the patterns of interaction. Focusing on patterns of strength and areas that may need to be adjusted provides a structure for reframing.

Models of Teams

One feature of teamwork is referred to as "role-release" within a **transdisciplinary model** (Linder, 1992/2007). Essentially, this involves team members with expertise in specific areas such as speech and language communicating with other team members about specific strategies and perspectives. When effectively implemented, this can increase the sense of self-efficacy of all team members. At the same time, when all members of a team increase their skill levels and capacities, they are less likely to feel anxious. **Interdisciplinary**, **multidisciplinary**, and **transdisciplinary** teams may have some overlap in features. There are some programs, however, that maintain specific distinctive features of certain models. Table 3.1 provides an overview of different elements of team models.

Importance of Avoiding Stereotyping

Team members are wise to avoid stereotyping each other or assuming that they know what others are thinking or feeling. Mutual involvement and shared decision making are integral to healthy team building (Stayton, Miller, & Dinnebiel, 2003). Understanding that each family is different, will react differently, and has different resources makes working with each child and family unique. Each family's intervention will therefore need to be tailored for that particular family's strengths, needs, and priorities (Bailey & Powell, 2005; McWilliam, 2005).

Overcoming Misconceptions About Professionalism

Anecdotally, it is not uncommon for new teachers to feel as though they have the answers to all the world's questions. If that is not possible, some teachers feel that at least they should know more than families. Family members may actually have much more information about their child's unique needs because they have a vested interest and also have the responsibility of caring for their child 7 days a week, 24 hours a day. Professionals sometimes mistakenly assume that they need to know more than the family members with whom they are working. Having unrealistic expectations can result in immobilizing anxiety and a sense of impossibility. Such distress is not useful or productive.

Professionals should try not to be threatened if parents use big words such as *mucopolysaccharidosis*. There may be many times when professionals actually do have more information than families, but such an imbalance in information is not a requirement for the role. Reducing defensiveness is important for all involved in order to avoid power differentials. It is, however, important that teachers know where to get information and understand well enough how service delivery is coordinated in order to navigate the systems. The following powerful statement from a parent speaks to these issues.

My son, Nick, was diagnosed with mucopolysaccharidosis at age 4 years, 8 months, after dozens of evaluations by medical and education professionals. I was shocked, heartbroken, and devastated, when I read what little information I could find about the disease. For Nick's type of MPS, the prognosis indicated death at a young age in severely demented, bedridden state. And what became clear almost immediately was that few professionals in either field had ever heard of or worked with a child with mucopolysaccharidosis type IIIa. Thus it became my mission to comb through medical textbooks and research articles, to track down and

TABLE 3.1   Models of Teams

Component	Multidisciplinary	Interdisciplinary	Transdisciplinary
Philosophy of team interaction	The importance of contributions from several disciplines is recognized	Responsibility for services among disciplines is shared among team members	Team members commit to teach, learn, and work across disciplinary boundaries to plan and provide integrated services
Family role	Families may meet separately with team members according to discipline	The family may or may not participate as an active team member. Representatives or the whole team may work with family	Families are always full members of the teams, determining their own team roles
Communication	Communication is often informal. Members may not think of themselves as part of a team	Regular team meetings are held for communication regarding children's progress	Regular team meetings are held to share information and to teach and learn across disciplines (for consultations, team building, etc.)
Staff development	Professional development is frequently focused on separate disciplines	Professional development is often shared across disciplines	Professional development across disciplines is essential to team development and role transition
Assessment process	Separate assessments are completed by specialists in different disciplines/ domains	Domain-specific assessment is conducted, with shared results	Arena assessment is conducted by team, observing and recording across disciplines
IEP/IFSP development	Separate plans for intervention are developed within each discipline	The team works together to develop goals by discipline, then the goals are shared with the team to form a plan	Staff and family develop a plan together based on family concerns, priorities, and resources
IEP/IFSP implementation	Team members implement their plan separately by discipline	Team members implement parts of the plan for which their disciplines are responsible	Team members share responsibility and are accountable for how the plan is implemented by one person, with the family

Sources: From Garland, C. G., McGonigel, J. J., Frank, A., & Buck, D. (1989). *The transdisciplinary model of service delivery.* Lightfoot, VA: Child Development Resources; and Woodruff, G., & Hanson, C. (1987). *Project KAI training packet.* Unpublished manuscript. Funded by the U.S. Department of Education, Office of Special Education Programs, Handicapped Children's Early Education Program.

speak with experts scattered throughout the US and other counties, so that I could learn about MPS type IIIa and share what I knew with others who treated and worked with him. I knew I could not save Nick's life, nor could I change the course of his illness. At the time, palliative care was the only option. But I believed with all my heart that helping others to understand him was the key to ensuring that, qualitatively, his life would be the best it could possibly be. To be sure, there were professionals who interpreted my attempts to communicate the knowledge I had gained as interference. But there were others who openly admitted their ignorance.

I will be forever grateful to the doctors, nurses and teachers who partnered me in this spirit of cooperation.

M. Lynn Castelli (2009)—Personal Communication

REFLECTION IN ACTION
MS. LIGHTBORNE

Ms. Lightborne often leaves school feeling the weight of the world on her shoulders, largely because of how very responsible she feels. One of the children in her class this year has significant challenges, and Ms. Lightborne genuinely feels sorry for this girl's family. The child's parents are young and have three children under 5 years. With the economic pressures intensifying, the child's father is working longer hours and worries that he will lose his job and, with it, the family's health insurance. Ms. Lightborne sometimes aches with wanting to "fix it" for this family, as well as all the others. Also, she worries that having the television on at home all the time was adding to this child's language delays, but she doesn't know how to address this with the family without sounding critical.

Over time, however, Ms. Lightborne began to realize that providing support, information, and resources to this family was genuinely helpful. She did not need to "rescue" or "fix" this family. As she grew to understand this more deeply through reflection, she also began to appreciate the strengths of the family and how they were learning to cope with their situation collectively. Ms. Lightborne began to notice how the family had fun and how they were increasingly able to manage their challenges. She also began to notice how she was internally adding one stressor on top of another and how that was contributing her feeling of being overwhelmed. She has begun to look at challenges differently, rather than just loading one on top of another.

Choice or No Choice?

When professionals choose to specialize in early childhood special education, they are expected to exhibit a willingness to address exceptionalities. Because early childhood education professionals are expected to address exceptionalities with the presumption of inclusion, some professionals must learn to be accepting and willing. In some ways, there may be emotional parallels between parents and professionals while they are learning to accept the developmental differences in some children. This process is supported by learning to focus on both strengths and needs.

Situations with Multiple Service Providers

In an ideal world, a child and family would receive services through a one-stop-shopping approach. Developing relationships with multiple service providers and possibly having to actually go to several different locations to obtain those services raise the likelihood that a family will not avail themselves of the service. In addition to the physical strain of

REFLECTION IN ACTION

MR. FRESHETTE

For the most part, Mr. Freshette communicates quite well with other team members. In fact, he has noticed that being the only male staff member can at times be an advantage. He does, however, admit to not feeling confident when interacting with the families. This is especially true with parents who are much older than he is. He just doesn't think he has much to offer and gets stuck beating himself up about this. There is no question that he wants to help. He just isn't sure where to start sometimes.

Over time, he has come to realize that no one besides himself expects him to have all the answers. He can be compassionate and resourceful, especially by accessing relevant information from the Internet. Fortunately, his supervisor is very skilled at using reflective supervision, and this process has helped him work through his own self-doubt. Transforming his insecurity into humility has worked well.

Family-centered practices provide opportunities for full participation on teams.

engaging in that kind of service procurement, the philosophy and interactive process with the family may be quite different from provider to provider. This could cause considerable problems. More paperwork, more professionals, conflicting schedules, and different methods of payment are issues that can be a real deterrent to actual participation in the services available. Coordination of services helps families greatly (Allred, Briem, & Black, 2003).

Need for Recordkeeping and Accountability

Recordkeeping is a crucial part of working within a collaborative process. Recordkeeping enhances accountability, engages everyone in the process, and serves as a constant reminder of what needs to be done for children and their families (Hanson & Lynch, 2004).

To be nonjudgmental, one must be committed to an ongoing process of reflection, questioning one's own assumptions and being willing to adjust as needed. One must be willing to observe, listen, and reframe situations to gain a better understanding. Although most would not proceed in a haphazard way, even professionals who are careful can have misunderstandings. How we address these misunderstandings matters greatly in the big picture. If we are able to clarify, regroup, and move on, then this behavior allows for healthy growth and the development of trust. Blaming, judging, and being defensive serve no productive or healthy purpose, but there are many times when these dynamics occur as unwanted side effects of challenge. The more team members can sustain shared goals, the more likely they are to work together in constructive ways. This may at times involve team members providing honest feedback and suggestions.

Transition Planning

An essential component of inclusion is transition planning (Rous & Hallam, 2007). As children make transitions to other programs and levels, team members should strongly consider inclusive options. This is extremely important when children move from an infant/toddler program to a preschool educational program. During the planning process, professionals should encourage visits to the available inclusive programs and frankly discuss the advantages and disadvantages of each option. This has huge implications for intervention. For students with exceptionalities to transition to appropriate inclusive settings, there needs to be a well-developed coordinating capacity among those involved, and the parents must be well informed and involved in determining all the options. Figure 3.3 is a simple sample consent form for release of information. Different programs usually have their own forms, with similar content, required by law.

EMOTIONS

The topic of families evokes emotions for people, whether they are professionals, parents, or siblings of children with disabilities. Because the topic of families is not a subject processed entirely on a cognitive level, team problem-solving and information, active engagement in team problem-solving and planning may be a motivating coping strategy for families. Being effective in accomplishing specific, attainable goals may make one

Take a few minutes to identify significant aspects of your own experience and/or family history. Are there sensitive issues, "sacred cows," you need to be aware of?

FIGURE 3.5 Personal Inventory

more comfortable processing and accepting difficult emotions. A fixed, single sequence of emotions and specific goals applicable to all families does not exist. Emotional responses vary from family to family and sometimes even within families. It helps when there is a structure in which family members are actively involved, making important decisions during an ongoing process of service coordination (Dunst & Bruder, 2006). It also helps for professionals to be in touch with personal feelings and have comprehensive support systems that make it possible for them to be psychologically available to families. It may be helpful to continue the personal inventory you began earlier in the book. Figure 3.5 provides some guidance as you continue with your personal inventory.

Self-Confidence

Working together with other team members can increase the perception of being able to do what is necessary, which is sometimes called self-efficacy, agency, or self-confidence. People may be extremely competent within other realms but may not have had the sorts of experience that would enable them to generalize those feelings to working with children who are "differently abled." For some team members, this lack of familiarity and experience may contribute to fear or anxiety, which can be immobilizing, or it can interfere with the healthy development of trust. Fears and anxieties can, however, be transformed into more constructive engagement, especially if they are acknowledged and validated without judgment. Using statements such as "I can appreciate that this may be uncomfortable," "Are you feeling apprehensive?" or "Do you want to talk about what is going on?" can help others feel acknowledged and validated. Professionals should not convey a disregard for the feelings of others or be dismissive, and they should avoid saying things like "There's nothing to be afraid of!" While such statements may be well intended, they can inadvertently communicate a lack of regard for the emotions of others. We can be reassuring without judging others' feelings and responses. You may find it helpful to think about what words would be comforting and supportive to you in a similar situation. Always putting yourself in the family's position helps to set the parameters of the relationship you will have with the family.

Personal Scan

Any consideration of roles and interactive patterns brings up the need for a personal scan of one's own patterns. This is a well-established practice in multicultural education, given a long and unfortunate legacy of discrimination, bias, and unequal treatment. When social structures are in transition to become more equitable, there is a simultaneous need to address attitudes, beliefs, and behavior (Wah, 2004). When people have grown up in the context of societies that have well-established patterns of discrimination and misunderstanding, the process of changing people's dispositions does not occur immediately. It is appropriate for us to start with ourselves and be willing to take a good, honest look at our own previous experiences and beliefs. Such a personal scan may be facilitated by someone with experience in group process, but it also can occur through individual initiatives. It is far better for us to acknowledge our misconceptions and/or trepidations about children who have challenging conditions than to proceed in a state of denial of our own perspectives. If we acknowledge our initial beliefs, we are in a better position to question them and, perhaps, be open to change.

Overcoming Obstacles

When one feels anxious and unsure about how to proceed, obstacles to resolution may emerge. Often, these obstacles are preventable. It is understandable that professionals might feel anxious, especially when they are just beginning to work with children who have disabilities. They may be unsure what to say and do, and they may have unrealistic expectations of themselves. Cooperatively developing realistic goals with family members helps to ensure that all members of the team stay focused on their shared motivation: the needs of the child. There are many strategies to facilitate flexibility in team interaction. Active listening, guidance, and group brainstorming contribute to a range of options. Given the often intense parental feelings evoked by having a young child with a disability, it is important that professionals feel prepared to address emotions and to provide support while family members are sorting out new and challenging circumstances. This is especially true with very young children because families may be in the process of adjusting to the idea that a child has potentially lifelong developmental disabilities. There is tremendous power in acknowledging what is challenging. Such confirmation makes it possible to fully commit to addressing needs. It is equally important for professionals to know when and how to make referrals and/or access additional resources rather than assume that they can provide the entire solution (Turnbull, Turnbull, Erwin, & Soodak, 2007; Turnbull, Turnbull, & Wehmeyer, 2007). Support groups and counseling can be helpful.

Processing a Range of Emotions

Emotionally, a whole range of feelings is possible, from intense sadness to joy, anger, resentment, fear, or an overwhelming feeling of unfairness. Parents may or may not articulate their feelings directly, and it is important that professionals not make assumptions about which feelings are emerging. One mother of a child with Down syndrome reported being astonished when her family received a condolence card acknowledging the birth of her son rather than a card of celebration and congratulation. Deep processing of emotion takes many forms and also takes time. While the coordination of services for children must be done efficiently, the process of adjusting to parenting a child with a disability may not fit tidily into a set of legal policies, procedures, and time lines. As stated earlier, many books and articles focus on family-centered services. Much of the most powerful advocacy work has been led by families, such as the Turnbulls (Turnbull, Turnbull, 2004 & Wehmeyer, 2007). The practices they have established and written about are now widely accepted.

Many family advocacy initiatives have been actualized through transformation of the emotions generated by their circumstances. The focus of this book is specifically on practical levels of preparation, with an emphasis on reflection and considering options. This book is process oriented, providing structure and support for engaging in reflection about your own family background and interactive style, as well as options for considering flexibility in your responses. Recognizing this dimension of work with children, families, and teams is important (Hanft, Rush, & Sheldon, 2004).

Empathy

The simplest form of empathy is emotional empathy, which occurs quickly, without prior intention. Controlled empathy is more often cognitive empathy, which may be equated with perspective taking. Cognitive empathy is effortful and difficult to achieve. The success of controlled empathy is dependent on an individual's ability to find some perspectives regarding the experience that will induce the empathic state of mind (Hodges & Wegner, 1997).

Empathy Without Projection

In an effort to establish rapport and express their support, professionals sometimes tell frustrated and vulnerable parents, "I know just how you feel!" Clearly, unless a professional is also the parent of a child with a disability, he or she cannot possibly know how the parents feel and should find other ways to communicate support. We must learn to listen deeply to ourselves and consider the messages we are conveying, whether intentionally or unintentionally.

Nonjudgmental Acceptance

Professionals need to know how to work with families, whose members may represent a whole range of perspectives. Some, for example, may be angry at the world, as part of an expression of grief. Support can be provided without stereotyping other people's emotional experiences. It should not be assumed that families are experiencing a fixed sequence of developmental stages of mourning over their child's diagnosis and losing the dream of having a son or daughter who will develop typically. Not all parents grieve over such diagnoses. When parents are experiencing extreme emotions, it is especially essential that others not be judgmental, not assume that they have to "fix it," and not take it personally. This requires that the professional have a considerable level of maturity, and it also implies that it is okay for professionals to interact with families in a way that includes emotional dimensions. Professionals must have a clear sense of when and how not to take things personally, while at the same time being accountable and responsible. Being aware of one's own patterns of interaction and family dynamics can make it easier to maintain boundaries and be aware of when a situation may be reminiscent of a past, personal occurrence that might trigger or restimulate a reaction.

Being open to support and feedback increases the likelihood that issues will be resolved. Historical beliefs which asserted that professionals needed to keep a strict distance add perspectives to the current focus on **family-centered services**. Current views do not assert that distance is a prerequisite for professionalism.

Respect for Boundaries

Families and professionals vary enormously in their personal boundaries. Beyond the differences in style, such as extroverted compared with introverted, there are countless differences in values, beliefs, and needs for privacy. While confidentiality must always be respected, as specified in federal laws, personal differences in interpretation are worth noting. For instance, some families are comfortable with blanket consent forms covering photographs, videotapes, and observations. Others may be highly sensitive about such consent. It is important for professionals to honor the wishes and preferences of each family's boundaries. Some families are relatively comfortable talking about their child's disability, while others may find it difficult to use words to describe all the complexities of their thoughts, feelings, and challenges (Bailey & Powell, 2005). There are times when these variations may be related to cultural differences. Language fluency may also be a factor. There are other times when people simply have different personalities and interactive styles.

Dynamics and Cultural Perspectives

All of the topics covered in this chapter refer to families and teams and involve cultural considerations. Specific aspects may be clarified and highlighted to enhance understanding of the cultural dimension of reflection. While all families are unique, there are also cultural patterns that may or may not be significant in family dynamics (Derman-Sparks & Olsen Edwards, 2010; Hanson & Lynch, 2004). When a family is second- or third-generation Japanese, Bosnian, Latino, or Afghani, the ways in which cultural traditions affect daily routines and beliefs may be different than for a family that has recently relocated. Professionals need to be willing to be lifelong learners, including learning about cultural traditions and beliefs that may be different from their own. It is wise to pick up on cues from others, letting them provide guidance and direction in terms of how cultural dynamics are relevant to each unique family.

Implications for Interventions

Many think of *inclusion* as an educational term only. Actually, inclusion in the early childhood years emphasizes full involvement of a child in family routines and social activities with relatives and friends, in addition to participating in the entire spectrum of educational and recreational opportunities that communities provide (Bruder, 2001; Dunst, 2001). Inclusion is not static or confined to one environment. Inclusion is fluid and should be the focus of everything planned for children with disabilities and their families. When working in inclusion settings, working with a child with disabilities is only part of the whole inclusion experience.

Working with a team that is involved with a child with disabilities is essential. The family is one very important part of the team. The remainder of the team may contain various specialists, including occupational therapists, physical therapists, speech and language therapists, and vision specialists. Organizing a functional working team that can communicate for the purpose of maximizing a child's potential is not an easy task. Building a team out of a group of professionals and parents takes time and great sensitivity. Working as part of that team means that each member must have equal voice, develop trust in the other team members, and listen to new ways of doing and being. To implement effective intervention, all participants need to be able to develop and use the same lens to view progress and pitfalls.

Shared goals and strategies must be put into action to create a team perspective. These shared goals need to attend to the child's academic development, social-emotional development, and physical growth; the effectiveness of the classroom environment; and the consistency of implemented strategies across multiple contexts such as school, home, recreational settings, social settings, and family groupings. Creating "communities of practice" has been a positive initiative (Buysse & Wesley, 2006; Winton, McCollum, & Catlett, 2007).

If a child has been through an early intervention program and is now entering a preschool program, new trust relationships must be developed between all parties responsible for providing the opportunity for inclusion (Rous & Hallam, 2007). Sometimes inclusion may not appear to be working because all relevant information is not being shared by all involved. In the absence of important information, the quality of parent–child transactions can be compromised. Inclusion is not a competition; it is collaborative and cooperative. If inclusion is effective, all involved are winners. Because each child and his or her family has different needs that require intervention based upon those needs, there is not a general recipe for intervention. One size does not fit all in terms of inclusion. Personalities of children, teachers, family members, and specialists need to be considered. Strengths and weaknesses of all involved need to be identified (Bailey & Powell, 2005). Common foci and purposes must be identified. Everyone on the team needs to serve as an advocate for each child and for the enhancement of inclusion opportunities and enriched services.

EXAMPLE 1   Meet the Children's Families

Karly's Family

Karly's parents have been very involved and supportive. Her parents decided to have a baby when they were older, after having been together as a couple for many years. Karly's extended family has been supportive and helpful. Karly's parents want her to have a full and happy social life as well as academic opportunities, so they are involved in many activities. They also schedule regular play dates with her friend. Karly's parents initiated the assessment process when she was 15 months old, based on observed language delays. They enjoy traveling, and that has been an important aspect of their family time. Karly is an only child.

Jessica's Family

Jessica has a large, lively family. She had three older siblings when she was born, ranging in age from 2 to 5, plus a loving dog, affectionately called Musty. Jessica's siblings and parents are very attentive to her needs. She is now the middle child with three younger siblings, aged 8 months to 3 years. Jessica's mother has a large extended family, many of whom live in the local community, within walking distance. Jessica's father lived with the family for 2 years after she was born and now lives in a nearby town. Jessica's mother has a live-in boyfriend who helps out with the children but also works two jobs so is not around much during the day and evening. Jessica is eligible for supplemental income because of her medical condition. She is also Medicaid eligible. She has a local pediatrician and also goes to routine clinic appointments at the children's hospital in a nearby city.

Sung Bin's Family

Sung Bin's birth family in Korea did not have the resources to support him. His adoptive family in the United States was devoted to providing optimal support. He was immediately enrolled in a high-quality early childhood program within the school system for 5 half-days per week. There he received physical, occupational, and speech and language therapies. He also attended a Montessori preschool program 5 half-days per week. The teachers at the Montessori school learned how to adapt the curriculum, use appropriate positioning, and integrate therapeutic techniques into the daily activities. There was full support from the director of special services in the local education agency. Over time, Sung Bin's family has been very supportive of his independence, including his current job, apartment, and engagement.

Resources

There are many excellent resources on the subject of early childhood inclusion. We strongly encourage you to explore those resources and develop your own sense of competence as you work with children and families. Your own ability to cope with unique and often unpredictable circumstances will surely be a support to families. Your perception of your competence and willingness to engage in continuing professional development regarding families and teams will greatly increase the likelihood that you will be effective in working with others. With appropriate support and resources, anxiety and uncertainty can be transformed into confidence.

Questions for Reflection

1. Through your reflection, note any aspects of working with families that may present challenges to you regarding belief systems or lifestyle. What strategies and resources might you use to address these issues?
2. How will you monitor your own progress as you work with families and children?
3. What recordkeeping strategies will be especially useful to you?
4. How will you express your empathy and support to families?
5. What roles have you played in teams?
6. Describe your interactive style.

Summary

We have discussed many important issues regarding working with families. Culture and belief systems play crucial roles in family styles and priorities. As practitioners, we must all incorporate ways to be lifelong learners. Developing and maintaining positive dispositions with respect for all families is central to the effectiveness of our work with children and their caregivers. Our effectiveness as we access and organize resources will greatly enhance our ability to advocate with families.

Key Terms

Family-centered practices   Multidisciplinary
Interdisciplinary   Transdisciplinary

Websites

Exceptional Parent
http://www.eparent.com

The Pacer Center, Minnesota
http://www.pacer.org/

The Waisman Center, University of Wisconsin
http://www.waismancenter.org

Center for Early Literacy Learning
http://www.earlyliteracylearning.org/pgparents.php

References

Allred, K., Briem, R., & Black, S. (2003). Collaboratively addressing the needs of young children with disabilities. In C. Copple (Ed.), *A world of difference.* (pp. 131–134). Washington, DC: NAEYC.

Anderson, W., Chitwood, S., Hayden, D., & Takemoto, C. (2008). *Negotiating the special education maze: A guide for parents and teachers* (4th ed.). Bethesda, MD: Woodbine House.

Bailey, D., & Powell, T. (2005). Assessing the information needs of families in early Intervention. In M. Guralnick (Ed.), *The developmental systems approach to early intervention* (pp. 151–184). Baltimore: Paul H. Brookes.

Banks, R., Santos, R. M., & Roof, V. (2003). Discovering family concerns, priorities, and resources: Sensitive family information gathering. *Young Exceptional Children, 6*(2), 11–19.

Barrera, I., Corso, R., & Macpherson, D. (2003). *Skilled dialogue: Strategies for responding to cultural diversity in early childhood.* Baltimore: Paul H. Brookes.

Batshaw, M. (2001). *When your child has a disability.* Baltimore: Paul H. Brookes.

Batshaw, M., Pelligrino, L., & Roizen, N. (Eds.). (2007). *Children with disabilities.* In M. Guralnick (Ed.), *The developmental systems approach to early intervention* (6th ed., pp. 151–184). Baltimore: Paul H. Brookes.

Bronfenbrenner, U. (1992). Ecological systems theory. In R. Vasta (Ed.), *Six theories of child development: Revised formulations and current issues* (pp. 187–248). Philadelphia: Jessica Kingsley.

Bruder, M. B. (2001). Inclusion of infants and toddlers: Outcomes and ecology. In M. J. Guralnick (Ed.), *Early childhood inclusion: Focus on change* (pp. 203–228). Baltimore: Paul H. Brookes.

Buysse, V., & Wesley, P. (Eds). (2006). *Evidence-based practices in the early childhood field.* Washington, DC: Zero-to-Three.

Cheatham, G., & Milagros Santos, R. (2005). A-B-Cs of bridging home and school expectations. *Young Exceptional Children, 8*(3), 3–11.

Corso, R., Santos, R., & Roof, V. (2002). Honoring diversity in early childhood education materials. *Teaching Exceptional Children, 34*(3), 30–36.

Derman-Sparks, L. & Olsen Edwards, J. (2010). *Anti-bias education for young children and ourselves.* Washington, DC: National Association for the Education of Young Children.

Dunst, C. J. (2001). Participation of young children with disabilities in community learning activities. In M. J.Guralnick (Ed.), *Early childhood inclusion: Focus on change* (pp. 307–333). Baltimore: Paul H. Brookes.

Dunst, C., & Bruder, M. B. (2006). Early intervention service coordination models and service coordinator practices. *Journal of Early Intervention, 28*(3), 155–165.

Erikson, E. (1962). *Childhood and society* (2nd ed.). New York: Norton.

Erwin, E., Soodak, L., Winton, P., & Turnbull, A. (2001). "I wish it wouldn't all depend on me:" Research on families and early childhood inclusion. In M. Guralnick (Ed.), *Early childhood inclusion: Focus on change.* Baltimore: Paul H. Brookes.

Garland, C. G., McGonigel, J. J., Frank, A., & Buck, D. (1989). *The transdisciplinary model of service delivery.* Lightfoot, VA: Child Development Resources.

Guralnick, M. (Ed.). (2001). *Early childhood inclusion.* Baltimore: Paul H. Brookes.

Guralnick, M. (Ed.). (2005). *The developmental systems approach to early intervention.* Baltimore: Paul H. Brookes.

Hanft, B., Rush, D., & Shelden, M. (2004). *Coaching families and colleagues in early childhood.* Baltimore: Paul H. Brookes.

Hanson, M., & Lynch, E. (2004). *Developing cross-cultural competence* (3rd ed.). Baltimore: Paul H. Brookes.

Hanson, M. & Lynch, E. (2004). *Understanding families.* Baltimore: Paul H. Brookes.

Harris, K. C., & Klein, M. D. (2002). The consultant's corner: Itinerant consultation in early childhood special education: Issues and challenges. *Journal of Educational and Psychological Consultation, 14,* 237–247.

Hodges, S. D., & Wegner, D. M. (1997). Automatic and controlled empathy. In W. Ickes (Ed.), *Empathic accuracy.* New York: Guilford Press.

Hyson, M. (Ed.). (2003). *Preparing early childhood professionals: NAEYC's standards for programs.* Washington, DC: National Association for the Education of Young Children.

Kalyanpur, M., & Harry, B. (1999). *Culture in special education.* Baltimore: Paul H. Brookes.

Linder, T. (1992). *Transdisciplinary play-based assessment.* Baltimore: Paul H. Brookes.

Lopez, E., Salas, L., & Flores, J. (2005). What about assessment and intervention? *Young Children, 60,* 48–54.

LaRocco, D., & Bruns, D. (2005). Advocacy is only a phone call away. *Young Exceptional Children, 8*(4), 11–18.

Maschinot, B. (2008). *The changing face of the United States: The influence of culture on early child development.* Washington, DC: Zero to Three.

McWilliam, P. J. (2000). *Lives in progress: Case stories in early intervention.* Baltimore: Paul H. Brookes.

McWilliam, R. (2005). Assessing the resource needs of families in the context of early intervention. In M. Guralnick (Ed.), *The developmental systems approach to early intervention* (pp. 215–234). Baltimore: Paul H. Brookes.

Meandan, H., Ostrosky, M., & Halle, J. (2006). "What? I Don't Understand;" and "Pardon?": Using communication breakdowns to encourage communication. *Young Exceptional Children, 9*(3), 2–9.

Ostrosky, M., & Lee, H. (2005). Developing culturally and linguistically responsive teams for early intervention: Promising practices. In Horn, E. & Jones, H. (Eds.), *Interdisciplinary teams.* Monograph Series No. 6. (pp. 21–32). Longmont, CO: Sopris West/DEC.

Pavri, S., & Fowler, S. (2001). *Child find, screening and tracking: Serving culturally diverse children and families.* Champagne, IL: Early Childhood Research Institute on Culturally and Linguistically Appropriate Services.

Pawl, J. (2000). The interpersonal center of the work we do. Washington, DC: *Zero to Three, 20*(4), 5–7.

Rous, B. & Hallam, R. (2007). *Tools for transition in early childhood.* Baltimore: Paul H. Brookes.

Sandall, S., Hemmeter, M. L., Smith, B., & McLean, M. (2005). *Recommended practice: A comprehensive guide.* Longmont, CO: Sopris West.

Stayton, V., Miller, P., & Dinnebeil, L. (2003). *Personnel preparation in early childhood special education: Implementing the DEC recommended practices.* Longmont, CO: Sopris West.

Thomas, R., Cooke, B., & Scott, M. (2005). Strengthening parent–child relationships: The reflective dialogue parent education design. *Zero to Three, 26*(3), 27–34.

Turnbull, A., Turnbull, R., Erwin, E., & Soodak, L. (2007). *Families, professionals, and exceptionality* (5th ed.). Upper Saddle River, NJ: Merrill/Pearson Education.

Turnbull, R., Turnbull, A., Shank, M., & Smith, S. (2004). *Exceptional lives* (4th ed.). Upper Saddle River, NJ: Merrill/Pearson Education.

Wah, L. M. (2004). *The art of mindful facilitation.* Oakland, CA: Stir Fry Seminars and Consulting Useful Resources.

Chapter 4

Assessment

OBJECTIVES

After reading this chapter, students will:

▪ Have a clear overview of major issues regarding assessment and the variety of available options;

▪ Identify ways in which reflection can be used during the process of assessment;

▪ Consider ways in which choices are made regarding types of assessment;

▪ Identify positive ways to communicate with families during assessment;

▪ Recognize and reflect on relevant cultural perspectives;

▪ Use reflection to interpret data from various sources, identifying current levels of **performance** for children;

▪ Recognize basic legal factors as they relate to assessment; and

▪ Identify personal strengths and areas of need in the implementation of assessment, along with resources to help.

INTRODUCTION

High-quality assessment is essential for all young children, those with exceptionalities and those who are developing typically. Assessment has many purposes and functions, including the implementation of appropriate curricular adaptations after the child's current performance level has been determined. Most important, assessment conveys a full, clear, and accurate representation of each child over time. This book addresses the issues of support and their relationship to adaptations during the reflective process of matching strategies to each child's characteristics. Assessment is at the heart of reflective process because a good match between child and adaptation cannot be made without an accurate and valid sense of each child's levels of functioning and abilities. The thrust of this chapter will be on ways in which reflection during assessment enhances the practical implementation of programs.

Assessment is essential and highlighted here are some of its more salient aspects. First, as professionals evaluate children and families, they should approach assessment from a strengths-based perspective. Although a child's area of concern is what makes him or her eligible for special services, it is not acceptable to focus primarily on deficits. Second, professionals should ensure that the assessment's representations of children are accurate and descriptive; this has a direct effect on how we can develop strategies to meet their needs. A young child's development is dynamic; what was true for a child a month ago may have now changed. Third, professionals must engage in ethical methods of assessment. This includes honoring confidentiality and legal protocol regarding accountability, roles, and responsibilities (Noonan & McCormick, 2006; Walsh & Taylor, 2006). Finally, professionals must understand that increasing the ability to assess the strengths and needs of young children and families can make them better at preventing complicating conditions, including the cycles of environmental risk (Farran, 2005; Hilliard, 1997; Stormont, 2007).

Some early childhood training programs have courses focused on early childhood assessment. Other programs cover the assessment of young children with developmental challenges in one session. If you have had the benefit of a more comprehensive

TABLE 4.1	Did You Know? Overview of Assessment	
Topic	**Relevant Factor**	**Reflective Elements**
Types of assessment	Continuum	Selection of types of assessment that best address the child's status/condition.
Family and team factors	Family centered; Different team models	Consideration of differences; Building trust; Communication
Cultural factors	Integration of and response to relevant information	Appreciation of and respect for diversity
Determination of current level of performance	Across all developmental domains	Accurately assessing, without bias
Determining eligibility; legal issues	Using data to identify	Identifying need and communicating status
Interpreting and summarizing results	Carefully consolidating and sharing information	Consideration of what is important, including strengths as well as needs.

opportunity, you may find it sufficient to scan some of the sections of this chapter. If you have had limited experience with the assessment of young children with challenges, you may want to supplement this chapter with some of the resources at the end of the chapter. There are many books and comprehensive resources available on the topic of assessment (Bondurant-Utz, 2002; McLean, Bailey, & Wolery, 2004; Meisels & Atkins-Burnett, 2005; Mindes, 2003; Popham, 2005). It would be helpful to use those comprehensive materials and to understand the context in which assessment is presented in this book. Table 4.1 provides an overview of topics covered in this chapter.

In this text, a developmental approach is used; team members with a background in typical development already have a framework from which to consider exceptionalities. Children who are eligible for special services are outside the range of what is considered typical in at least one domain of development (Guralnick, 2005; Hyson, 2003). Those who have a solid conceptual framework in exceptional development can build on that foundation, studying the characteristics of children with different conditions (Batshaw et al., 2007; Neisworth & Bagnato, 2005). Through a focus on reflective process, this book encourages the reader to observe, develop hypotheses regarding a child's challenges, create and implement ways to test the hypotheses, and interpret data. This book uses response to intervention (RTI), or scientifically based instructional strategies.

At its best, assessment is a dynamic process through which we can determine each child's current level of performance, adjust what we are doing, and use formative measures to document children's progress. The cycle of assessment and intervention provides the basis for active planning to address each child's unique pattern of strengths and needs to support optimal development.

Readers can use this book as a resource that can be adapted for an individual's own level of expertise, supporting the process of considering programmatic options and reflecting on the child in question. Beginning special education teachers may doubt their own ability. Given the tremendous complexity of each child's unique developmental patterns and the many variables affecting the dynamic of development, it is wise to approach assessment with a balanced combination of confidence and humility. It is not necessary to have all the answers, but it is dangerous to assert that which is not true.

To fully benefit from this chapter you should actively participate in applying the principles and practices as you read. It would be helpful for you think of one child with whom you have worked, and focus on this child as you actively reflect while reading. You can start by identifying characteristics of the child, including strengths and areas of concern.

Questions for Reflection Regarding Your Focus Child:

1. What are some of the more evident developmental issues for this child?
2. What are some of this child's interests and motivations?
3. What do you know about this child's family? Have you met them?
4. Are you familiar with the family's belief system, values, and culture?

When we are committed to high-quality assessment, then we are willing and able to work toward a deeper understanding of each child's strengths and needs. Over time, assessment can increase our collective understanding of what is occurring during the dynamic process of development. High-quality assessment ensures that we will do much more than just get a snapshot of the child's development upon which to base our knowledge of the child. Early childhood professionals should continue to consider the child's current level of performance over time. Professionals also assess other relevant elements, such as how a child approaches new tasks and whether he or she is actively problem solving and adjusting as needed.

Through documentation of developmental risks, the environment can be adjusted to intercept the negative trajectory, which may have long-term positive effects on a child's development. Rather than assume that there are going to be long-term developmental challenges, professionals can identify and address risk factors. There is strong research to support the belief in the power of healthy opportunities in early childhood (Shonkoff & Phillip, 2001). This long-term research has been substantiated over time and has made it possible for educators to work closely with policy makers and legislators to enhance the quality and quantity of early childhood education available to young children and families through programs such as Head Start and Family Resource Centers (Zigler & Styfco, 2004). Many terms have been used to describe the process of intervention as we gather information about children. In early childhood special education, the term "recognition and response" has been widely used (Buysse & Wesley, 2006).

Results-Based Accountability

Data-driven decision making, or **results-based accountability**, uses relevant assessment information about students to design or adjust programs. This can be done for groups as well as individuals. If the performance of a group of preschool children indicates that they have not yet mastered a particular concept such as patterns then teachers can adjust the experiential curriculum to include more of a focus on that concept. If results indicate that the group of preschool children understand and can demonstrate that concept, then this assessment can inform the teachers' practices, so instruction focuses on other concepts that need extra support.

Professionals and families collaborate in planning and implementing assessment.

Assessment is individualized and appropriate for the child and family.

Assessment provides useful information for intervention.

Professionals share information in respectful and useful ways.

Professionals meet legal and procedural requirements and meet Recommended Practice guidelines.

Source: Information from Sandall, Hemmeter, Smith, & McLean, 2005

FIGURE 4.1   DEC's Recommended Practices: Assessment

While understanding the development of a child who is experiencing difficulties can be daunting, it is extremely important that early childhood professionals make a commitment to do their very best. They should also feel comfortable seeking and advocating for support as needed. If a specialist, such as a speech and language therapist or occupational therapist is required, then a professional with advanced expertise should be involved in the process. Sometimes all that is needed is a consultation with the specialists. For other cases, a specialist might be a full member of the team.

Division for Early Childhood, Council for Exceptional Children

The Division for Early Childhood, Council for Exceptional Children (DEC/CEC) has identified a number of recommended practices regarding assessment. Among these practices is the use of multiple measures and being as free as possible of bias. An overview of DEC's A list of Recommended Practices for assessment is presented in Figure 4.1, with more complete information integrated into all chapters.

Historical Perspectives on Assessment

Special education assessment and research has changed over time. Increased information about disabilities has developed and clarified the **diagnoses** of syndromes. Technology has dramatically increased understanding of conditions, such as autism, through brain scans. Positron emission tomography (PET), magnetic resonance imaging (MRI), and computerized tomography (CT) scans have created many new ways to assess biological aspects of development . Increasingly, early childhood programs are using technology for assessment, especially with software that makes it possible to manage data. As more is learned about how the developing central nervous system is affected by environmental factors (Bailey, Bruer, Symons, & Lichtman, 2001), new horizons expand the ability to provide supports for young children. While the advent of new methods does not replace the value of high-quality observation and clear perspectives, we can enhance our understanding with new dimensions.

Reflection

Reflection during the process of assessment plays a central role and contributes to the results. Using reflection to consider issues and to problem solve can help professionals learn more about the sometimes complex characteristics of young children. Even when a child has a diagnosis of conditions such as autism or Down syndrome, early childhood professionals must still consider the characteristics of the individual child. When we engage in reflection during assessment, we step back from our presumptions. Instead of proceeding with an automatic, mechanical script, professionals can continually consider possibilities. Through reflection, observations are filtered and processed, which enhances their validity. Reflection can increase one's ability to thoughtfully consider a variety of factors that may affect a child's development, and to think about which factors might be the most important contributions to the outcome (Losardo & Notari-Syverson, 2001; Noonan, & McCormick, 2006). Such consideration, with an exploration of many variables, has the potential to yield a fuller understanding of each child, and ultimately a more reliable assessment of the child's development. Increased **reliability** also provides increased accountability. Increased accountability can enhance a professional's confidence in how he or she represents developmental outcomes and presents them to other team members. From the start, reflection can help to sort out multiple variables.

TYPES OF ASSESSMENT

There are many types of assessment from which to select multiple measures. Some of these are listed in Table 4.2, which represents a continuum of assessments ranging from informal, naturalistic measures to those that are more structured and formalized. Methods such as observation (Jablon, Dombro, & Dichtelmiller, 2007) are used

TABLE 4.2 Purposes and Types of Assessment: Overview

Assessment Type	Role(s) of Reflection
Observation	Importance of reducing bias and/or projection during process
Anecdotal records	Selection of relevant anecdotes
Work samples	Identification of samples and clear description of significance
Portfolios	Organization and selection so the documents are demonstrative of individual children
Running records/rubrics	Selection of salient features; recording information
Event sampling	Decisions regarding selection of events
Frequency counts	Importance of remaining astute, especially with behavior that may be relatively subtle.
Developmental inventories/surveys Criterion-referenced	Need for accurate reporting by all members of team.
screening instruments	Need for efficient development of rapport with children, to ensure best performance.
Functional behavioral assessment	Importance of interpreting information so it reflects the underlying contributing factors.
Play-based assessment	Use of reflection to efficiently engage children in activities.
Standardized instruments: **norm-referenced**	Importance of using observation during process of administering assessment.

with all children. Other methods, such as **standardized instruments**, are generally used systematically to identify eligibility for special services and gather more comprehensive information about a child's performance and potential (Guralnick, 2005). Table 4.2 provides an overview of multiple types of assessment.

Multiple Measures

When young children who are developing typically are assessed, multiple measures are chosen to gather and organize information including performance in different developmental domains. In contrast, with children whose development may be challenged, multiple measures of assessment are required by law (Guralnick, 2005; Losardo, & Notari-Stevenson, 2001; Neisworth & Bagnato, 2005). In addition to an inventory of quantitative data documenting strengths and areas of concern, documentation of qualitative factors must also be used.

Reflection can be especially useful when considering how various areas of a child's competence and difficulty impact each other, as well as how best to describe a child's attributes and dispositions. These perspectives balance out the quantitative data that is collected and analyzed. Formative and summative measures contribute to this balance.

Formative Assessment

Formative assessment includes any methods that involve gathering performance information in ways that directly inform intervention or teaching. In formative assessment, professionals identify areas of children's strengths and needs, include specific areas that warrant extra support, and adjust programs based on that information. Reflection is especially important during **formative assessment** because given the informal nature of these measures, one must be very careful to avoid preconceived expectations, bias, or subjectivity.

Observation

Observation has long been recognized as an essential process through which we can increase our understanding of children (Jablon, Dombro, & Dichtelmiller, 2007). Developing inter-rater reliability is very important to ensure that perspectives that are free from bias. When early childhood professionals observe, they need to document their perceptions, articulating what they see and hear (Jablon, Dombro, & Dichtelmiller, 2007; Losardo & Notari-Syverson, 2001). Observation can be done in various contexts, including structured and unstructured classroom activities as well as home environments. Some instruments such as the Early Childhood Environmental Rating Scale (ECERS), the Infant Toddler Environmental Rating Scale (ITERS), and Classroom Assessment Scoring System (CLASS) have been developed to guide observation in various settings (Harms & Clifford, 1980; Pianta, La Paro, & Hamre, 2007).

While observation may be viewed as a basic form of assessment, its power should not be underestimated. Given its open structure, it is especially important that team members are effectively able to monitor themselves and question. Observers must know developmental benchmarks as well as qualitative shifts and factors such as coping strategies that serve as internal compasses. They need to have a sense of how to ensure that their blind spots are addressed. Attunement increases the degree to which perspectives on each child are valid and reliable.

Anecdotal Records

Anecdotal records are important as we collect information using a variety of strategies (Losardo & Notari-Syverson, 2001). Anecdotal records include notes gathered from a range of contexts that document and demonstrate current level of performance and significant interactions. Anecdotal records can contribute valuable insights about children's development. Professionals use reflection to choose anecdotal records that might be used. Using anecdotal records to document a child's development is widely accepted. The decision, however, about what to include or not to include moves into a much deeper realm.

Initially, significant variables may not be obvious to observers. Professionals may observe events that seem to be developmentally significant, while events with more significance remain effectively obscured. Sometimes what is most obvious is not most developmentally significant. For instance, if a child is feeling extremely vulnerable and afraid, he or she might compensate by behaving in ways that hide his or her emotions. Boys are often given messages that say it is not okay to be afraid, and they may compensate by acting tough. It is important for early childhood professionals to tap into underlying emotions rather than to assume the behavior that is most apparent tells the whole story.

Work Samples

Work sampling is well-established protocol in the assessment of children who are developing typically, and increasingly it is being used with children who have exceptionalities. Meisels (1992) and Jablon, Dichtelmiller, and Dorfman (1994) have created a system for gathering and organizing work samples, which includes careful descriptions of each sample, elaborating on its significance and relevance as documentation of the performance level and style of each child. These samples can provide rich evidence of a child's strengths and needs. Work samples are especially useful in demonstrating change over time. Work samples might range from examples of a child's art to photo or video documentation of block building or play.

Event Samples

When a child demonstrates certain behaviors that require monitoring across contexts, a professional may create an event sample where he or she can observe and record that particular behavior in different settings. An event sample is a matrix that makes it possible to document occurrences of a specific behavior, such as using physical aggression instead of verbal requests.

Portfolios

Portfolios have been widely used with children across a developmental continuum. Portfolios include a variety of documents as evidence of development in many areas. They can include work samples, running records, event sampling, photographs and other measures of a child's performance. The documentation presented in the portfolio is generally gathered over time and provides an excellent opportunity to show growth. Professionals should carefully select the documents for the portfolio and ensure that it is organized. Organization and careful selection will contribute to the effectiveness of the portfolio as authentic assessment; (Lynch & Struewing, 2002). With advancing technology, electronic portfolios can include video clips of children engaged in activities, which can greatly enhance the potential for teachers and parents to communicate with each other about the strengths and needs of children.

Screening Instruments

Screening instruments provide a relatively efficient way to determine whether a child is performing within an expected range for his or her age across developmental domains (Gilliam, Meisels, & Mayes, 2005; Meisels, & Atkins-Burnett, 2005; Miller, 1993). Screening instruments are designed to be administered in 15 to 45 minutes, in contrast to a full-scale assessment which takes longer. If a child has difficulty with a screening instrument, it may not mean that he or she has a significant developmental delay or disability, but his or her performance would be considered a red flag and would warrant more in-depth assessment to explore areas of strength and concern.

A child's scores on a screening instrument are not necessarily representative of a child's true capability. If he or she has not had enough sleep, is not feeling well, or is intimidated by an unfamiliar setting, his or her performance might not represent skills he or she has mastered. Checking in with parents or familiar caregivers can be helpful in distinguishing between an accurate score and an inaccurate one. If a child performs well on a screening instrument this is usually indicative of healthy development. Reflection during the screening process can be very useful in establishing rapport and gathering information that best represents a child's true capability.

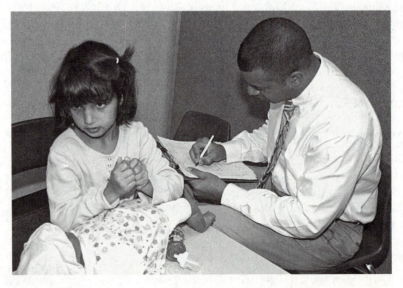

A variety of measures are used, based on children's characteristics and needs.

Generally, if a child does not perform well on a screening instrument, a more in-depth assessment is justified. An in-depth assessment sometimes is a comprehensive instrument addressing all developmental domains. However, if the screening process indicates a significant delay in one area, such as speech and language, the follow-up assessment may focus specifically on that area, and be done by a specialist (Gilliam, Meisels, & Mayes, 2005).

Ecological Assessment and Natural Environments

Early childhood professionals must consider the context in which we assess children's development. Historically, children were usually assessed exclusively in clinical contexts, which implied that the situation in which the assessment occurred was irrelevant. Increasingly, the assessment of children occurs in natural environments. These can be in the comfort of a child's home, in an early childhood center, or in a setting as representative as possible (McCormick & Noonan, 2002). There are many documented benefits of assessment in natural environments. One benefit is the opportunity to gather information that is authentically representative of a child's abilities (Ostrosky & Horn, 2002). Unfamiliar or intimidating situations can interfere with a child's optimal performance (Linder, 2008).

In ecological assessment, professionals carefully document environmental factors that may contribute to a child's performance such as structure, organization of room, interactions with other children, and the degree to which adults are responsive compared with directive (Ostrosky & Horn, 2002). The environment includes availability of appropriate toys as well as caregiving practices.

Play-Based Assessment

Play-based assessment creates an environment in which we can intentionally observe and document a child's performance in various contexts, such as structured play, unstructured play, play with a peer, and snack time (Linder, 2008). Assessment of children during play has evolved over many years, with play therapy providing valuable perspectives on children during the mid-20th century.

Reflection During Formative Assessment

While early childhood practitioners use various measures and methods to gather information about children's current levels of performance, they should also use reflection and deep-level integration as they notice how children solve problems. Reflective practices during assessment increase the potential to identify key issues and patterns in performance. Professionals' willingness to develop and sustain attunement enhances the clarity with which they perceive individual patterns of development in children. Reflection involves a continual process of sorting, shedding, and sloughing-off misconceptions. It involves not being judgmental and not jumping to conclusions. Using reflection makes it possible to consider what is actually going on with each child, especially regarding underlying factors and interpretation of presenting symptoms. Reflection can help to identify the best methods and measures to document the unique patterns of a child's development, such as running records or work samples.

Reflection can help to identify the best methods and measures, such as running records or work samples, to document the unique patterns of a child's development.

SUMMATIVE ASSESSMENTS

Standardized Instruments

Standardized measures are named based on statistical information gathered from the performance of representative samples, to determine the distribution of the overall population's performance. This information or **standardization** is used to compare the performance of individual children with statistical averages of the other children's performance. When an individual child's performance falls outside a given range, the child's eligibility for special services is established.

Standardized assessment instruments have provided a tool for educators and other social scientists, but there have been major concerns about the use of standardized assessment, especially for purposes such as measuring the effectiveness of educational practices. Early childhood educators have long challenged the value of standardized tests and have raised questions about their usefulness (Kohn, 2001).

Psychometricians have responded by trying to improve the **validity** and reliability of the tests that are used and to make them more representative of the groups being assessed. Concerns about bias relating to gender, culture, and socioeconomic status have been specifically addressed.

Because of an increased focus on **standardized testing** with legislation such as No Child Left Behind (NCLB), it is important for teams to consider the individual child's results to determine validity and reliability. Sometimes children may perform less well on standardized instruments than they do on other measures. If this is the case, such discrepancies can be documented.

Selection of Instruments

Practitioners should be familiar with a broad range of instruments and make selections based upon the unique needs of the child. If a child appears to have a learning style that would be especially well assessed using a specific instrument, a practitioner might choose that instrument accordingly. For a child who demonstrates concepts in the context of play, a play-based assessment would be valuable. For a child who has a visual impairment, it would be important to use methods that engage other senses. Given budgetary constraints in schools, it is common for programs to have access to a single instrument or a small sampling of instruments that are used for all children in the program. It is helpful, however, for practitioners to be aware of where they might access a broader range of instruments, such as a state resource center (http://www.nectac.org/chouse/).

Educational Reports

An educational report is an example of a **summative assessment** that includes information from a variety of sources, including information that has previously been attained through formative methods. This information is integrated and consolidated into a description of each child's current level of performance in all developmental domains and is coupled with the perspective of how the child has developed over time. **Baseline data** as well as change of time is generally included.

Reflection and Summative Assessment

As practitioners gather information from a variety of sources, including both qualitative and quantitative measures, they should consolidate results so that the results are understandable to others. A full **summative** assessment for children with disabilities must also serve the basic purpose of providing teams with specific descriptions of characteristics to help develop appropriate adaptations.

Presenting Information

Once practitioners have information about a child's current level of performance, they can integrate the information from a variety of sources into a coherent report that covers all domains. The report should be clear, relatively free of jargon, and written in a way that conveys a positive portrayal of each child. It should be carefully organized and present areas of concern as well as strengths in ways that are family-centered and constructive. In addition to a written report, professionals also need to be prepared to share information in meetings with families. Setting a positive tone in the meeting and sharing information that in ways that contribute to effective communication is helpful in a way that contributes to effective communication.

Practitioners should state clearly if they do not yet have enough information to fully understand why a child is behaving or performing a certain way; this is better than making a seemingly authoritative statement that is inaccurate. Children are sometimes **misdiagnosed**. It is important that complex developmental issues are considered and contextualized. We are advocating for the prevention of such mistakes as much as possible, through the practitioner's willingness to reflect, communicate, and listen to different points of view. Practitioners should not immediately assume that they have all the answers but rather work within the team to further the mutual progress toward assessment of young children. When we write reports with input from parents and other team members, we must be willing to edit and revise as much as necessary to convey reliable and trustworthy perspectives on children's development. What we choose not to include in a report is sometimes as significant as what we include.

THE CHANGING ROLES OF FAMILIES AND TEAMS IN ASSESSMENT

Historically, parents were often not valued as team members and reliable sources of information about their children. The assumption was often made that parents' perceptions of their children were inherently distorted, biased, and subjective in ways that made them less valid (Turnbull, Turnbull, & Wehmeyer, 2007). The role of the professional was to present a clear, objective, and unbiased view of a child's development. With time and many years of advocacy, one of the major changes has been that parents are encouraged to share their valued perspectives and understandings of their child's challenges as well as abilities (Gallagher, Fialka, Rhodes, & Arceneaux, 2002; McWilliam, 2005; Turnbull, & Turnbull, & Wehmeyer, 2007). This is clear progress in early childhood special education because parents' perceptions are informed by knowing their children well at all hours of the day and night. Fortunately, parental perspectives are now considered an integral core of assessment of young children and measured through formal instruments.

Professionals should recognize the unique strengths and needs of each family as they assess young children (Jung, 2007; McWilliam, P. J., 2000). The roles of professionals can be determined by the needs of the family. Some families have more information about their child's condition than the teachers, particularly if it is a very rare syndrome that may be genetic because the family may have had previous experience dealing with it. Families may become experts as well as advocates for their children, especially because ample information is available through the Internet. There are times when family members may use complex terminology, such as "mucopolysaccharidosis" (Castelli, personal communication; November 11, 2009).

Importance of Teamwork

During the assessment process, families and professionals should work together as a team, building trust and increasing understanding of each child's strengths and needs. It helps to have a shared developmental framework from which to consider each child's performance and progress, to help determine whether or not the child needs special services and which types of services and support.

Documenting Multiple Perspectives

When observation or anecdotal records are used instead of or in addition to formal assessment instruments, it is not necessary that everyone agrees or presents the same view of a child's development. It is, in fact, quite common for children to behave and perform differently in varied contexts. These different perspectives should be documented. For example, a practitioner might note, "According to Justin's mother, he is able to put on his own shoes. This has not yet been observed at school." Such differences in perspective do not usually represent a substantial conflict or disagreement over a child's capabilities, but they should be documented. Children performance often varies in different contexts.

Reflection in Teams: Multiple Perspectives

Federal law requires that assessment represents multiple disciplines, and there are different ways to accomplish that goal. With teams comprised of people in many roles, there is potential for a variety of perspectives. Parents are central in the team, and their views are crucial in helping to establish a full sense of each child's development. Paraprofessionals and teacher assistants often spend considerable time with children and may have additional perspectives to share. With their professional expertise and preparation, teachers, both general education and special education, are able to observe, interact, and reflect on significant factors. Specialists, school psychologists, and social workers will all bring their own valuable insights to the team. An occupational therapist may be more inclined than others to include issues such as sensory processing to a reflective process, and he or she can share understandings of important dimensions with the rest of the team. Communication is an integral aspect of the reflective dynamic in teams.

The placement of children in inclusive settings has increased, and it is imperative that professionals who do not have extensive expertise in special education know they should consult with specialists instead of assuming they should be able to complete a full-scale assessment themselves. When programs are administered by school systems, this is generally understood. With private early childhood programs, however, it is necessary for administrators and teachers to forge connections with the local public schools.

Seeking Help from Specialists

Once a teacher has documented that a child is performing outside a range of what would be considered normal, it is appropriate to make a referral and request assessment from a specialist. Hearing, vision, and general health screenings are typically part of assessment of physical development. There is increasing evidence that dental health is important in its impact on other domains of development. Screening for lead may be warranted in physical assessment. Information about possible chronic health issues including diabetes, sickle cell disorder, asthma, allergies, or epilepsy is important (Batshaw, Pelligrini, & Roizen, 2007; Platt & Sacardote, 2002).

Inter-Rater Reliability

When more than one perspective is shared, it is important to consider the alignment and congruence between team members. Inter-rater reliability refers to the extent to which team members agree as they report on the performance of a child. Instruments are designed to minimize ambiguity and to be clear in ways that enhance the inter-rater reliability (McLean, Bailey, & Wolery, 2004).

Communicating with Families During Assessment

Practitioners must be open to the range of responses when families consider the possibility their child has a disability or delay. If professionals assume families will be upset, their bias can affect the quality of communication . Professionals also should not assume that families confronted with a relatively mild delay will be able to take things in stride. Some families may cope very well with the identification of significant challenges. Professionals should be able to listen well, share accurate information, and approach situations without assumptions or prejudice. This will help to establish healthy working relationships with families (Bailey & Powell, 2005; Turnbull, Turnbull, & Wehmeyer, 2007).

The Importance of Rapport

When professionals establish rapport with a child and family, they increase the likelihood that the child will demonstrate characteristics and behavior that are representative of his or her capabilities. If professionals are unresponsive and cold in interactions, they can inadvertently intimidate a child, potentially inhibiting his or her responses. Interacting with a child in ways that convey encouragement and support is preferable to less-responsive modes. Professionals can use their facial expressions, tone of voice, and body language to communicate that they can be trusted. A feeling of trust usually contributes to a more representative performance on the part of the child and more valid perspective on the part of the assessor.

While most young children have not had the negative life experience to establish deeply ingrained patterns of test phobia, adults engaging in assessment may have their own residual issues regarding tests. Unfortunately, these can be conveyed through facial expression, intonation, and gestures. Professionals should not create and perpetuate negative dynamics regarding assessment. Setting a positive, encouraging tone is more likely to elicit an optimal performance from each child. Positive feedback can be shared in many ways.

Use of Active Listening During Assessment

With any communication, there is a need to check-in with the child and family to see if what has been received or understood is what was intended. The use of active listening methods, such as saying, "It sounds like you are feeling frustrated. Are you?" may be especially helpful in making sure there is effective communication. The language used to check-in needs to be adjusted for individual children and families.

Reading Cues

Interpretation of children's cues is an essential, but not always easy, aspect of assessment (Sheridan, Foley, & Radlinski, 1995). Children often provide cues and signals that are relatively clear, unambiguous, and easy to decode. In turn, they may respond to the cues of others, so reciprocity is a natural process and outcome. When children have cues that are difficult to interpret, it is more challenging to use those cues as evidence of current level of performance. If a child has clear gestures, facial expressions, and/or words, we may readily be able to identify what he or she comprehends and intends to communicate.

When the signals and cues from a child are difficult to read, there is often more uncertainly about the child's intent and level of comprehension. It is often necessary to interpret cues cautiously and use open-ended phrasing such as "it appears that . . . " and "it is likely that . . ." rather than making definitive statements about a child's current level of performance. As professionals become familiar with each child, they can more fully and clearly articulate a child's motivation, strengths, and areas of concern or need. Increasingly, we are able to appreciate and convey unique configurations beyond the general patterns we have learned through the study of typical development.

Sometimes the process of assessment is upsetting to families, especially if they experience the emerging reality of their child's condition as an assault on their previous worldview. It helps when professionals can maturely appreciate the need for adjustment and be supportive without conveying a sense of pity. When professionals exhibit genuine acceptance of people with disabilities it can be easier for them to convey support in natural, sincere ways (Hanson & Lynch, 2004).

Although it was once assumed that denial was a stage through which families of children with disabilities passed, that concept has recently been challenged. Not long ago it was often assumed that families would go through the stages of grieving when their children were identified as having developmental disabilities. While for some families this may still occur, intervention services have improved the process and potentially made it less traumatic (Gallagher, Fialka, J., Rhodes, C., & Arceneaux, C., 2002).

Communication, Confidentiality, and Coordination

Within teams, there must always be a focus on communication, confidentiality, and coordination. Team members need to discuss important issues regarding children's assessments. Sometimes this is done during meetings, both formal planning and placement team meetings and child study team meetings. At other times, communication occurs informally, through conversations in various contexts. Regardless of how a conversation occurs, confidentiality must be respected. It is important for professional team members to remember that information shared in any context may still be considered privileged, and the assumption should not be made that it is okay to share it with others. Coordination of communication is essential, especially when there are multiple perspectives. While it is helpful to have information from many sources, there can also be fragmentation. Pulling perspectives together and organizing them is necessary. Assessment of children with special needs must be a collaborative process.

CULTURAL PERSPECTIVES ON ASSESSMENT

Professionals must consider cultural values and beliefs to better understand the development of young children. Early childhood education has made tremendous progress toward the full appreciation of cultural perspectives. There have been many initiatives, ranging from the anti-bias curriculum (Derman-Sparks, 1989; Derman-Sparks & Olsen Edwards, 2010) to the work of the Children's Defense Fund and Head Start, that have thoroughly infused multicultural perspectives into programs with young children. All major organizations have played leadership roles with this initiative.

Interpretation of Dynamics Related to Cultural Factors

Cultural factors are significant in determining eligibility for a number of reasons. First, different cultures perceive disability differently. A family acclimating to the developmental status of their child may need to sort through a whole range of emotions and cultural beliefs about their child's condition (Cheatham & Milagros-Santos, 2005). For instance, in some cultures perceive disability as a sign of a curse or blessing. A child's disability may be perceived as a punishment. One mother reported that when her son with Down syndrome was born, she received a condolence card from some well-intentioned acquaintances.

Professionals do not need to assume that there will be issues related to the family acceptance of children with disabilities, it is just helpful to be aware that there may be issues. We do not want to create self-fulfilling prophecies; at the same time, if issues emerge, we want to be prepared to address them.

Overrepresentation of Children from Culturally Diverse Groups in Special Education

Unfortunately, there is a disturbing statistical trend in special education that children from culturally diverse groups, especially those who are of color, are overrepresented in special education (Pavri & Fowler, 2001; Shealey & Lue, 2006). Conversely, they are underrepresented among those who are identified as having gifts and talents (Cartledge, Gardner, & Ford, 2009). This must not be interpreted as an indicator that children from diverse cultural groups are more vulnerable.

These statistics must be contextualized in the social systems that perpetuate unequal opportunities. Poverty, not ethnicity, is the paramount risk factor. Poverty is not equally distributed among all ethnic groups. Children from culturally diverse groups in the United States are much more likely to be living in poverty than their

Caucasian counterparts (Farran, 2005). Low socioeconomic status is a primary predictor of developmental challenge (Ziegler & Styfco, 2004). As a risk factor, it is often associated with many other risks, such as lack of appropriate medical care, lack of nutrition, and lack of opportunities for activities that support healthy development (Cooney et al., 2007; Hilliard, 1997; Shealey & Lue, 2006). Thus, a compelling case can be made that the increased rates of developmental challenges among children from culturally diverse groups living in poverty are largely preventable (Pavri & Fowler, 2001). As we work together to assess young children, we must keep this in mind and always be willing to reflect on and reconsider possible assumptions. This includes understanding how individual situations mirror social systems, some of which have unfortunately perpetuated unequal opportunities. Through assessment, we have the potential to change those dynamics (Farran).

Confronting Stereotypes

Race, culture, ethnicity, and economic factors may potentially influence the assessment of young children. Cultural stereotypes may inadvertently influence expectations. It is very important that we look at statistical trends and disaggregate variables such as poverty. Is it ethnicity or poverty that contributes to developmental challenges? There is plentiful research indicating that it is poverty rather than race or ethnicity that negatively influences development (Shonkoff & Phillips, 2001). Certain conditions, however, such as Tay-Sachs disease, sickle cell anemia, and thalassemia are more prevalent among those from specific ethnic groups (Batshaw, Pelligrini, & Roizen, 2007).

English Language Learners

A child who is not fluent in English is unlikely to score well on an assessment done in English. Professionals must know and demonstrate appropriate and ethical representation of each child's development by avoiding being too hasty or by jumping to conclusions. Professionals should gather information about the developmental context of the child to ensure that the child has not been misidentified as needing special education. Children who are English language learners need support for the acquisition of English and/or to be assessed in their primary language. Certainly children who are learning English as a second language need and deserve supports, but that is different from having a developmental disability. Teachers must be able to consider various factors as they affect a child's progress (McLean, 2002).

When appropriate standards have been set which do not lower expectations for children growing up in poverty, we can align these standards with a system-wide commitment to support students in their optimal outcomes. Organizations such as the Children's Defense Fund led by Marian Wright Edelman have long advocated for support and services for children to decrease the negative effects of poverty for children who were born into challenging circumstances. Rather than noting the negative effects of poverty on development and lowering our expectations of students growing up with such risks, we can acknowledge the risk and create ways in which those factors can be alleviated (Farran, 2005).

We may think of culture as often involving a specific set of filters for experience. Such perspectives may help us better understand the many ways in which we need to make sure we are clearing and checking our own process as we assess children's development. Our first impressions may be affected by what we think we know, or what we think is important. Certain aspects of development may be incongruous with what we are used to, so it is imperative that we are willing to reflect, reconsider, and hear a variety of perspectives. Having a firm foundation regarding multicultural issues will help us reflect and increase our ability to appreciate patterns and nuances associated with diverse values, beliefs, and customs (Barrera & Kramer, 2009; Cheatham & Milagros Santos, 2005; Hilliard, 1997; Pavri & Fowler, 2002).

Our ongoing willingness to scan our own views and beliefs is developed through increasing our understanding of multicultural perspectives. Such scanning and willingness to reflect on our own assumptions is very helpful in reducing bias.

EXAMPLE 1   **Vignette: Joel**

In Puerto Rico, a boy who was almost 5 with very limited expressive language and a recent diagnosis of autism was drinking out of a baby bottle filled with a milk-cereal mix. A professional consultant questioned why he was allowed to drink from a bottle, when there was documented evidence he was capable of eating solid food independently. She expressed concern that allowing him to continue to drink from a baby bottle would encourage his ongoing infantilization, instead of nurturing autonomy and independence considered more typical for his chronological age. The consultant's interpretation would make sense under certain circumstances, but a significant piece of information was missing from her assessment: in the Puerto Rican culture, it is not unusual for children across the developmental continuum to drink from baby bottles long after they have begun to eat solid food. Given such relevant information, the behavior of this child with autism would be interpreted differently. Furthermore, if there were actual developmental concerns about the child engaging in this behavior, it would be helpful to have it come from the perspective of someone very familiar with the cultural traditions.

Questions for Reflection:
1. Based on your own experiences, what feeding practices are most familiar to you?
2. How can you ensure that you gather the information you need about a variety of cultures?
3. If this child were in your care, how might you communicate with Joel's mother regarding his patterns?

DETERMINING CURRENT LEVEL OF PERFORMANCE

Professionals must determine a child's current level of performance in all domains of development in order to write an **Individualized Education Program (IEP), or Individualized Family Service Plan (IFSP)** which identifies goals and desired outcomes based on what appears to be attainable for each child. Children's performances are assessed using certain benchmarks. Through data collection and careful reflection, professionals develop a clear sense of the child's current capabilities, not just whether or not they have attained certain benchmarks, but how they learn. The professional can then design strategies that match each child's needs. As an example, a child who has

TABLE 4.3 Benchmarks and Adaptations	
Benchmark	**Adaptations**
Pincer grasp	Hand-over-hand assistance
Two-word phrases	Prompts; modeling; requests
Initiation of interaction with another child	Scaffolding, support, modeling
Sorting objects by color	Prompting; demonstration; verbal guidance
Use of problem-solving strategies with manipulatives	Verbal guidance; demonstration
Walking with support	Physical support; equipment as needed; accessible environment

difficulty shifting to a new approach to a problem, verbal feedback and/or demonstration can be part of scaffolding. Table 4.3 provides some perspectives on the ways in which scaffolding can be used when children have difficulty in certain areas.

Assessment Across Domains

Development across domains is usually integrated instead of fragmented, especially when children are developing normally. In practice, however, we separate assessments into different domains. This is especially useful in order to focus on areas that need extra intervention. Information regarding different areas of development is reported separately, with the understanding that for young children there is significant overlap between domains. If a child has language delays, social interaction is usually affected. When there are cognitive challenges, language development is often affected. A report on a child's current level of performance may or may not include root causes that are contributing factors. Essentially, the presenting symptoms, developmental benchmarks, and characteristics become the focus of a report on a child's current level of performance.

Benchmarks and Milestones: Indicators

Through research, benchmarks or milestones for a normal range of development have been identified in all domains (Gesell & Ilg, 1949). Children performing within a certain range would be considered typical. Practitioners must remember the unique qualities of children who are considered typical, even if they are not eligible for special services. Children significantly outside the range of what would be considered typical are eligible for special services. Benchmarks can be helpful in determining eligibility and planning **individualized programs.** There is significant variability in typical development especially regarding pace of growth and skill acquisition, so the difference between typical and exceptional development is not always clear-cut.

As the study of child development has changed over time, there is a deeper understanding of how experiences affect children's skill acquisition and concept development. Many sources on typical development are available. Specific skills such as sitting without support, taking first steps, and saying first words are relatively measurable. While there may be some differences regarding when children attain these benchmarks, there is a shared understanding about the sequence and developmental progression.

For some children, using a developmental checklist, assessment instrument, or assessment framework to report on performance may be sufficient. We can identify the skills attained along with areas that need to be enhanced. Reporting this information may be done directly through simple statements about accomplishments such as specific fine motor skills. With other children, the process is more complex. You will find a section in each of this book's curricular adaptation chapters that addresses specific factors related to each domain.

STANDARDS   Any consideration of assessment must include a discussion of standards. Organizations such as the National Association of the Education of Young Children (NAEYC), the DEC, and the National Head Start Association (NHSA) have all established standards. It is important to understand the role that standards play in all aspects of education, including evaluation. Benchmarks and standards represent a shared vision of what we hope children will accomplish, based on realistic expectations and grounded, evidence-based development information. There have been many reform initiatives centered around standards, notably those that include creativity (Hyson, 2003). In addition to the standards of different professional organizations in various areas of concentration, NAEYC has a standard for assessment, Standard 3, as does DEC/CEC Standard 8.

Focus on Characteristics

Months may go by during which even a full team of well-prepared and experienced professionals can be confounded by characteristics that elude a clear diagnosis.

Careful record keeping is an important element in using informal assessment methods in natural settings.

Situations such as these illustrate how essential it is for us to focus on characteristics and match patterns of strengths and needs with adaptation strategies. Professionals can develop and implement intervention strategies without confirming a diagnosis for young children. Many states have regulations that allow young children to be served if they are identified as having developmental delays. This term refers to delays that are measurable and observable, but which may not confirm a categorical diagnosis. They may eventually be diagnosed as having other conditions, or they may not need long-term services. Some states permit serving children who are identified as at risk, even though the child may not have significant enough delays to be eligible for services under the Individuals with Disabilities Education Act (IDEA). Providing such services can be cost-effective over time, but it also requires certain resources.

Documenting Areas of Need

Identifying an area of need is not a criticism of a child. An inventory of skills can help to guide the team in providing appropriate supports. Professionals are not doing the child a favor by indicating that he or she has mastered skills when actually those skills are still emerging. If we overestimate a child's current level of performance, we may inadvertently mismatch the intervention needed with what is actually provided.

Qualitative Indicators

Qualitative indicators are very important as we assess young children. These include children's coping abilities, interactive styles, and problem-solving strategies. Variables and developmental features such as temperament are additional aspects of the complex dynamic (Neisworth, Bagnato, Salvia, & Hunt, 1999; Williamson & Anzalone, 2001). Some children may be especially susceptible to environmental factors such as distractions, noise levels, general organization, or structure of an environment. Some of these qualitative characteristics can contribute to children performing inconsistently in different settings or at different times. Difficulties with **self-regulation** may manifest in performance problems (Bronson, 2001; Chandler & Dahlquist, 2002). Because these qualitative differences may be symptomatic of difficult-to-**diagnose** neurological conditions, professionals may be perplexed by them during the assessment process (Als, 1986; Bronson, 2001; Chandler & Loncola, 2008; Shonkoff & Phillips, 2001).

A related constellation of characteristics that may affect the qualitative aspects of a child's development involves difficulty with **sensory processing**. Such difficulty can have an impact on development in many other areas. Difficulty with sensory integration is usually part of the characteristics that affect children with autism, but it also can affect performance in children whose development is not on the continuum of pervasive developmental disorders.

Interpreting Children's Lack of Progress

Two children with virtually the same quantitative results on assessment instruments may progress significantly different from each other over time. Given developmentally appropriate practices as well as individual support, if a child makes less progress over time it is certainly not a definitive sign that the teacher is ineffective. It may be a sign that the child has intellectual disabilities (mental retardation) rather than developmental delays. When a child is initially assessed and referred for special services, professionals may not be able to determine the child's potential for future progress in terms of rate and quality. It is important to note that professionals with extensive preparation and appropriate credentials can exercise and articulate **clinical opinion** regarding the developmental status of children." It is generally not expected that classroom teachers would conduct full **diagnostic evaluations** of children.

Documenting Children's Competence

Professionals must not underestimate a child's competence based on his or her performance. Professionals should acknowledge glimmers of potential, so that they do not inadvertently contribute to lower expectations, which may lead to interventions that provide fewer positive challenges. This cascading dynamic can perpetuate assumptions about children's limits. Ultimately, the early childhood professional's purpose should be to provide supports that equalize opportunities for all children to perform to the best of their abilities. If children's abilities and potential are underestimated through reduced expectations, professionals unintentionally create obstacles to children's progress.

Children Actualizing Potential

At times, it may be less clear how the child will progress, given appropriate intervention. A child with developmental delays that are secondary to a lack of environmental opportunity and developmentally appropriate practice may make phenomenal progress within a relatively short period of time. Given the opportunity, children may demonstrate gains of more than one developmental year in less than a 12-month span of time. In those instances, the developmental delay can be addressed and alleviated significantly through child and family-centered programs.

Questions for Reflection:

1. Think of your focus child. What developmental benchmarks has this child attained in all domains of development?
2. How did you determine if the child had attained specific skills? What measures did you use?
3. How did you determine if the measures you used were accurately assessing this child's competence?
4. Are there aspects of this child's development that warrant special adjustment of measures?

Forming Hypotheses

Professionals may formulate many hypotheses regarding a child's developmental progress, and then follow up to see if the hypotheses are accurately representing the child's performance and abilities. Because professionals use different measures to assess achievement, they must keep in mind that children do not always demonstrate the skills that they have attained. They may be capable of skills that they have not yet mastered, especially if the environment in which they are growing up does not offer opportunities for developmentally appropriate practice.

LEGAL FACTORS IN ASSESSMENT

All major special education laws have included requirements for assessment. These legal guidelines provide clear parameters for children with special needs. This is a brief overview, with the understanding that practitioners should know where to go for more information. Practitioners should know what questions to ask about legal mandates, as well as knowing one's own limits. Practitioners who have a basic concept of legal mandates can use reflection to guide their practices.

Referral Process and Establishing Eligibility

The federal laws establish eligibility through a significant delay. This may be 2 standard deviations from the mean (30th percentile) in one developmental domain or 1.5 standard deviations in at least two developmental domains. While the criteria for eligibility has changed over time, and continues to be reconsidered with reauthorizations of the IDEA, the need for documentation of significant delays continues. In early childhood, practitioners can identify children who have developmental delays, not just those with identified diagnoses. When children do not have quantitative delays as measured by standardized tests but who manifest behaviors that are a concern, it is possible for qualified professionals to use their judgment or informed opinion to determine eligibility. Such a decision would need to be supported with ample documentation of developmental concerns.

During evaluation, professionals must gather and present information to be used in a planning and placement team meeting to make a decision about whether or not a child will receive special services, and in what context. It is imperative that professionals understand and convey to families that identification of eligibility is not an indictment or a judgment. When young children are identified as eligible for special services, it does not mean they have a one-way ticket into the world of special education. Eligibility is based on current level of performance, and there are many times when children make significant progress given appropriate intervention. Families may be afraid of having their children identified, but if they truly understand that their children are not being "labeled," then teams can work together to provide appropriate accommodations and help the child address developmental challenges in meaningful contexts. It is important for professionals to remember that determining eligibility for young children with special needs can be an emotional process for families (Bailey & Powell, 2005). Setting a supportive tone can make a major difference in a child's adjustment. In optimal interaction, a climate of mutual trust is built between families and professionals, with a clear focus on what is best for each child.

When working with young children, it is not unusual for teachers and other team members to observe children who have not been identified as eligible for special services and wonder if they are progressing normally. Sometimes such concerns are warranted based on a child's behavior, but are not necessarily long term. Children's behavior may be affected if there has been a change in the family structure, a loved one has been ill, or a new sibling has been born. Many life circumstances may result in changes of behavior or performance. In other cases, team members may observe behavior or characteristics that lead to full assessment and identification of eligibility for special services. When children have received birth-to-3 services and are transitioning to preschool services, assessment information from the early years should be shared with new teachers and team members.

Summary

In our advocacy for including the reflective process in assessment, we want to be careful to clarify that we are not recommending over-thinking or excessive analysis, which can sometimes detract from the basic patterns that exist and potentially interfere with developing a course of action.

Young children's characteristics may be complex in ways that make it very difficult to be certain about contributing factors. When this is the case, a team should move beyond trying to establish a full understanding and instead state clearly what the on-going questions will be, so subsequent assessment may continue to monitor those variables. After deep and thorough consideration of the information available, as well as extra probing to explore the areas of question, it is okay to summarize the current level of performance based on available information, even if there are remaining questions. To continue to reflect beyond an increase in understanding is not likely to yield greater insight. In practical applications, appropriate adaptations may be developed and implemented based on a child's current level of performance across domains, even when there is not a confirmed understanding of underlying diagnoses. Adaptations can be designed to match and respond to symptoms and characteristics.

Key Terms

Baseline data
Clinical opinion
Diagnoses
Diagnostic evaluation
Formative assessment
Individualized Education
    Program (IEP)

Individualized Family Service
    Plan (IFSP)
Norm-referenced
Performance
Reliability
Results-based accountability
Self-regulation

Sensory processing
Standardization
Summative assessment

Website

The National Early Childhood Technical Assistance Center
http://www.nectac.org/chouse

References

Als, H. (1986). A synactive model of neonatal behavioral organization: Framework for the assessment of neurobehavioral development in the preterm infant and for the support of infants and parents in the neonatal intensive care environment. *Physical and Occupational Therapy in Pediatrics.* 6, 613–653.

Bailey, D., Bruer, J., Symons, F., & Lichtman, J. (Eds.). (2001). *Critical thinking about critical periods.* Baltimore: Paul H. Brookes.

Bailey, D. B., & Powell, T. (2005). Assessing information needs of families in early intervention. In M. J. Guralnick (Ed.). *The developmental systems approach to early intervention* (pp. 151–184). Baltimore: Paul H. Brookes.

Banks, R. A., Milagros Santos, R., & Roof, V. (2003). Sensitive family information gathering. *Young Exceptional Children, 6*(2), 11–19.

Barrera, I., & Kramer, L. (2009). *Using skilled dialogue to transform challenging interactions.* Baltimore: Paul H. Brookes.

Batshaw, M., Pellegrino, L., & Roizen, N. (Eds.). (2007). *Children with disabilities* (6th ed.). Baltimore: Paul H. Brookes.

Bayley, N. (1993). *Bayley Scales of Infant Development–II.* San Antonio, TX: Psychological Corporation.

Beaty, J. (2010). *Observing the development of the young child* (7th ed.). Upper Saddle River, NJ: Merrill/Pearson Education.

Bonderant-Utz, J. (2002). *Practical guide to assessing infants and preschoolers with special needs.* Upper Saddle River, NJ: Merrill/Pearson Education.

Brainard, M. B. (1997). Assessment as a way of seeing. In A. Lin Goodwin (Ed.), *Assessment for equity and inclusion.* London: Routledge.

Brazelton, T. B. (1973). *Neonatal behavioral assessment scale.* Philadelphia: B. Lippincott.

Bricker, D., & Pretti-Frontczak, K. (Eds.). (2002). *Assessment, evaluation, and programming system (AEPS) for infants and children (Vol.3) AEPS measurement for three to six years.* Baltimore: Paul H. Brookes.

Bricker, D., & Squires, J. (1999). *Ages and stages questionnaire.* Baltimore: Paul H. Brookes.

Bronfenbrenner, U. (1977). Toward an experimental ecology of human development. *American Psychologist, 32,* 513–531.

Bronson, M. (2000). *Self-regulation in early childhood.* New York: The Guilford Press.

Buysse, V., & Wesley, P. (Eds.). (2006). *Evidence-based practices in the early childhood field.* Washington, DC: Zero-to-Three.

Cartledge, G., Gardner, R., & Ford, D. (2009). *Diverse learners with exceptionalities.* Upper Saddle River, NJ: Merrill/Pearson Education.

Chandler, L., & Dahlquist, C. M. (2002). *Functional assessment: Strategies to prevent and remediate challenging behavior in school settings.* Upper Saddle River, NJ: Merrill/Pearson Education.

Chang, D., & Demyan, A. (2007). Teachers' stereotypes of Asian, black, and white students. *School Psychology Quarterly, 22,* 91–114.

Cheatham, G., & Milagros Santos, R. (2005). A-B-Cs of bridging home and school expectations. *Young Exceptional Children,* 8(3), 3–11.

Cooney, M., Buchanan, M., Dombrowski, S., Noonan, K., & Martin, R. (2007). Low-birth weight and cognitive outcomes: Evidence for a gradient relationship in an urban, poor, African American birth cohort. *School Psychology Quarterly,* 22(1), 26–43.

Derman-Sparks, L., & Olsen Edwards, J. (2010). *Antibias education for young children and ourselves.* Washington, DC: National Association for the Education of Young Children.

Dunst, C. J, Bruder, M. B., Trivette, C., Hamby, D., Raab, M., & McLean, M. (2001). Characteristics and consequences of everyday natural learning opportunities. *Topics in Early Childhood Special Education,* 21(2), 68–92.

Farran, D. (2005). Developing and implementing preventive intervention programs for children at risk: Poverty as a case in point. In M. J. Guralnick (Ed.), *The developmental systems approach to early intervention* (pp. 267–304). Baltimore: Paul H. Brookes.

Foley, G., & Hochman, J. (Eds.). (2006). *Mental health in early intervention.* Baltimore: Paul H. Brookes.

Fraiberg, S. (1977). *Insights from the blind: Comparative studies of blind and sighted infants.* New York: Basic Books.

Gallagher, P., Fialka, J., Rhodes, C., & Arceneaux, C. (2002). Working with families: Rethinking denial. *Young Exceptional Children,* 5(2) 11–17.

Gardner, H. (2000). *The disciplined mind.* New York: Penguin Books.

Gessell, A., & Ilg, F. L. (1949). *Child development.* New York: Harper & Row.

Gilliam, W., Meisels, S., & Mayes, L. (2005). Screening and surveillance in early intervention services. In M. J Guralnick (Ed.), *The developmental systems approach to early intervention.* Baltimore: Paul H. Brookes.

Goodwin, A. Lin. (Ed.). (1997). *Assessment for equity and inclusion.* London: Routledge.

Guralnick, M. J. (Ed.). (2005). *The developmental systems approach to early intervention.* Baltimore: Paul H. Brookes.

Hanson, M., & Lynch, E. (2004). *Developing cross-cultural competence* (3rd ed.). Baltimore: Paul H. Brookes.

Harms, T., & Clifford, R. M. (1980). *Early childhood environment rating scale.* New York: Teachers College Press.

Hilliard, A. G. (1997). Language, culture, and the assessment of African American children. In A. Lin Goodwin (Ed.), *Assessment for equity and inclusion.* London: Routledge.

Hyson, M. (2003). (Ed.). *Preparing early childhood professionals: NAEYC's standards for programs.* Washington, DC: NAEYC.

Jablon, J., Dombro, A., & Dichtelmiller, M. (2007). *The power of observation* (2nd ed.). Washington, DC: NAEYC.

Jung, L. (2007). Writing individualized family service plan strategies that fit into the routine. *Young Exceptional Children. 10*(3), 2–9.

Kohn, A. (2001). Five reasons to stop saying "Good job!" *Young Children, 56*(5), 24–28.

Linder, T. (2008). *Transdisciplinary play-based assessment* (2nd ed.). Baltimore: Paul H. Brookes.

Losardo, A., & Notari-Syverson, A. (2001). *Alternative approaches to assessing young children.* Baltimore: Paul H. Brookes.

Lynch, E., & Hanson, M. (2004). *Understanding families: Approaches to diversity, disability, and risk.* Baltimore: Paul H. Brookes.

Lynch, E. M., & Struewing, N. (2002). Children in context: Portfolio assessment in the inclusive early childhood classroom. In M. Ostrosky & E. Horn (Eds.), *Assessment: Gathering meaningful information. Young Exceptional Children Monograph Series No. 4.* Longmont, CO: The Division of Early Childhood/Sopris West.

McCormick, L., & Noonan, M.J. (2002). Ecological assessment and planning. In Ostrosky, M. & Horn, E. (Eds.), *Assessment: Gathering meaningful information* (pp. 47–60). Longmont, CO: Sopris West/ DEC.

McEvoy, M., Neilsen, S., & Reichle, J. (2004). Functional behavioral assessment in early childhood settings. In M. McLean, D. B. Bailey & M. Wolery (Eds.), *Assessing infants and preschoolers with special needs* (3rd ed., pp. 236–261). Upper Saddle River, NJ: Merrill/Pearson Education.

McLaughlin, J., & Lewis, R. (2001). *Assessing students with special needs.* Upper Saddle River, NJ: Merrill/Pearson Education.

McLean, M. (2002). Assessing young children for whom English is a second language. In M. Ostrosky & E Horn (Eds.), *Assessment: Gathering meaningful information. Young exceptional children monograph series No. 4.* Longmont, CO: The Division of Early Childhood/Sopris West.

McLean, M., Bailey, D. B., & Wolery, M. (Eds.). (2004). *Assessing infants and preschoolers with special needs.* Upper Saddle River, NJ: Merrill/Pearson Education.

McWilliam, P. J. (2000). *Lives in progress: Case stories in early intervention.* Baltimore: Paul H. Brookes.

McWilliam, R. (2000). It's only natural . . . to have early intervention in the environments where it's needed. In S. Sandall & M. Ostrosky (Eds.), *Young exceptional children monograph series No.2: Natural environments and inclusion* (pp. 17–26). Denver, CO: The Division for Early Childhood of the Council for Exceptional Children.

McWilliam, R. (2005). Assessing the resource needs of families in the context of early intervention. In M. J. Guralnick (Ed.), *The Developmental Systems Approach to Early Intervention* (pp. 215–234). Baltimore: Paul H. Brookes.

Meisels, S. (1992). *The work sampling system: An overview.* Ann Arbor, MI: University of Michigan.

Meisels, S., & Atkins-Burnett, S. (2005). *Developmental screening in early childhood* (5th ed.). Washington, DC: NAEYC.

Meisels, S., & Fenichel, E. (1996). *New visions for the developmental assessment of infants and young children.* Washington DC: Zero to Three.

Miller, L. (1993). *First STEP screening test for evaluating preschoolers.* San Antonio TX: Psychological Corporation.

Mindes, G. (2003). *Assessing young children.* Upper Saddle River, NJ: Merrill/Pearson Education.

Neisworth, J. T., & Bagnato, S. J. (2005). DEC recommended practices: Assessment. In S. Sandall, M. L. Hemmeter, B. Smith, & M. McLean, *DEC recommended practices.* Longmont, CO: Sopris West.

Odom, S. (2009). The tie that binds: Evidence-based practice, implementation science, and outcomes for children. *Topics in Early Childhood Special Education, 29*(1), 53–61.

Ostrosky, M., & Horn, E. (Eds.). (2002). *Assessment: Gathering meaningful information. Young Exceptional Children Monograph Series No. 4.* Longmont, CO: The Division of Early Childhood/Sopris West.

Pavri, S., & Fowler, S. (2001). *Child find, screening, and tracking: Serving culturally and linguistically diverse children and families.* Champagne, IL: CLAS, University of Illinois Urbana-Champagne.

Pianta, R., La Paro, K., & Hamre, B. (2007). *Classroom assessment scoring system.* Baltimore: Paul H. Brookes.

Platt, A. F., & Sacerdote, A. (2002). *Hope and destiny: A patient's and parent's guide to sickle cell diseases and sickle cell trait.* Roscoe, IL: Hilton Publishing Company.

Popham, W. J. (2005). *Classroom assessment: What teachers need to know.* Boston: Allyn & Bacon/Pearson Education.

Sandall, S., Hemmeter, M. L., Smith, B., & McLean, M. (2005). *DEC recommended practices.* Longmont, CO: Sopris West.

Shealey, M., & Lue, M. (2006). Why are all the black kids still in special education? Revisiting the issue of disproportionate representation. *Multicultural Perspectives, 8*(2), 3–9.

Sheridan, M., Foley, G., & Radlinski, S. (1995). *Using the supportive play model: Individualized intervention in early childhood practice.* New York: Teachers College Press.

Shonkoff, J., & Phillips, D. (2001). *From neurons to neighborhoods.* Washington, DC: National Academy of Sciences.

Suzuki, L. A. (2002). *Handbook of multicultural assessment.* San Francisco: Jossey-Bass.

Turnbull, R, Turnbull, A., & Wehmeyer, M. (2007). *Exceptional lives* (5th ed.). Upper Saddle River, NJ: Merrill/Pearson Education.

Walsh, S., & Taylor, R. (2006). *Understanding IDEA: What it means for preschool children with disabilities and their families.* Reston, VA: Council for Exceptional Children.

Williamson, G. G., & Anzalone, M. E. (2001). *Sensory integration and self-regulation in infants and toddlers: Helping very young children interact with their environment.* Washington, DC: Zero to Three.

Wolraich, M., Gurwitch, R., Bruder, M. B., & Knight, L. (2005). The role of comprehensive interdisciplinary assessments in the early intervention system. In M. Guralnick (Ed.), *The developmental systems approach to early intervention* (pp. 133–150). Baltimore: Paul H. Brookes.

Zigler, E., & Styfco, S. J. (Eds.). (2004). *The Head Start debates.* Baltimore: Paul H. Brookes.

Chapter 5

Introduction to Curricular Adaptations

OBJECTIVES

After reading this chapter, students will:

- Demonstrate an understanding of developmentally and individually appropriate curriculum;
- Demonstrate how an early childhood curriculum may be adapted to meet individual needs using a continuum of **strategies**;
- Identify the match between specific characteristics in children and positive options for **adaptations**;
- Become familiar with embedding differentiated instructional methods into general curriculum; and
- Identify effective **evidence-based practices**.

ADAPTING CURRICULUM TO MEET INDIVIDUAL CHILDREN'S NEEDS

The change toward inclusion in early childhood special education requires that teachers and all team members working with young children with disabilities be adept, competent, and confident in their ability to adapt curriculum for the individual needs of children. Proficiency in addressing the unique needs of children with disabilities within inclusive classrooms may be enhanced by the general qualities of good teachers. Good teachers have the ability to establish and maintain rapport with children, to instinctively adapt to individual needs even among children in the typical range, and to encourage children as they engage in learning experiences.

Part of any teacher's success in guiding and supporting children is having faith that children can learn, even if they are momentarily challenged or confused. Reassuring teacher feedback can express understanding and confidence about children's development and their acquisition of new skills. It is understood that certain aspects of learning may be inherently frustrating, just as mastery of concepts and skills is intrinsically rewarding. Effectiveness in adapting curricular activities for young children with disabilities is an extension of those well-recognized best practices in early childhood. Techniques alone, however, without the ability to relate positively to young children, are not likely to be effective if they are implemented in mechanical ways.

Evidence-Based Practices: Curricular Adaptations

This book discusses evidence-based practices. This theme is especially relevant in considering how to adapt curriculum, because professionals need to have methods to determine which strategies are effective. In some instances, there is research that certain general strategies are often effective for children with certain clusters of characteristics. In other instances, evidence for effectiveness comes in the form of an individual child's positive response to certain intervention. In such a circumstance, we need to document such evidence through the collection of data. Teacher reflection while making decisions can include the consideration of many factors. Table 5.1 provides some examples of possible strategies for teachers to consider as they make choices about how to adapt curriculum for the unique needs of individual children. Some of these strategies, such as provision of a predictable environment, may be integrated into what is routinely offered. A predictable environment does not reduce the potential for spontaneity and may actually increase everyone's comfort level.

TABLE 5.1   Strategies

Possible Strategy	Rationale
More time	Child's process is slower
Clear expectations	Child may have trouble figuring out what is expected
Clear boundaries	Child may not have healthy boundaries
Simple directions	Child may have trouble processing complex or unclear directions
Routines	Predictable, consistent routines can be anticipated by child
Predictable environment	Child can gain a sense of organization from predictable environment
Meaningful organization	Systems for organization that make sense to children enhance their ability to comply
Consistent structure	Children gain a sense of stability from schedules and systems that are consistent
Scaffolding and support, as needed	Adult or peer guidance, as needed, ensures a match between child's level of difficulty and level of intervention offered
Adapted materials, as needed	Materials that are smaller, larger, or different in some way may increase function and participation
Opportunities for peer interaction	Peers provide role models and motivation for children with challenges
Provision of positive feedback	Increases the likelihood that children will continue with active engagement
Coordinated team	Lack of coordination can lead to fragmentation and mixed messages
One to one and facilitated peer interaction, as needed	When more focused intervention is needed it will be available

Identification of Explicit Elements of Interaction

Tremendous progress has been made in early childhood education in identifying explicit elements of interaction that facilitate optimal development. Understanding specific aspects of interaction makes it possible for teachers to enhance communication strategies in natural ways. The scientific understanding of these interactive elements has grown from processes that, in healthy development, occur naturally. While we recognize the possibility for incidental learning among children who are typical, children with exceptional developmental challenges need specific supports to learn. For example, taking turns in conversations progresses naturally in typical development, but children with developmental challenges may need more guidance in recognizing how to engage in a conversational exchange.

Reading Interactive Cues

One example of a crucial variable is the cue reading that is found in healthy attachment and relationships. The reciprocity of eye contact, expressions, and vocalizations creates the context for connections and communication with others. Sometimes caregivers exhibit certain characteristics that compromise the quality of basic connections. For instance, mothers who are depressed and/or unresponsive may not respond to the cues and signals shared by children, so the potential for mutuality and synchrony is jeopardized (Birch, 2009). Sometimes children's characteristics make it difficult for others to read their cues. For example, when a child is blind his or her expressions generally do not reflect the nuances of mutuality with others, even if he or she is attuned to other factors such as auditory and tactile stimulation.

Variety of Curricular Models

Some curriculum models may have more "scripted" methods specifically for certain children (LaRocque & Darling, 2008). The majority of children being served in general, inclusive classrooms are using the same curriculum as children without disabilities, but need adaptations to those activities to be able to fully participate (Dunst et al., 2001). Whether a practitioner is a family member, a teacher's assistant, or a physical therapist, once he or she has successful experience working in inclusive programs, choosing and implementing appropriate, effective adaptations often becomes second nature. Together, practitioners figure out what works for an individual child, and then they do it.

Practitioners problem solve, carefully consider options, and arrive at possible solutions. Then, they implement solutions. They evaluate their strategies as they use them, and adjust, as needed (Filler & Xu, 2007; Ostrosky & Cheatham, 2005). Sometimes even people with a good deal of experience working with young children with disabilities find themselves looking for new ways to adapt environments. With changing technology, changing laws, and innovative programs, early childhood education is a dynamic field in which ongoing professional development is imperative (Bruder, 2009; Stayton, 2009).

Responsiveness and Intentionality

Implementing curricular adaptations in inclusive early childhood settings involves a careful planning process as well as the ability to think on one's feet. Responsiveness, positive dispositions, and the ability to anticipate what children might do or need next are all qualities widely recognized as being important for early childhood educators (Epstein, 2007). Children are full of surprises, and learning to maintain one's bearings while also staying on course is an ongoing process just as is being able to effectively observe the changing developmental needs of any child (Katz & McClellan, 1997). Maintaining an inner compass enhances the likelihood that practitioners will be able to figure out what will be helpful in different situations and intentionally adjust. It is important to note that responsiveness does not mean teachers just "go with the flow" and compromise consistency.

Adjusting as Needed

Intelligence includes the ability to solve problems and adjust coping strategies, as needed (Sternberg, 2003). Rather than continuing with attempts that do not work, an effective problem solver of any age will adjust and try different strategies until one works. This ability to be flexible rather than rigid in solving problems is a very important attribute in effective teaching with young children who have disabilities.

When teachers engage in power struggles with children, it is not unusual for difficulties and behavioral issues to escalate. Successful teaching is not predicated on adults

REFLECTION IN ACTION

MS. LIGHTBORNE

Ms. Lightborne has been teaching for almost 20 years and has realized many times that the need for professional development is ongoing. Every year, her groups change. Children enter her class with unique needs, and each year questions emerge regarding appropriate strategies for children who are identified as being eligible for services or those who have not yet been identified but demonstrate challenges. This year she has a child with the characteristics of Asperger syndrome in her class, so she is concentrating on learning as much as possible about that condition, along with methods that may be effective.

She has found that one of the most difficult aspects of effectively implementing strategies has been considering multiple environmental factors from many perspectives. Her classroom is typically busy, with the happy buzz of children talking and being purposefully engaged. She has noticed that Jordan acts out much more in her classroom than he does when he is next door, where there are fewer children and a calmer atmosphere. Ms. Lightborne has always enjoyed creating a classroom climate in which there was much busyness, so it has been challenging for her to acknowledge that this might be overstimulating to Jordan, who has sensory-processing difficulties. She is learning not to take it personally. At the same time, she recognizes the need to adjust the level of stimulation within the room. Jordan cannot say, "This is too much for me!" The adults need to be able to figure this out and make necessary adjustments. Figure 5.1 provides a visual representation of this reflective process on the part of Ms. Lightborne.

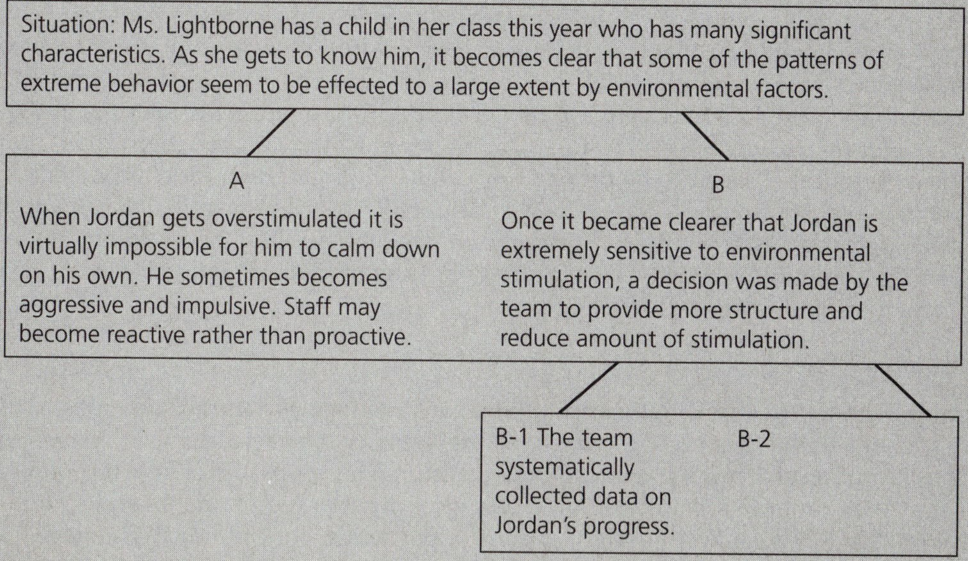

Situation: Ms. Lightborne has a child in her class this year who has many significant characteristics. As she gets to know him, it becomes clear that some of the patterns of extreme behavior seem to be effected to a large extent by environmental factors.

A

When Jordan gets overstimulated it is virtually impossible for him to calm down on his own. He sometimes becomes aggressive and impulsive. Staff may become reactive rather than proactive.

B

Once it became clearer that Jordan is extremely sensitive to environmental stimulation, a decision was made by the team to provide more structure and reduce amount of stimulation.

B-1 The team systematically collected data on Jordan's progress.

B-2

FIGURE 5.1 Decision Tree

having power over children. Successful teaching emerges from effectively negotiating mutually agreed-upon solutions (Paley, 1999).

Characteristics

When working with children who have exceptionalities, practitioners must have some functional knowledge of potentially disabling conditions, their characteristics and effective strategies for intervention. A diagnosis alone does not yield a formula for intervention because each child is unique and has a different configuration of symptoms.

For instance, each child with autism is a distinctive person. Understanding underlying patterns and contributing factors can be very helpful in creatively solving problems about possible interventions. Understanding that most people with autism also have difficulty with sensory processing can be essential in designing curricular adaptations. If practitioners know that people with autism may have tactile defensiveness and experience touch and sensation differently, they can plan for social situations in which hugging may be experienced as aversive.

Even though each individual has his or her own configuration of symptoms, certain conditions can have a somewhat predictable cluster or constellation of characteristics. Specific and accurate information on conditions can be attained through resources such as the National Dissemination Center for Children and Youth with Disabilities (http://www.nichcy.org; Paasche, Gorrill, & Strom, 2004).

Starting with Developmentally Appropriate Curriculum

There are many specialized curriculum models for children with exceptionalities (Squires & Bricker, 2007). This book is primarily focused on adapting developmentally appropriate curriculum, as recognized by the National Association for the Education of Young Children (NAEYC) and other leading early childhood organizations. While there are many potential definitions, interpretations, and variations for the term *inclusion* in early childhood classrooms, the one unifying factor is that inclusive classrooms are places where children with disabilities participate along with peers who are developing typically. It is imperative that the educational opportunities be appropriate for the children who are typical, as well as those who are eligible for special services. Increasingly, standards and practices have referred to "all children" to express the intent of addressing developmental diversity (Hyson, 2003; Stayton, Miller, & Dinnebeil, 2003). Early childhood educators need to be prepared to adjust their practices for children across a developmental continuum (Watson & McCathren, 2009). More explicit clarification of terminology, such as "including children with disabilities," has ensured that efforts to deflect the spotlight from those with disabilities has not inadvertently glossed over differences that need to be acknowledged.

Constructivism

Starting with a developmentally appropriate constructivist curriculum provides a cohesive framework that has been documented and supported by research over many years. A constructivist curriculum provides a basic structure for groups of children. If professionals start with programs that meet NAEYC's accreditation requirements and standards (Hyson, 2003, 2008), and they design learning opportunities for children that engage them in meaningful activities through which their development is enhanced, then they are off to a good start (Jalongo & Isenberg, 2008; LaRocque & Darling, 2008; Winter, 2007).

Given such opportunities for children, professionals can then address the unique patterns of development evident in some children who may or may not be eligible for special services under IDEA, Section 504 of the Rehabilitation Act, or the Americans with Disabilities Act (Rab & Wood, 1995; Walsh & Taylor, 2006; Wood & Youcha, 2009).

CHARACTERISTICS OF CHILDREN: IDENTIFICATION OF STRENGTHS AND NEEDS

Professionals can use assessment to identify individual patterns of strengths and needs. Characteristics of each child, not just his or her diagnosis, contribute to a professional's understanding of his or her current performance level. This is important because not only do individual children have unique configurations of characteristics, but also because diagnoses are not always necessary in early childhood in order to determine eligibility for special services.

While federal law currently makes it possible for young children to be identified as eligible for special services without a categorical diagnosis, some states do not recognize the non-categorical identification of 'developmental delay' for eligibility determination.

Non-Categorical Eligibility Determination Based on Delays

Changes in federal law permits the determination of a young child's eligibility to be based upon a developmental delay (Walsh, 2006). In some cases, a diagnosis may be made at a later date. For example, a child who is performing below an expected level when they are in preschool may be identified as eligible for special services based on the documentation of developmental delays. Then in first grade, this child is identified as having learning disabilities. This is not uncommon. Adaptations need to be made for preschool children whether or not they have a diagnosis of a specific condition. This can be done by identifying the characteristics of each child and matching strategies to those characteristics.

This non-categorical eligibility determination makes it possible to access intervention without needing a specific diagnosis. This is especially helpful with young children because there are many times when they may exhibit behaviors or symptoms associated with certain diagnoses, but they may not actually have the syndromes or conditions. Sometimes children make great progress when they are very young. Children who are 3 in April might demonstrate certain characteristics, but in February of the following year they may have progressed so much that they are no longer officially eligible for special services, based on federal guidelines. The flexibility in determining eligibility is very helpful with young children.

When professionals focus on characteristics, it makes it possible for them to clearly outline each individual child's patterns of strengths and needs or concerns. Such a summary then leads directly to the identification of desired outcomes, objectives, or goals for the child in different domain areas.

Identification of Outcomes Based on Children's Needs

To a large extent, practitioners identify appropriate outcomes for children based on their needs. Sometimes this is relatively easy to figure out, but other times it is more complex. If a young child is having difficulty using a pincer grasp, which is an underlying skill used in many fine motor tasks, it is appropriate to identify mastery of the pincer grasp as

TABLE 5.2   Matching Strategies with Children's Characteristics

Child's Characteristic	Possible Strategies
Difficulty with pincer grasp	Hand-over-hand assistance; different materials
Difficulty sustaining attention	Use of manipulatives; topics of interest to child
Limited expressive language	Plentiful opportunities to talk; use of cues and prompts
Intellectual disabilities; slower acquisition of concepts	More time; use of objects
Frequently disengaged	Adult facilitation of engagement; use of materials focusing on child's interests
Limited engagement in play	Plentiful opportunities to play with other children; adult scaffolding/facilitation, as needed
Disorganized; trouble following directions	Clear, explicit directions, routines, and predictable environment; picture schedules

an objective/outcome for the child. Curricular adaptations such as scaffolding and hand-over-hand assistance can be used to help the child attain this outcome, and the adaptations can be embedded in daily activities to offer many opportunities for practice. If the child has the potential to attain mastery of the pincer grasp, then this would be a realistic outcome. If the child does not have the potential to attain it, then support for generalized use of a palmer grasp would be more appropriate. Subsequent chapters will address this crucial dynamic in all domains of development.

Matching Strategies and Adaptations to Children's Characteristics

Once practitioners have a concept of how to determine appropriate adaptations, they can become proficient in the process. Table 5.2 presents some examples of apparent matches between children's characteristics and possible strategies. While this table focuses on characteristic needs of children, practitioners should also remember strengths. Please note that the column on the right presents options, not requirements.

The crucial match between a child's developmental level and need to the educational methods and intervention is central to its effectiveness. The use of a problem-solving model is integral to effectively determining which strategies match well with a child's specific needs (Ostrosky & Cheatham, 2005). Figuring out what works and planning to incorporate those elements into the intervention for children with developmental challenges is important. Sometimes a reflective process is part of that planning and implementation. Consideration of underlying factors, as with a functional behavioral assessment, enhances intervention by providing meaningful assistance based on what is needed.

Embedding or Integrating Objectives into Activities: Theory

Once the Individualized Family Service Plan (IFSP) or Individualized Education Program (IEP) has identified realistic outcomes, the objectives can be embedded or integrated into activity plans and daily activity schedules. This model of integrating outcomes and strategies is well-established and supported by research (LaRocque & Darling, 2008; Odom, 2000; Ostrosky & Sandall, 2001; Pretti-Frotczak, Grisham-Brown, & Hemmeter,

2005; Sandall & Schwartz, 2009). It is important to note that the methods and adaptations that are used are not random. They are carefully planned, implemented, and monitored to ensure effectiveness with each child. Thus, a system is created through which intervention strategies are integrated into developmentally appropriate curriculum.

Levels and Types of Support

The tiered model of levels of support for children offers a continuum of options. Response to intervention, also known as **recognition and response** (Buysse & Wesley, 2006; Winton, McCollum, & Catlett, 2008), presents three levels of support. The first is available to all children and includes general support strategies. In early childhood, small groups are considered part of the general classroom organization, in addition to the provision of scaffolding, as needed. Level 2 involves more intentional provision of specific strategies that are geared and tailored for the needs of individual children. Level 3 involves the provision of much more focused interventions.

We have discussed the many motivating factors regarding inclusion. Some have supported inclusion because of evidence that it can be effective (Buysse & Wesley, 2006; Dunst & Trivett, 2009; Dunst et al., 2001; McWilliam, Wolery & Odom, 2001; Odom, 2009). Others have supported it because it is believed to be the "right thing" to do, based upon principle (Pearpoint & Forest, 1992; Pruitt, 1997). The tremendous variation in children as well as educational systems has contributed to challenges in implementation. If there is evidence of what is effective for a given child, then the adaptations should be based on the practices that work. Professionals should start by having a repertoire of strategies from which to select a good match for each individual child's needs.

It is more challenging to address the needs of children whose characteristics and/or conditions may be more complex or rare. In such situations, teachers must be

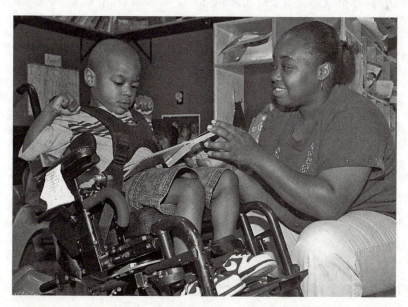

Adults can support developmentally appropriate activities with children.

TABLE 5.3   What Teachers Need to Know

Patterns of typical and exceptional development, including characteristics

Information about and sensitivity to families, cultures, and communities

How to identify and use a variety of assessment measures

How to adapt developmentally appropriate curriculum to address the needs of children on a continuum of developmental levels

How to demonstrate professionalism in a variety of contexts

Source: Information from CEC/DEC Standards.

able to adapt strategies from a repertoire, and then adjust them to the individual needs of the child to the greatest extent possible. Table 5.3 summarizes some of the key competencies necessary for teachers of young children with exceptional development.

While there are some curriculum models that provide relatively prescribed sets of methods, this text focuses on tailoring intervention strategies to individuals with learning differences, without using formulaic approaches. For adapting curricular activities in the context of inclusive classrooms, this text focuses primarily on the active process of reflection and decision making, including levels of support, when the match for individual children and their characteristics is less obvious or predictable. Each of the following chapters will focus on development in different domains.

The match between each child's developmental needs and the presentation of his or her educational opportunities has long been recognized as central to effective educational practices. When children have developmental challenges, matching the child's unique needs with approaches is based on the same educational principle, but it involves a more complex degree of tailoring to meet each child's current level of performance as well as processing style (Gardner, 2000).

Some adaptations are relatively logical. With experience, practitioners can make adaptations with proficiency. For instance, if a child is slower in processing, he or she will need more time. If a child has difficulty manipulating very small objects, they will need larger objects to manipulate. A child in a wheelchair will need extra space to move from one area to another to make all parts of the classroom environment accessible. If a child has trouble processing verbal directions, providing simpler directions makes sense, along with picture cues and/or demonstration. When children are easily disorganized and have trouble sorting things out in less-structured environments, it is helpful to provide more structure and predictability in the environment.

Professionals should have not only a repertoire of potential strategies to use when children have developmental differences, but they also should have the ability to create a match between each child's needs and methods that are used in order to effectively address the needs of all children within inclusive classrooms. This ability is based on knowing about typical and exceptional development. It is also based on having insight into one's own interactive and teaching styles, ranging from highly structured to more spontaneous.

IDENTIFICATION OF EFFECTIVE PRACTICES

How do effective teachers address children's unique needs? What do they do to connect with each individual child? We asked some well-established effective teachers, both with and without special education certification. Ms. Carrie, who has been teaching preschool special education for over 25 years, wisely reflected that it is necessary to be a lifelong learner, because each child is different. It is important to get to know each child, and determine what works well for him or her. Mr. Freshette works in a supportive team and also has significant experience teaching preschool special education within inclusive settings. He has an extraordinary ability to remain calm with children, even when they are very upset. He is clear, empathic, and steady in his responses to children, without caving in to them when their behaviors are escalating.

Both teachers and children are unique, each with personal styles, interests, and motivations. Teachers have strengths and needs. Some seasoned teachers have had many years to develop their own styles and methods before teaching children with exceptionalities within inclusive classrooms. For some, this can be a major adjustment. For others, it may be a natural progression.

Integrated Supports

When important elements such as administrative support, healthy teamwork, coordinated efforts, time for communication, and opportunities for professional development are in place, it is possible for experienced teachers to extend their skills to address the unique needs of children with challenging conditions. This has been the case for Ms. True, who has taught kindergarten for over 30 years, and does not have special education certification.

Continuum of Program Options

In the past, children with special needs were in separate self-contained classrooms, resource rooms, or special schools, unless they were able to meet certain criteria to make them eligible for mainstreaming into "regular" kindergarten (Bricker, 2000). With recent inclusion initiatives, however, Ms. True has had more children with exceptionalities fully included in her kindergarten classes, and she has adjusted her repertoire of strategies accordingly. Among those with more significant challenges have been children with Down syndrome, autism, and neurological impairment. The least restrictive environment is relevant, when considering a continuum of options.

Importance of Administrative Support and Professional Development

In addition to participating in professional development activities, it has been very helpful for Ms. True to have administrative support and collaboration with a special education teacher who intermittently visits the kindergarten class for consultation and support in the inclusive context. This support in situ has made it possible for Ms. True to develop her own ability to tailor the match between a child's developmental needs and effective strategies. Research has supported this dynamic (Leiber et al., 2000). Her ability to reflect and consider not just what she and other team members are doing, but also *how* it is being done, has been crucial for effectiveness.

Classroom Atmosphere and Environment

Ms. True has been able to sustain a classroom atmosphere that is creative, accepting, and child-centered, without having an exaggerated, unnecessary focus on the children with disabilities. All the children in her classroom are productively and positively engaged in meaningful activities. The children with disabilities are purposefully engaged, and their peers are accepting of them. Opportunities for constructive engagement have been recognized as significant in extensive research (Dunst et al., 2001; McWilliam & Casey, 2008; Pianta, LaParo, & Hamre, 2008).

One method Ms. True has used to enhance this climate of developmental diversity is to encourage children to focus on what they are doing rather than worrying about other children. Essentially, she has created an atmosphere in which the expectations are clear and children learn to monitor their own behavior, so the role of the teacher is not to be authoritarian, but rather to be supportive. This includes the opportunity for the teacher to work one-to-one or in small groups, providing more potential for individualization. Establishing predictable routines has been very important. The noise level in the room has also been significant. If it is necessary, Ms. True uses a variety of strategies to monitor and give feedback to the children about volume of noise in room. Using consistent signals helps them to be more in charge of themselves and what they do, and enhances the overall opportunities for concentration. She considers having a positive classroom climate a very high priority for all children.

EMBEDDING OR INTEGRATING STRATEGIES AND OUTCOMES: APPLICATIONS

When professionals plan for an inclusive classroom, the strategies and the tone they use can make a big difference. There is a natural progression of identifying individual children's characteristics and patterns, identifying effective strategies, and embedding those strategies into daily routines and activities. Professionals should use a systematic approach while also evaluating the effectiveness of what they do; this can increase the likelihood of success (Watson & McCathren, 2009). The following examples will help clarify this progression.

EXAMPLE 1   Karly

When she was very young, Karly had language delays and sensory processing dysfunction that affected her fine motor development. It was helpful to have a full and rich sense of Karly as a person, especially in terms of her creativity and comprehension, in order to identify outcomes and strategies that were a good match for her. Her sensitivity, humor, and artistic flair made it possible to focus on motor skills and sensory integration during activities that were motivating and meaningful to her. Because she took great pleasure in painting the outside of ceramic bowls with special paint that could be glazed, she was far more likely to persist with the fine motor activity and want to repeat it, expanding her own skills and strategies. Thus, the degree of Karly's motivation increased the likelihood that she would gain practice through repetition in a meaningful context. This was a far better strategy than implementing "drill and practice" methods mechanically.

Structuring Adapted Activity Plans

Activity plans provide a structure and organization to facilitate the implementation of activities. While the formats may vary, there are some common elements such as a clear statement of objectives, materials, initiation, procedure, and closure. Some states have developed their own preferred activity plan format. Having clearly stated

Purpose of Activity:	Sensory experience
	Language development
	Social interaction with peers
	Concepts (measurement, etc.)
Materials:	Sand table
	Choice of manipulatives, figures; measuring spoons and cups
Procedure:	Teacher introduces the activity
	Provides an overview of focus and materials
	Teacher provides verbal guidance regarding number of children

FIGURE 5.2 Sample Activity: Sand Table

outcomes/objectives is essential. It is helpful if they are well integrated with IEP outcomes. In some cases, plans include sections for differentiated instruction tailored for the identified needs of children who are gifted and talented, as well as those who have delays. Formats vary, but generally there is some similarity in the basic content. The sand table activity presented in Figure 5.2 is an example of a simple child-centered activity often available in early childhood programs.

Integration of Individualized Strategies

Individualized, differentiated strategies can be integrated throughout the activity plan or listed at the end. When they are integrated throughout, the adaptations for individual children can be color-coded for easy reading. If they are typed on a computer, italicizing and/or printing in bold can enhance accessibility. If there are several children in a group who need differentiated instruction, a variety of fonts may be used. Proposed strategies for Karly appear in italic bold, embedded into the activity in Figure 5.3.

Purpose of Activity:	Sensory experience ***Karly may be sensitive to the texture of sand*** Language development ***Karly will be paired with a verbal peer***
	Social interaction with peers ***Facilitation of peer interaction will be available, as needed***
	Concepts (measurement, etc.)
Materials:	Sand table ***Texture of sand may be adjusted, as needed, or Karly can wear gloves. She may also use utensils (spoons, scoops) if touching the sand irritates her.***
	Choice of manipulatives, figures; measuring spoons and cups ***Materials that are especially motivating to Karly and her friend will be available.***
Procedure:	Teacher introduces the activity
	Provides an overview of focus and materials
	Teacher provides verbal guidance regarding number of children ***Teacher will be available to help children engage, but will make a point of stepping back as soon as they are independently involved with activity.***

FIGURE 5.3 Sample Adapted Activity: Sand Table

TABLE 5.4 Characteristics, Strategies, and Opportunities Within Environments		
Characteristics	**Strategies**	**Opportunities**
Problems manipulating small objects	Use of larger objects	Centers; Snack; Play
Use of a wheelchair	Accessible environment	Throughout the day
Difficulty processing verbal directions	Clear, explicit directions; picture cues. Simple, clear directions.	Environmental cues; Scaffolding and support from adults, other children, in all contexts
Child is disorganized	Structure, predictability	Monitoring throughout the day, in all contexts. Guidance and support for self-regulation.

Whatever approach is used, the adaptations should be clearly accessible and reader friendly, so the teacher and all other team members are able to easily figure out what strategies might be used. Some states have adopted activity plans used in all districts, which include a section for differentiated instruction. Table 5.4 provides some samples of how strategies to address specific challenges may be integrated into the schedule and activities.

PLANNING DIFFERENTIATED INSTRUCTION BASED ON UNIQUE CHARACTERISTICS

Sometimes characteristics in a child are complex and compounded enough that practitioners need to sort out which factors are most important and also determine which strategies are most effective. Strategies should not be randomly implemented based on trial and error. Teachers and other team members should work together in intentional ways to determine which strategies appear to be likely to be effective and then collaborate further to evaluate their success. Consistency is important, especially once an appropriate plan has been established (Epstein, 2007).

Use of Specific Strategies

There are times when a decision is made to try a specific strategy with a child, such as giving the child a choice of two options during a transition to center time. This can be a very good method for most children. As simple as the transition may seem, it can potentially trigger an emotional outburst from a child who wants to do something else. If an objective for a child is that he or she will expand his or her repertoire of play themes, he or she may resist being guided away from the only center he or she ever voluntarily chooses. This happened one morning when Delia, a girl who will be turning 4 in a few months, was told by Mr. Freshette, her teacher, that she could play with computers or tangrams, but not play in the area that had become a fixation for her. Offering a choice of two other activities did provide her with some sense of being in control, but that might have been initially obscured by her wish to remain in her preferred area.

Strategies to Expand Children's Repertoire

Offering options is a well-established strategy to broaden a child's repertoire of play themes, and is often used when children become fixated upon one, or a narrow range of

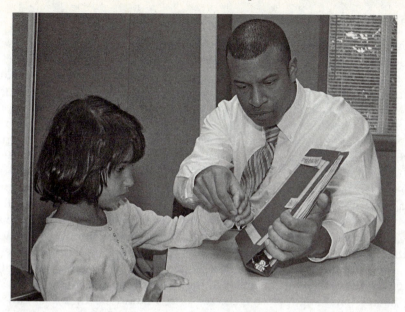

The level of intervention is determined based on each child's individual needs.

themes (Linder, 1993, 2008). The term *perseveration* is sometimes used to describe the repetitive actions of children who may need intervention to increase their range of engagement.

Intentional Selection of Strategies

When team members understand that it is possible to make intentional decisions about which strategies to use, it adds leverage to educational opportunities within classrooms. It is helpful to consider options in an organized way. Figure 5.4 provides a sampling of possible strategies organized by the type of adaptation.

Type of Adaptation	Sample
Environmental	Noise level
	Amount of Stimulation
	Room arrangement
	Accessibility
Materials	Different size
	Adaptive (e.g., scissors)
	Special equipment
	Positioning
Adjustments to instruction	Scaffolding
	Prompts
	Cues
	Questioning strategies

FIGURE 5.4 Types of Strategies for Adaptations

REFLECTION: ADJUSTING APPROACHES TO INTERVENTION

It is important to consider not just *what* is done during adaptations, but also *how* it is done. In the scenario with Delia and Mr. Freshette, it was significant that Mr. Freshette used a clear, matter-of-fact tone of voice, while being empathic and supportive. Significantly, he did not react to Delia's outburst with an escalated tone of voice or launch into a power struggle. Calmly, but firmly, he said, "I'm sorry, but you need to choose something else to do this morning. I will help you choose, if you wish." He also did not cave in or alter his initial request, given Delia's escalation. After approximately one minute of intense emotional outburst, Delia calmed down, and was guided toward using the computer. Thus, it was not just *what* Mr. Freshette did but *how* he did it.

Reflection can be a very powerful tool in helping teams, professionals as well as parents, adjust what they do to become more effective. Reflection requires a well-established repertoire of possible strategies and responses to situations, with an ability to quickly size up a situation and select an option for intervention. Sometimes this occurs intuitively. Practitioners might do something spontaneously that matches a child's needs, demonstrating a good fit. Sometimes when caregivers respond so intuitively, it is a challenge for them to plan for and use the same strategies intentionally. Teachers should consider what is effective to increase the likelihood that they can use those strategies intentionally, not just incidentally (Epstein, 2007). Balancing these with predictable routines is also central to providing environments that support optimal interaction for all children.

Multiple Perspectives from Team Members

When team members discuss a child's response to a situation and what seemed to work, they can determine what is most effective for that child. Team communication is essential to the coordination and implementation of high-quality inclusive programs

CEC/DEC Standard 4: Instructional Strategies	
CC4S4	Use strategies to facilitate maintenance and generalization of skills across learning environments.
CC4S6	Use strategies that promote successful transitions for individuals with exceptional learning needs.
EC4K1	Concept of **universal design for learning**
EC4S1	Plan, implement, and evaluate developmentally appropriate curricula, instruction, and adaptations based on knowledge of individual children, the family, and the community.
EC4S2	Facilitate child-initiated development and learning.
EC4S3	Use teacher-scaffolded and initiated instruction to complement child-initiated learning.
EC4S4	Link development, learning experiences, and instruction to promote educational transitions.
EC4S5	Use individual and group guidance and problem-solving techniques to develop supportive relationships with and among children.
EC4S6	Use strategies to teach social skills and conflict resolution.
EC4S7	Use a continuum of intervention strategies to support access of young children in the general curriculum and daily routines.

FIGURE 5.5 DEC (CEC/DEC Standards).

(Allred, Brien, & Black, 2003). Communication can yield information about important cultural factors as well (Corso, Santos, & Roof, 2002).

Adjusting Along the Way

Effective reflection can be a very useful process when practitioners have both an internal ability to consider various options and an external support system. Reflection is a process through which one can consider options. Adaptations can also involve a bit of invention. For instance, if a child is attempting a fine motor activity, but is having difficulty maneuvering the pieces of a puzzle, a practitioner who has a basic concept of fine motor skill acquisition and a sense of adaptation principles may adjust the position of the puzzle so that it is easier to manipulate on a slant. The teacher may also look for puzzles with handles on them. Sometimes puzzles may be adapted for ease of handling in cost-effective ways (Milbourne & Campbell, 2007). Using reflection to generate such relatively simple solutions implies an ability to think about possibilities when children are having difficulty.

INTEGRATING GOALS AND OBJECTIVES WITH CHILDREN'S CHARACTERISTICS AND CURRICULAR ADAPTATIONS

To engage in the active process of solving problems and exploring options, teachers need to have information about each child's current level of functioning. If a child's current performance has not already been assessed, assessment would be an initial step. Given a child's current developmental performance level, the next step would be determining reasonable outcomes. This is part of the IFSP or IEP (Filler & Xu, 2007). Clear, attainable, and relevant objectives should be based on what a child is not currently achieving and the child's zone of proximal development. This makes it possible to develop intervention strategies that guide or "scaffold" the child toward acquiring new skills or developmental abilities (Vygotsky, 1967).

During the implementation phase of intervention, practitioners are faced with the task of matching what a child needs, from moment to moment. Sometimes the intervention has been pre-planned, and a consistent response is used, no matter who is interacting with the child. This is very important because more than one adult is frequently in a classroom, and predictable responses and consequences are essential for success. Predictable responses and consequences are elements of social environments that have long been recognized as crucial to the success of young children in inclusive settings (Bruder, 1993).

For instance, if a child has a language delay and is getting very upset and frustrated because he is trying to express something but cannot find the right words, an effective strategy could be pre-planned. The teacher might gain physical proximity, look directly at the child, and model a simple statement, such as asking the child if this is what he or she wants. A simple request to the child, with modeling of possible replies, creates an opportunity for the child to successfully express what he or she wants. The intervention builds in the option for the child to provide feedback. It is worth noting that this method is often used when children who are developing typically are first acquiring language and may be frustrated over their inability to generate words as quickly as they may want.

Exercising Professional Judgment

Teachers need to be encouraged to rely on their own professional judgment when thinking about their next steps in designing interventions for all children in a classroom. A teacher with a classroom assistant might feel very isolated in terms of support and feel vulnerable when trying to determine what is right for an individual child and what makes sense for all children within the context of the classroom. This teacher should use the opportunity to form a professional development circle, a relationship with a mentor, or an ongoing dialogue with a colleague in that school or another school, which would make exercising professional judgment easier. The opportunity to present data to another professional and to engage him or her in communication about teaching and intervention ideas is one way to grow as a teacher and to empower oneself to be more comfortable exercising professional judgment.

Informing Practice with Formative Assessment

An essential element of effective reflection is the determination of success through formative assessment. Ongoing observation, running records, and other forms of data collection provide valuable information about each child's progress in ways that inform practice. If a certain approach or strategy is working, it makes sense to continue to use it. Professionals and parents can use children's performance as one measure of whether an intervention strategy is working. Acknowledging and celebrating children's accomplishments can provide the momentum for continued success.

Data Collection over Time

Some forms of progress, however, are not immediately evident. Professionals may need to use an approach over time, before expecting to see any demonstrable results. In such instances, keeping careful records of what methods are used and how a child responds is important over time. If, after a reasonable amount of time, a strategy has had no apparent positive effect, then it is probably important for the team to reconsider variations on the strategy.

Child Outcomes

The outcomes for each child provide essential data and information about the effectiveness of the intervention. The determination of an intervention's effectiveness based upon children's performance and progress is contingent upon a reliable perspective on the whole child, including innate factors as well as environmental conditions. Professionals know that the rate at which children progress varies significantly even without disabilities. Professionals should be careful as they assess the process and outcomes that they take into consideration the initial characteristics of each child, the baseline, as well as the child's pace of development and progress.

The following chapters provide the opportunity to consider the applications of curricular adaptations in all domains of development. These adaptations will also be applied in the context of different curricular areas, addressing all early childhood standards.

Questions for Reflection

When you are working with a child, are you aware of your own observations of what the child is doing? Are you aware of how he or she is responding to the situation and to interaction?

1. What system do you use to keep track of the child's ongoing engagement?
2. How do you adjust to changing interactions with children? Please be as specific as possible.
3. Do you adjust your tone of voice? Your position? Your volume?
4. Do you rephrase questions or statements if children appear non-responsive?
5. When you relate to children from culturally and/or linguistically diverse groups, are you aware of how you might adjust your interaction? If so, how?

Summary

This chapter has provided an overview of the progression from the identification of characteristics of individual children, to the identification of possible strategies and finally to the integration or embedment of those strategies into daily routines and activities. The following chapters will guide you through application of interventions within specific areas.5

Key Terms

Adaptations
Evidence-based practices

Recognition and response
Strategies

Universal design for learning

Websites

The Circle of Inclusion
http://www.circleofinclusion.org

Frank Porter Graham Child Development Institute, University of North Carolina, Chapel Hill
http://www.fpg.unc.edu

The Division for Early Childhood, Council for Exceptional Children
http://www.dec-sped.org

The National Association for the Education of Young Children
http://www.naeyc.org

The National Dissemination Center for Children and Youth with Disabilities
http://www.nichcy.org

References

Allred, K., Briem, R., & Black, S. (2003). Collaboratively addressing the needs of young children with disabilities. In C. Copple (Ed.), *A world of difference* (pp. 131–134). Washington, DC: National Association for the Education of Young Children.

Birch, M. (Ed.). (2009). *Finding hope in despair.* Washington, DC: Zero to Three.

Bricker, D. (2000). Inclusion: How the scene has changed. *Topics in Early Childhood Special Education, 20*(1), 14–19.

Bronfenbrenner, U. (1992). Ecological systems theory. In R. Vasta (Ed.), *Six theories of child development: Revised formulations and current issues* (pp. 187–248). Philadelphia: Jessica Kingsley.

Bruder, M. B. (1993). The provisions of early intervention and early childhood special education within community early childhood programs: Characteristics of effective service delivery. *Topics in Early Childhood Special Education, 13*(1), 19–37.

Bruder, M. B. (2009). The national status of in-service professional development systems for early intervention and early childhood special education. *Infants and Young Children, 22*(1), 13–20.

Buysse, V., & Wesley, P. (Eds.). (2006). *Evidence-based practices in the early childhood field.* Washington, DC: Zero to Three.

Copple, C., & Bredekamp, S. (2009). *Developmentally appropriate practices* (3rd ed.). Washington, DC: National Association for the Education of Young Children.

Corso, R., Santos, R., & Roof, V. (2002). Honoring diversity in early childhood education materials. *Teaching Exceptional Children, 34*(3), 30–36.

Dunst, C., Bruder, M. B., Trivette, C., Raab, M., & McLean, M. (2001). Natural learning opportunities for infants, toddlers, and preschoolers. *Young Exceptional Children, 4*(3), 18–22.

Dunst, C., & Trivette, C. (2009). Using research evidence to inform and evaluate early childhood intervention practices. *Topics in Early Childhood Special Education, 29*(1), 40–52.

Epstein, A. (2007). *The intentional teacher.* Washington, DC: National Association for the Education of Young Children.

Filler, J., & Xu, Y. (2007). Including children with disabilities in early childhood education programs: Individualizing appropriate practice. *Childhood Education, 83*(2), 92–98

Foley, G., & Hochman, J. (Eds.). (2006). *Mental health in early intervention.* Baltimore: Paul H. Brookes.

Gardner, H. (2000). *The disciplined mind.* New York: Penguin Books.

Grisham-Brown, J., Hemmeter, M. L., & Pretti-Frontczak, K. (2005). *Blended Practices.* Baltimore: Paul H. Brookes.

Guralnick, M. (Ed.). (2001). *Early childhood inclusion: Focus on change.* Baltimore: Paul H. Brookes.

Hemmeter, M. L. (2000). Classroom-based interventions: Evaluating the past and looking to the future. *Topics in Early Childhood Special Education, 20*(1), 56–60.

Hyson, M. (Ed.). (2003). *Preparing early childhood professionals: NAEYC's Standards for Programs.* Washington, DC: National Association for the Education of Young Children.

Hyson, M. (2008). *Enthusiastic and engaged learners.* New York: Teachers College Press.

Jalongo, M. R., & Isenberg, J. P. (2008). *Exploring your role as a reflective practitioner.* Upper Saddle River, NJ: Merrill/Pearson Education.

Katz, L., & McClellan, D. (1997). *Fostering children's social competence: The teacher's role.* Washington, DC: National Association for the Education of Young Children.

LaRocque, M., & Darling, S. (Eds.). (2008). *Blended curriculum in the inclusive classroom.* Boston: Allyn & Bacon/Pearson Education.

Leiber, J., Hanson, M. J., Beckman, P. J., Odom, S. L., Sandall, S. R., Schwartz, I. S., et al. (2000). Key influences on the initiation and implementation of inclusive preschool programs. *Exceptional Children, 67*(1), 83–98.

Linder, T. (1993/2008). *Transdisciplinary play-based intervention.* Baltimore: Paul H. Brookes.

McGuire-Schwartz, M., & Arndt, J. (2007). Transforming universal design for learning in early childhood teacher education from college classroom to early childhood classroom. *Journal of Early Childhood Teacher Education, 28,* 127–139.

McWilliam, R., & Casey, A. (2008). *Engagement of every child in the preschool classroom.* Baltimore: Paul H. Brookes.

McWilliam, R., Wolery, M., & Odom, S. (2001). Instructional perspectives in inclusive preschool classrooms. In M. Guralnick (Ed.), *Early childhood inclusion: Focus on change* (pp. 503–530). Baltimore: Paul H. Brookes.

Milbourne, S. A., & Campbell, P. H. (2007). *CARA's kit: Creating adaptations for routines and activities.* Philadelphia: Child and Family Studies Research Programs. Thomas Jefferson University.

Miller, R. (1996). *The developmentally appropriate inclusive classroom.* New York: Delmar.

Odom, S. (2000). Preschool inclusion: What we know and where we go from here. *Topics in Early Childhood Special Education, 20*(1), 20–27.

Odom, S. (2009). The tie that binds: Evidence-based practice, implementation science, and outcomes for children. *Topics in Early Childhood Special Education, 29*(1), 53–61.

Ostrosky, M., & Cheatham, G. (2005). Teaching the use of problem-solving process to early childhood educators. *Young Exceptional Children. 9*(1), 11–20.

Ostrosky, M., & Sandall, S. (2001). *Teaching strategies: What to do to support young children's development.* DEC Monograph #3. Longmont, CO: Sopris West.

Paasche, C., Gorrill, & Srom (2004). *Children with special needs in early childhood settings.* Clifton Park: NY: Thompson/Delmar.

Paley, V. (1999). *The kindness of children.* Cambridge, MA: Harvard University Press.

Pearpoint, J., Forest, M., & Snow, J. (1992). *The inclusion papers.* Toronto, Ontario, Canada: The Inclusion Press.

Pianta, R., La Paro, K., & Hamre, B. (2007). *Classroom assessment scoring system.* Baltimore: Paul H. Brookes.

Pickard-Kremenitzer, J., & Miller, R. (2008). Are you a highly qualified, emotionally intelligent early childhood educator? *Young Children, 63,* 106–112.

Pruitt, P. L. (1997). Inclusive practices for preschoolers with disabilities. In P. Zionts (Ed.), *Inclusion for students with learning and behavior problems* (pp. 329–390). Austin, TX: PRO-ED.

Rab, V., & Wood, K. (1995). *Child care and the ADA.* Baltimore: Paul H. Brookes.

Sandall, S., Hemmeter, M. L., Smith, B., & McLean, M. (2005). *Recommended practices: A comprehensive guide.* Longmont, CO: Sopris West.

Sandall, S., & Ostrosky, M. (Eds.). (2000). *Natural environments and inclusion.* DEC Monograph # 2. Longmont, CO: Sopris West.

Sandall, S., & Schwartz, S. (2009). *Building blocks* (2nd ed.). Baltimore: Paul H. Brookes.

Smith, B. J., McLean, M. E., Sandall, S., Snyder, P., & Broudy-Ramsey, A. (2005). Recommended practices: The practices and evidence base used to establish them. In S. Sandall, M. L. Hemmeter, B. J. Smith, & M. E. McLean (Eds.), *DEC recommended practices* (pp. 27–44). Longmont, CO: Sopris West.

Squires, J., & Bricker, D. (2007). *An activity-based approach to developing young children's social emotional competence.* Baltimore: Paul H. Brookes.

Stayton, V. (2009). State certification requirements for early childhood special educators. *Infants and Young Children, 22*(1), 4–12.

Stayton, V., Miller, P., & Dinnebeil, L. (2003). *Personnel preparation in early childhood special education: Implementing the DEC recommended practices.* Longmont, CO: Sopris West.

Sternberg, R. J. (2003). A broad view of intelligence: The theory of successful intelligence. *Consulting Psychology Journal: Practice & Research, 55,* 139–154.

Tertell, E., Klein, S., & Jewett, J. (Eds.). (1998). *When teachers reflect: Journeys toward effective, inclusive practice.* Washington, DC: National Association for the Education of Young Children.

Turnbull, R., Turnbull, A., & Wehmeyer, M. (2007). *Exceptional lives* (5th ed.). Upper Saddle River, NJ: Merrill/Pearson Education.

Vygotsky, L. (1967). Play and its role in the mental development of the child. *Soviet Psychology, 5,* 6–18. (Original work published in 1933).

Walsh, S., Smith, B., & Taylor, R. (2000). *IDEA requirements for preschoolers with disabilities.* Reston, VA: The Council for Exceptional Children.

Walsh, S., & Taylor, R. (2006). *Understanding IDEA: What it means for preschool children with disabilities and their families.* Reston, VA: Division of Early Childhood, Council for Exceptional Children.

Watson, A., & McCathren, R. (2009). Including children with special needs. Are you and your program ready? *Young Children, 64*(2), 20–26.

Winter, S. (2007). *Inclusive early childhood education: A collaborative approach.* Upper Saddle River, NJ: Merrill/Pearson Education.

Winton, P., McCollum, J., & Catlett, C. (2008). *Practical approaches to early childhood professional development.* Washington, DC: Zero-to- Three.

Wolery, M., & Sainato, D. M. (1996). General curriculum and intervention strategies. In S. L. Odom & M. E. McLean (Eds.), *Early intervention/early childhood special education: Recommended practices* (pp. 125–158). Austin, TX: PRO-ED.

Wood, K., & Youcha, V. (2009). *The ABC's of the ADA.* Baltimore: Paul H. Brookes.

Chapter 6
Play and Social Development

OBJECTIVES

After reading this chapter, students will:

- Be familiar with an overview of typical and exceptional social-emotional development;

- Understand the importance of play, curriculum, and the environment on early intervention for children who have short- or long-term social-emotional challenges;

- Demonstrate an understanding of how characteristics of children can be effectively matched with intervention strategies;

- Demonstrate an understanding of how risks and protective factors contribute to and alleviate challenging behaviors;

- Recognize ways in which an active reflective process may be used to enhance the effectiveness of inclusion of children with social and emotional challenges.

DEVELOPMENTALLY APPROPRIATE CURRICULUM THAT SUPPORTS SOCIAL-EMOTIONAL DEVELOPMENT

Laying the Groundwork

Social and emotional difficulties in young children pose unique challenges to caregivers because of the complexity and potential subjectivity of the social-emotional area. Even when social development progresses within a typical range there are seemingly infinite individual variations of temperament, personality, and interactive styles.

Theories of social development also range from psychosocial, as explained by Erik Erikson (1963) to approaches that are more behavioral (Sandall & Ostrosky, 1999). It is imperative that caregivers be familiar with the complexity of normal social development in order to differentiate the characteristics of children that are outside that range.

Of all the domains, social-emotional development is perhaps the most complex. It is also at the heart of performance in all developmental realms. Normal social-emotional development involves a tremendous interplay of dynamics on multiple levels. Scientists are studying social and emotional development with advanced technology, which can measure chemical and electrical responses to certain stimuli in the brain and cells throughout the body (Shonkoff & Phillips, 2001; Shore, 1997). Even with these scientific advances, there is still considerable mystery involved, especially in the interactions that occur between people.

It is well recognized that attachment is an essential building block for healthy emotional development (Riley, San Juan, Klinkner, & Ramminger, 2008). The interaction between the individual and his or her environment plays a significant role in all domains of development. This has long been recognized on a psychobiological level (Shore, 1997; Zigler & Styfko, 2004) and now has also found its way to social policies (Shonkoff & Phillips, 2001). This phenomenon is especially important in social and emotional development, not just in terms of the complexity of neurological development, but also in terms of the complexity of understanding group dynamics and social patterns. As most teachers know from personal experience, disruptive behavior in a class has the potential of altering the quality of everyone's interaction. Just as a good laugh shared can set a tone for a group, more negative interactions can create a context for escalating challenges.

RISK AND PROTECTIVE FACTORS: RESILIENCE

While considering atypical development and the characteristics of children who may need intervention, professionals should remember the concept of risks and protective factors, as they impact the dynamic of development (Stormont, 2007). Early childhood educators have learned much about resilience and children's amazing ability to overcome the challenges that face them. While some risks, such as poverty, may affect development across developmental domains, some risk factors have the potential to be especially damaging to social and emotional development. Factors that can negatively impact relationships include maltreatment, abuse, or neglect. Factors affecting the central nervous system (CNS) can contribute to sensory processing issues and difficulty with self regulation. Factors such as temperament can impact a child's ability to cope and adjust, given the many unpredictable elements in a typical early childhood classroom.

When practitioners lack information about child development it can negatively affect attachment, especially if the lack of information results in expectations that cannot be actualized or are a mismatch for the child's capabilities at his or her current age. Some examples would be a child's ability to calm himself or herself down or figure out what the expectations are when he or she is being given inconsistent messages and expectations. Parental mental health issues such as untreated postpartum depression can be a significant risk factor. Family dynamics may also be risk factors (Birch, 2009; Zeanah, 1993).

The markers or indicators of healthy attachment include gaze, synchrony, and reciprocity. Individual children vary infinitely; the pacing, temperament, and rhythm of each relationship is as unique as the individuals involved. There are general relationship patterns we acknowledge, not so much as formulas to follow in cookbook fashion, but as guidelines that help us recognize shared humanity. Recognizing these patterns may also be helpful during moments of doubt, which can present themselves even with robustly healthy relationships. Table 6.1 provides an overview of significant social developments in early childhood.

Setting the Stage for Healthy Social and Emotional Development

There are many environmental elements that support healthy social and emotional development that would ideally be found in all early childhood programs. These elements are recognized in the accreditation through the National Association for the Education of Young Children (NAEYC), as well as the Head Start Association and other indicators, such as those in the Early Childhood Environmental Rating Scale (ECERS) and The Classroom Assessment Scoring System (CLASS).

These healthy environmental elements should be universally available in responsive, supportive environments where all individual differences are recognized and respected. In a positive school environment, there is an atmosphere of regard for a variety of perspectives. There are both implicit and explicit understandings about how people should treat each other. In early childhood practitioners should ensure that all children have opportunities for a variety of interactions—individualized, small-group, and whole-group activities. Figure 6.1 provides some perspectives on environments that support healthy social and emotional development.

TABLE 6.1   Significant Social Developments in Early Childhood

Developmental Feature	Specific Indicators	Relevance
Attachment	Connections with others; trust	Relationship development
Separation	Autonomous action; self-esteem; confidence	Autonomy enhances quality of social interaction and responsibility.
Individuation	Ability to differentiate	Children are able to process and act as individuals
Perspective taking	Ability to see and understand situations from a variety of perspectives	Difficulty with perspective taking contributes to difficulty with interaction
Empathy	Expression of concern for others	
Social problem solving	Coping strategies; negotiation; arriving at mutually acceptable resolutions	Contributes to healthy coping in a variety of situations
Conflict resolution	Verbal negotiation; asking for assistance; identifying possible solutions; verbal expression of feelings.	Makes it more possible for children to reconcile differences
Self-regulation	The ability to calm and self-soothe, as well as sustain engagement	Difficulties can have pervasive impact on interaction and engagement; functioning
Engagement in play	Many aspects of healthy development emerge in the context of play	Spontaneous interaction supports healthy development; difficulties can have significant impact

Positive learning environments are welcoming and accepting. Children are actively engaged and participating together. There are also places in the classroom where children can go to be quiet, either alone or with others. The atmosphere is child-centered and accessible. Children with and without challenging conditions are equal members of the classroom community. The tone is not overwhelming and/or overstimulating. There is an atmosphere of mutual respect. Adults are available to support children as needed, but there are also many child-centered activities and opportunities for independence. Clear expectations, structure, and predictable schedules provide a sense of security to children. Clear limits provide healthy boundaries.

FIGURE 6.1   High-Quality Inclusive Social Environments: What Do They Look Like?

PLAY, CURRICULUM, AND SOCIAL-EMOTIONAL ISSUES

The Importance of Play

Play progresses through stages. Positive play experiences can unite and blend all aspects of development, and benefit the child in a variety of areas, including social, emotional, language, physical, cognitive, creative, moral, and cultural (Tsao, 2002; Van Horn, Nourot, Scales, & Alward, 2007).

Play Stages

Parten (1932) looked at play through the social interaction lens. She suggested looking at the social interaction among children that takes place during their play. Parten categorized play into the several types. When children achieve the level of cooperative play, they still enjoy

TABLE 6.2   Types of Play

Type of Play	Child Characteristics
Solitary play	Child acts alone
Onlooker play	Child watches others
Parallel play	Child individually plays with toys and materials that are similar to those used by other children in geographic proximity.
Associative play	Child engages in the same activity as other children but in an unorganized, disassociated way.
Cooperative play Pretend play Sociodramatic play Outdoor play Object play	Child organizes in a group (small or large) for some purposes and with other children; shares equipment, materials, ideas, and purposes.

engaging in the other types of play from time to time. Other theorists have also conceptualized types and **stages of play**. Table 6.2 provides an overview of different stages of play.

Benefits of Play

There are many benefits to play. Play promotes cognitive development and skills. It facilitates both divergent and convergent thinking. Play helps children to develop and improve their communication skills and to enhance their language and literacy development. Both fine and gross motor skills are enhanced through play. Play encourages positive emotional development and provides the opportunity for children to develop social interaction skills.

The Role of Play

Developmentally appropriate curriculum for supporting social-emotional development is all encompassing. Play is key to social-emotional development. Play is the socializing experience that allows young children to develop positive and caring behavior toward peers. A classroom ripe with opportunities for creative play will enhance developmental opportunities for the children. Fostering play in a classroom does not hinge solely on the materials and equipment. Certainly having a variety of play materials enhances the potential for quality play, but it is not totally necessary. Children have the potential to engage in their best play when there are minimal materials to channel the direction of their play. What really helps to increase the potential for developing play in a classroom is the philosophy and value of play held by the teachers and the leadership in the school. This is manifested through interactions during which adults are available to scaffold and facilitate play and social interaction as needed (Kaiser & Rasminsky, 2003; Sandall & Ostrosky, 1999).

Different Types of Play and Activities

Both the areas and the flow of the day in an early childhood classroom has potential for enhancing social-emotional development. There are activities that even further encourage social-emotional growth. Dramatic play, puppet play, and some types of block play can all foster socialization. Outdoor play, art, music, and movement activities are also areas that are rich with social development opportunity. Initially, children may engage in play as onlookers and not active participants. If this happens it is important to note that children are still learning. If a child does not move beyond the onlooker stage, it might be time to consider a more direct intervention and/or to consider why this is happening. For instance, a child with the characteristics of post-traumatic stress disorder (PTSD) may be fearful, and he or she may benefit from reassurance. A child with a nonverbal processing disorder may have trouble reading the cues of other children, and may benefit from assistance as he or she attempts to interpret what other children are doing, to find a way to enter the play. A child with sensory processing dysfunction may find the spontaneous and tactile aspect of play unnerving. Children may have characteristics of reactive attachment disorder, anxiety, depression, or phobias.

Research on Play

There is considerable research on the development of play and the role of play in various aspects of child development (Bretherton, 1989; Bretherton, O'Connell, Shore, & Bates, 1984; Fein, 1981; Fisher, 1992; Kinsman & Berk, 1979; Rubin, 1982). Elias and Berk (2002) posited that there is a role for socio-dramatic play in the self-regulation in children. Bronson (2000) further explored the significance of self-regulation. If children have neurological risks, they may especially need predictability and organization within the classroom. They may be especially susceptible to decompensating in an environment that is chaotic or disorganized.

Pretend Play

Children begin to engage in pretend play, develop receptive and expressive language, and use mental representation at approximately the same time in their development. It is understandable that researchers have hypothesized strong relationships among these processes. Pretend play requires the ability to transform objects and actions symbolically; it is carried out through interactive social dialogue and negotiation; and it involves role taking, script knowledge, and improvisation. Lillard (1998) stated that pretend play involves negotiation between players with differing views, simultaneous representation of objects in two ways (real and pretend), role play requiring acting out others' thoughts and actions, and portrayal of emotions appropriate to varied situations and actors. These are all actions that suggest that the pretenders have mental representation abilities. However, substantial research on how children understand other's thinking indicates that even though children can pretend through actions earlier, they do not gain the ability to understand that others may not have the same knowledge as they do until age 4 or 5. Taking this perspective is referred to as the "theory of mind".

Communication and Cognition in the Context of Play

Pretend play uses language and takes place in social contexts. Some recent studies of pretend play provide some insight on the social and linguistic competence vital for school success. In an observational study of pretend play, Sawyer (1997) found that preschool children's pretend play involved improvisational exchanges, rather than following a script. He also found that these exchanges were more successful when they were implicitly included in the play scenario rather than when children stopped the play to make explicit suggestions. He provides rich examples of the skill children exhibit in using improvisation in pretend play.

Nonsocial Play Behaviors

Movement from simple to complex social pretend play does not occur smoothly for some children. Rubin and Coplan (1998) reported about a series of studies that followed children who exhibited nonsocial or "withdrawn" play behaviors during preschool. They found that early social withdrawal is a strong predictor of peer rejection, social anxiety, loneliness, depression, and negative self-esteem in later childhood and adolescence. Nonsocial play behaviors also seem to have negative implications for academic success. The researchers stated that the consequences of social withdrawal might vary by culture; there may be more negative consequences for boys in the U.S., compared to boys in other cultures where passive, controlled, and reticent behavior is valued (e.g., China). Gender differences in play may also affect kindergarten adjustment, with boys who have solitary-passive play behaviors and girls who have solitary-active play behaviors rated as more poorly adjusted by teachers (Coplan, Gavinski-Molina, Lagace-Seguin, & Wichmann, 2001).

Socioeconomic Factors

Pretend play development may also be affected by socioeconomic factors. In observations of 22 classrooms for two periods of play, children who participated in Title I preschool programs did not show the same increase in social pretend play in a similar time period that is typically found in most preschool studies (Farran & Son-Yarbrough, 2001). This finding is disturbing because this study found that associative play, in which children interact briefly, had the most positive relationship to quantity of verbal behaviors, but over the two time periods associative play decreased while parallel play, in which children play alongside others but do not interact, showed an increase.

This trend was most evident in Title I preschool classrooms with the largest proportions of children from low socioeconomic backgrounds. In the study, there was also no increase in the total amount of verbal interaction over the two time periods, which is incongruent with most research. Because an increase in social pretend play and language use were not observed, the researchers express concern that such preschools may "facilitate the behavioral introduction to the expectations of the public school environment but may not provide the foundational understandings and experiences to keep those early successes from disappearing once the curriculum becomes more demanding" (Farran & Son-Yarbrough, 2001, p. 259).

CHILDREN WITH DISABILITIES

Research demonstrates that social pretend play is important for the development of children with disabilities. Children with disabilities, however, often have difficulty engaging in social pretend play. Odom, McConnell, and Chandler (1993) found that teachers reported that about 75% of children with disabilities need assistance with social skills. Guralnick and Hammond (1999) found that children with mild disabilities exhibit play transition patterns (i.e., from solitary to parallel to social) that are congruent with those of typical peers. On the other hand, the social and pretend play patterns of children with autistic disorders are likely to differ from those of other children. Children with autistic disorders may lack the mental representation and language competencies needed for pretend play, or lack skill in spontaneously generating ideas for pretend play (Jarrold, Boucher, & Smith, 1996).

Complexity of Diagnosis

Sometimes the intensity, duration, and frequency of characteristics are significant enough to ensure a relatively clear diagnosis by professionals trained in specialized areas. At other times, a definitive diagnosis determining eligibility for special services may be more difficult, and careful observation over time in a variety of contexts may be necessary. Family involvement and careful consideration of cultural factors are essential aspects of the assessment and treatment of social and emotional development (Barbarin, 2006; Bowman & Moore, 2006). It is not currently necessary in many states to have a definitive diagnosis of a social-emotional condition to determine eligibility for services. The professional judgment of a licensed psychologist, for example, is often sufficient. The use of **positive behavioral supports** and documentation of response to intervention using a tiered approach may also provide appropriate intervention. This tiered approach offers a viable structure for differentiating instruction based on the degree of challenge experienced by children.

It is important that professionals match intervention strategies with individual characteristics while addressing children's social and emotional challenges. This chapter focuses on some characteristics of atypical social development and matching those characteristics with intervention strategies, along with careful assessment to determine responses to intervention (Sugai & Horner, 2002).

CURRICULUM IMPLEMENTATION AND SOCIAL DEVELOPMENT

One curriculum delivered the same way does not fit the needs of all the children. Each child in an early childhood classroom is a unique individual whose skills, knowledge, level of development, and needs will evolve and become known to the teacher over time. Curriculum development and implementation is an ongoing process that is nurtured through child observations, trial and error, and knowledge of child-specific preferences and capabilities. Children with social and emotional development issues typically have difficulties in verbal and nonverbal communication, social interactions, getting involved in play, and maintaining interest in leisure or play activities. A basic expression of a range of emotions may be challenging for some children, especially if they have received negative messages about sharing their feelings. For example, many boys are given a specific message about crying, and many girls are given a specific message about asserting their anger. Other gender differences and patterns of socialization have long been recognized as relevant to the topic of emotional development (Kinsman & Berk, 1979).

Adaptations in Dramatic Play

Many of the materials and activities found in the dramatic play area are familiar to children. If a child has a special need, it is possible that either the family or the therapist(s) working with the child has addressed how to make dramatic play materials and activities available. Adaptive devices, adaptive furniture, and a realistic approach to the feasibility of the child engagement in certain according to have possibly been addressed. General modifications should be developed according what initially makes the experience inaccessible to a child.

Physical equipment in the dramatic play area can create a barrier for some children, depending on the child's size. When a child has a physical disability and cannot reach the table or the floor or shelves in the dramatic play area, environmental modifications can be made as indicated. The child might engage in play while standing. This may seem like a very simple modification, but it is one that may make considerable difference to the child. When choosing roles to play, the child with a physical disability needs to be encouraged to select roles that do not require sitting down or getting from a standing to a sitting position. The child achieves greater mobility by standing because if the child is in a mobile stander, this position allows him or her to be moved to another part of the dramatic play area more easily by a teacher or a peer, so he or she can work on a tray or adaptive chair. Incorporating an adaptive chair into the play makes sense while playing certain themes. If the children are playing restaurant, bakery, library, or store, the surface can become a logical part of the play. While it is preferable that children with special needs use the same surfaces as all the other children in the class, the other children may use a tray surface as well.

Visual Impairments

Children with visual impairments are usually very interested in dramatic play and require few modifications. For a child with minor impairments, allowing the child to get as close to the materials and the play situation as possible works best. This child may initially need help in finding the materials and learning cues to where the materials belong. Once the child is familiar with these situations, there are usually few modifications necessary. Children with visual impairments enjoy the stimulation of dramatic play because it is not exacting and does not tax them visually.

Peer interactions are powerful motivators.

Social-Emotional or Behavior Disorders

Dramatic play activities are sometimes frustrating for children who display behaviors that are challenging to peers and/or adults. Some children may have developed few coping skills. In other activity areas, these children react negatively if something does not fit together perfectly on the first try, or he or she has not had prior experience with the activity. This may also happen in the dramatic play area. This negative response happens because the child does not have the social skills or the emotional stamina to take a risk in social interaction or role-play. Children who are emotionally fragile may not have the correct perceptions of peer responses to their behaviors or dress-up clothes choices. The very unstructured nature of dramatic play that appeals to many children can also be exactly what frightens the child with special social or emotional needs. The teacher can spend some time with the child observing the play and commenting on it prior to any attempt by the child to join in. Once the child appears to be ready to enter the play, the teacher needs to facilitate the entry and remain involved or supportive until the child is really comfortable. If the teacher exits prematurely, the child is bound to follow the teacher, and the play episode will be over for that child. Regardless of whether the child is prone to acting out or is usually withdrawn, the same supportive facilitation may be necessary to ease the child into a positive play situation.

An example of this type of interaction involves a child with a very disturbing, hoarse quality to his voice and some fairly extreme acting-out behaviors. This child had difficulty getting children to pay positive attention to him. Although he was very bright, highly verbal, and skilled in describing how he felt when he was rejected by his peers, he was not aware of the impact of his behavior on the peers in the class. His teacher worked slowly and carefully to point out instances where he could join in the play, and told him exactly how and what he might say to converse with his peers, so they would positively respond to him. He was supported to use a sweet voice instead of his usual high-pitched raspy voice. This change resulted in the other children welcoming him to play. His family was very supportive about reinforcing the use of his sweet voice, and they found that they all loved listening to him. Not only did the reminder to use a different voice alter his voice quality, but it also altered the nature of what he said. His verbalizations became more positive, less accusing, and more loving.

As pointed out in the discussion about manipulative materials, the socially immature child who also has language delays will benefit from being surrounded by the conversation that takes place in the dramatic play area. Although a child with language delays may not yet play cooperatively, the child may engage in solitary play in the proximity of children who provide high potential for language involvement. As children engage in dramatic play, whether it is parallel or cooperative, they may narrate their activity and use a wide variety of vocabulary. In addition to real words, they may invent words to describe their actions.

Learning Challenges and Intellectual Disabilities

Modifications that would enable the child with learning challenges to participate in dramatic play activities might include having a teacher situated within the activity area in order to model appropriate play behaviors and to support the development of interaction between the child and the other children in the area. Demonstrations of the use of materials may be of benefit to the child because the child may have had limited exposure to certain materials and experiences due to developmental delay. A child with learning difficulties may not have the entry behaviors necessary to begin to interact with others. The child may not know how to play a certain role. If this is the case, the teacher might want to establish a routine in which the child's day begins with the dramatic play area. This may be very helpful because if the child is among the first children to enter dramatic play, it is not as overwhelming to the child as attempting to join play in progress. The teacher might ask the child what he or she plans to do in the dramatic play area as a means of prompting behavior. If a peer can be supported to help the child with learning difficulties, then teacher dependency can be diminished or avoided.

Children with developmental challenges may need to have modified materials made available to them in order to participate in dramatic play. If a child cannot manage the small play dishes, cups, and silverware these should be replaced with regular size plastic picnic dishes that are larger and easier to grasp. If the dolls are heavy, one or two lighter dolls may need to be added to the family. If all the dolls are made of hard plastic, a cloth doll or rubber doll would also be a welcome addition. Some of the dress-up clothes need to have Velcro fasteners instead of small buttons or zippers. Play fruits and vegetables may need to be collected in several smaller baskets instead of one large basket. If a child cannot manage the large wooden blocks, the addition of a wagon may allow the child to transport blocks to the construction site. Teachers may also develop the guideline of two children carrying each large wooden block as a safety precaution. These are simple modifications to make.

CHARACTERISTICS OF CHILDREN WITH SOCIAL-EMOTIONAL CHALLENGES

Autism

WHAT IS AUTISM?   Autism is a complex developmental disability that typically appears during the first three years of life. Currently recognized as the result of a neurological disorder that affects the brain's function, autism and its associated behaviors have been challenging to estimate. Estimating the prevalence of autism is difficult and controversial due to differences in the ways that cases are identified and defined, differences in study methods, and changes in diagnostic criteria. One study reported the prevalence of autism in 3- to 10-year-olds to be about 3.4 cases per 1,000 children (Yeargin-Allsopp, Rice, Karapurkar, Doernberg, Boyle, & Murphy, 2003), while other sources cite a prevalence rate of about 1 in 500 (NICHCY, 2009). Some recent research indicates a prevalence rate of 1 in 150. Autism is about four times more common in boys than girls. Girls with the disorder, however, tend to have more severe symptoms and greater cognitive impairment. Autism appears to know no racial, ethnic, or social boundaries. Family income, lifestyle, and educational levels do not affect the chance of autism's occurrence.

Autism impacts the normal development of the brain in the areas of social interaction and communication skills. Children and adults with autism typically have difficulties in verbal and nonverbal communication, social interactions, leisure, or play activities. Children and adults with autism may also have sensory processing dysfunction and difficulty with perspective taking. The disorder makes it hard for them to communicate with others and relate to the outside world. In some cases, aggressive and/or self-injurious behavior may be present. Children with autism may exhibit repeated body movements such as hand flapping or rocking, unusual responses to people or attachments to objects, and resistance to changes in routines. Individuals may also experience sensitivities in sight, hearing, touch, smell, and taste. The prevalence rate of autism makes it one of the most common developmental disabilities, yet most of the public, including many professionals in the medical, educational, and vocational fields, are still unaware of how autism affects people and how they can effectively work with individuals with autism.

Types of Autism

IS THERE MORE THAN ONE TYPE OF AUTISM?   Several related disorders are grouped under the broad heading of pervasive developmental disorder or PDD—a general category of disorders that are characterized by severe and pervasive impairment in several areas of development (American Psychiatric Association, 1994). A standard reference is the *Diagnostic and Statistical Manual* (DSM-IV), (Fourth Edition,1994) a diagnostic handbook in its fourth edition. The DSM-IV lists criteria for a specific diagnosis under the category of pervasive developmental disorder. Diagnosis is made when a specified number of characteristics listed in the DSM-IV are present. Diagnostic evaluations are based on the presence of specific behaviors indicated by observation and through parent consultation, and should be made by an experienced, highly trained team. When professionals or parents are referring to different types of autism, they are often distinguishing between autism and one of the other pervasive developmental disorders.

Individuals who fall under the pervasive developmental disorder category in the DSM-IV exhibit commonalties in communication and social deficits, but differ in terms of the severity of their disorder. Table 6.3 highlights some major points, (from the Autism

TABLE 6.3   Did You Know? Different Types of Pervasive Developmental Disorders

Autistic disorder	Impairments in social interaction, communication, and imaginative play prior to age 3 years. Stereotyped behaviors, interests, and activities.
Asperger's disorder	Characterized by impairments in social interactions and the presence of restricted interests and activities, with no clinical significant general delay in language, and testing in the range of average to above average intelligence.
Pervasive developmental disorder-not otherwise specified (commonly referred to as atypical autism)	A diagnosis of PDD-NOS may be made when a child does not meet the criteria for a specified diagnosis, but there is a severe and pervasive impairment in specified behaviors.
Rett's disorder	This is a progressive disorder which, to date, has occurred only in girls. Period of normal development and then loss of previously acquired skills, loss of purposeful use of the hands replaced with repetitive hand movements beginning at age 1–4 years.
Childhood disintegrative disorder	This is characterized by normal development for at least the first 2 years and then significant loss of previously acquired skills (American Psychiatric Association, 1994). Autism is referred to as a spectrum disorder. This means that the symptoms and characteristics of autism can present themselves in a wide variety of combinations, from mild to severe. Although autism is defined by a certain set of behaviors, children and adults can exhibit any combination of the behaviors in any degree of severity. Two children, both with the same diagnosis, can act very differently from one another and have varying skills. Therefore, there is no standard "type" or "typical" individual with autism.

Society of America, http://www.autism-society.org; http://www.autismsociety.org), that help distinguish the differences between the specific diagnoses used.

Clarifying Terminology

Many terms may create confusion for parents of children with autism. Parents may hear different terms used to describe children within this spectrum, such as autistic-like, autistic tendencies, autism spectrum, high-functioning or low-functioning autism, more-abled, or less-abled. Whatever the diagnosis it is very important to understand that children can learn and function productively and show gains from appropriate education and treatment beginning as soon as possible.

What Causes Autism?

Researchers from all over the world are devoting considerable time and energy to finding the answer to this critical question. Medical researchers are exploring different explanations for the various forms of autism. Although a single specific cause of autism is not known, current research links autism to biological or neurological differences in the brain. In many families, there appears to be a pattern of autism or related disabilities which suggests there is a genetic basis to the disorder. At this time, no gene has been directly linked to autism (2009). Stanford University Medical Center (2009, October 16). Mechanism Of Gene Linked To Autism, Schizophrenia Pinpointed. *ScienceDaily*. Retrieved November 15, 2009, from http://www.sciencedaily.com/releases/2009/10/091012225541.htm

Several outdated theories about autism's causes have been proven to be false. Autism is not a mental illness, children with autism are not children who choose not to

REFLECTION IN ACTION
MS. LIGHTBORNE

Ms. Lightborne has been grappling, trying to get services for Jordan, who has significant language delays as well as behavioral challenges. He frequently spends time by himself, relatively isolated. It is not clear whether his isolation is a function of language delays, sensory differences, or underlying factors related to social-emotional development. He meets some of the autism criteria identified by the DSM-IV, but he also sometimes spontaneously interacts with others.

Through her conversations with specialists, Ms. Lightborne realized it was not necessary to have a definitive diagnosis for Jordan in order to recommend services. She realized through discussions with a consultant and through her own reflections that she had assumed a diagnosis was a necessary prerequisite for further intervention. She came to understand that she had been focusing on trying to confirm a diagnosis rather than determining what Jordan's areas of strength and concern might be.

behave, autism is not caused by bad parenting, no known psychological factors in the development of the child have been shown to cause autism.

Did You Know?

The following information is from the *Diagnostic and Statistical Manual of Mental Disorders*, Fourth Edition (DSM-IV):

DIAGNOSTIC CRITERIA FOR 299.00 AUTISTIC DISORDER

A total of six (or more) items from (1), (2), and (3), with at least two from (1), and one each from (2) and (3).

1. *Qualitative impairment in social interaction, as manifested by at least two of the following:*
   a. *Marked impairments in the use of multiple nonverbal behaviors such as eye-to-eye gaze, facial expression, body posture, and gestures to regulate social interaction*
   b. *Failure to develop peer relationships appropriate to developmental level*
   c. *A lack of spontaneous seeking to share enjoyment, interests, or achievements with other people, (e.g., by a lack of showing, bringing, or pointing out objects of interest to other people)*
   d. *Lack of social or emotional reciprocity (note: in the description, it gives the following as examples: not actively participating in simple social play or games, preferring solitary activities, or involving others in activities only as tools or "mechanical" aids)*
2. *Qualitative impairments in communication as manifested by at least one of the following:*
   a. *Delay in, or total lack of, the development of spoken language not accompanied by an attempt to compensate through alternative modes of communication such as gesture or mime)in individuals with adequate speech, marked impairment in the ability to initiate or sustain a conversation with others; stereotyped and repetitive use of language or idiosyncratic language*
   b. *Lack of varied, spontaneous make-believe play or social imitative play appropriate to developmental level; restricted repetitive and stereotyped patterns of behavior, interests and activities, as manifested by at least two of the following: encompassing preoccupation with one or more stereotyped and restricted patterns of interest that is abnormal either in intensity or focus apparently inflexible adherence to specific, nonfunctional routines or rituals*
   c. *Stereotyped and repetitive motor mannerisms (e.g., hand or finger flapping or twisting, or complex whole-body movements)*
   d. *Persistent preoccupation with parts of objects*
3. *Delays or abnormal functioning in at least one of the following areas, with onset prior to age 3 years:*
   1. *Social interaction*
   2. *Language as used in social communication*
   3. *Symbolic or imaginative play*
      The disturbance is not better accounted for by Rett's Disorder or Childhood Disintegrative Disorder.

The following definition is from the Autism Society of America:

Autism is often a severely incapacitating lifelong developmental disability that typically appears during the first three years of life. It occurs in approximately fifteen out of every 10,000 births and is four times more common in boys than girls. It has been found throughout the world in families of all racial, ethnic and social backgrounds. No known factors in the psychological environment of a child have been shown to cause autism.

The symptoms are caused by physical disorders of the brain. They include:

1. Disturbances in the rate of appearance of physical, social and language skills.
2. Abnormal responses to sensations. Any one or a combination of senses or responses are affected: sight, hearing, touch, pain, balance, smell, taste, and the way a child holds his body.
3. Speech and language are absent or delayed while specific thinking capabilities might be present; Abnormal ways of relating to people, objects and events.

Autism occurs by itself or in association with other disorders that affect the function of the brain such as viral infections, metabolic disturbances, and epilepsy. It is important to distinguish autism from mental retardation or mental disorders since diagnostic confusion may result in referral to inappropriate and ineffective treatment techniques. The severe form of the syndrome may include extreme self-injurious, repetitive, highly unusual and aggressive behavior. Special educational programs using behavioral methods have proven to be the most helpful treatment with many children who have such characteristics. Innovative combinations of highly structured programs using Discrete Trials and more inclusive opportunities have been successful for some children.

The definition of the syndrome listed above is oriented to children, but such children do not outgrow their autism. Much of the literature on autism deals with children because educating children with autism is such a big issue that more research, education, and writing about autism is centered on children rather than adults.

Current Issues in Autism

Autism spectrum disorder is one of the fastest-growing disability categories. It is also one of the most challenging. It is currently estimated that from 1 in 500 to 1 in 150 children have autism, and it affects boys at a 4-to-1 ratio over girls. The recent explosion in the number of children diagnosed with autism has created considerable interest in the possible causes of autism. Theories include genetics, environmental factors such as pesticides, infections, hormone imbalance, and mercury in vaccines. The Centers for Disease Control and Prevention, the Food and Drug Administration, the Institute of Medicine, the World Health Organization, and the American Academy of Pediatrics have all largely dismissed the notion that thimerosal causes or contributes to autism. Major studies have found no link. Despite all evidence to the contrary, the number of parents who blame thimerosal for their child's autism has only increased. The issue has become one of the most fractious and divisive in pediatric medicine. Because the composition of the vaccines have been modified, there should be a decrease in the number of autism cases if there is indeed a link between the mercury in vaccines and autism. There has been no decrease in numbers.

Serious Emotional Disturbance

Did You Know?
Many terms are used to describe emotional, behavioral, or mental disorders. Currently, children with such disorders are categorized as having a serious emotional disturbance, which is defined under the Individuals with Disabilities Education Act (IDEA),

P.L. 101-476 (http://www.ed.gov/policy/speced/leg/idea/history.html; http://www.ed.gov/policy/speced/leg/idea/history.html) as

> A condition exhibiting one or more of the following characteristics over a long period of time and to a marked degree that adversely affects educational performance:
>
> A. An inability to learn that cannot be explained by intellectual, sensory, or health factors;
> B. An inability to build or maintain satisfactory interpersonal relationships with peers and teachers;
> C. Inappropriate types of behavior or feelings under normal circumstances;
> D. A general pervasive mood of unhappiness or depression; or
> E. A tendency to develop physical symptoms or fears associated with personal or school problems. (IDEA, C.F.R. § 300.7(b)(9), 2004).

As defined by the IDEA, serious emotional disturbance includes schizophrenia but does not apply to children who are socially maladjusted, unless it is determined that they have a serious emotional disturbance (IDEA, C.F.R. § 300.7(b)(9), 2004).

What Are the Indicators of Emotional Disturbance?

There are several widely accepted characteristics associated with serious emotional disturbance. These characteristics may at times occur in the overall population, but to a lesser degree. Some elements of defining characteristics follow:

• An inability to learn which cannot be explained by intellectual, sensory, or health factors. The child is learning significantly below what is expected based on the information available. This is observed over a significant period of time. The child is capable of learning based on intellectual/ability tests scores, and classroom performance. No evidence of visual or hearing problems exist. There is no explanation for learning problems.

• An inability to build or maintain satisfactory interpersonal relationships with peers and teachers. The child has poor communication skills, interrupts class, has difficulty taking turns, has poor eye contact, cannot stay on topic, has inappropriate conversation, and may not tell the truth. There may be evidence that the child is not able to differentiate between what is real and what is imagined. A child may exhibit inappropriate touching, offensive behaviors (spitting, cussing, etc.), be non-compliant, and have difficulty sustaining friendships for long. These behaviors or manifestations interfere in working with others and affects their own educational performance.

• Inappropriate types of behavior or feelings under normal circumstances. The child does not react with appropriate behaviors when compared with age peers in similar settings and circumstances. Examples include: school phobia, behavioral or emotional reactions not expected in given situations.

• A general pervasive mood of unhappiness or depression. Young children show their unhappiness by displaying aggressive or withdrawn behaviors. We cannot accept aggressive or withdrawn behavior at school because they affect the child's performance. Practitioners care if a child is unhappy for long periods of time, and may seek to convey this to parents. Sometimes children will cry often for no reason and appear to be depressed. These children need our services. Practitioners should support parents, so they can accept this need is important.

- A tendency to develop physical symptoms or fears associated with personal or school problems. Fears may include those of separation from parents during a time that is not age appropriate or continues over an extended period of time. Students may be afraid to join or participate in group situations. Physical symptoms include ticks, self-abuse, chronic stomach complaints, excessive requests to visit the nurse, and persistent crying when no physical symptoms are evident.

Characteristics

Some of the characteristics seen in children who have emotional disturbances include:

Hyperactivity (short attention span, impulsiveness)

Aggression/self-injurious behavior (acting out, fighting)

Withdrawal (failure to initiate interaction with others; retreat from exchanges of social interaction, excessive fear or anxiety)

Immaturity (inappropriate crying, temper tantrums, poor coping skills)

Learning difficulties (academically performing below grade level)

Children with the most serious emotional disturbance may exhibit distorted thinking, excessive anxiety, bizarre motor acts, and abnormal mood swings. Many children who do not have an emotional disturbance may exhibit these same behaviors from time to time during their development. When children have a serious emotional disturbance, these behaviors do not go away and may be displayed over an extended period of time. The behavior signals that the child is not coping with his or her environment or peers and may be attempting to process an unusually high degree of stress.

Secondary Psychosocial Conditions

Sometimes children with other conditions such as physical challenges, sensory impairments, or medical conditions may have secondary psychosocial difficulty. These might include extreme frustration, depression, low self-esteem, or what has sometimes been called "learned helplessness." Sometimes children need extra support to develop the coping strategies they need. It should be noted that such secondary conditions may be highly treatable given appropriate supports. Optimally, children learn to advocate for themselves and adjust to their conditions in constructive ways making it possible to lead meaningful lives.

Other Factors That May Impact Social-Emotional Development

Other factors that may negatively affect social and emotional development relate to biological risks. If there are temperamental vulnerabilities such as hypersensitivity and/or hyper-reactivity, these may become part of a cascading pattern of escalating risks associated with difficulties in self-regulation. Difficulties with sensory processing may further exacerbate these patterns, unless specifically addressed through intervention (Schore, 1994; Zeanah, 1993). Some patterns of biological vulnerability related to

Children learn from each other in natural environments.

neurological risk may be secondary to prenatal exposure to toxic substances, including drugs and/or alcohol. Information about this as it relates to individual children may not be available to teachers. Even when it is, it is very important that the risk not be compounded by negative judgments and potential self-fulfilling prophesies. Children with biological risk may be more susceptible to challenging behavior, but they may also respond very well to appropriate intervention.

SELF-REGULATION AND SOCIAL INTERACTION   There are times when children who are impulsive and have difficulty controlling themselves need extra support in order to exercise the self-control that others may effortlessly have. Children with sensory processing disorders may have this sort of difficulty. The "invisibility" of the conditions may actually contribute to cascading complications through misunderstandings and the misinterpretation of children's cues (Schore, 1994; Zeanah,1993). Teachers can offer supports in unobtrusive, soothing ways. When the staff recognize the patterns of children who are easily overstimulated, they can provide opportunities to help children with personal integration.

MATCHING CHARACTERISTICS WITH INTERVENTION: THE IMPORTANCE OF REFLECTION

Outcomes and Intervention

In order to determine effective intervention strategies, teachers should be as clear as possible about the specific problems. What are the specific characteristics that need to be addressed? When do they occur? In what contexts do they occur? Are they consistent or intermittent issues? What has been done already to try to address the challenging behaviors? Our starting point for determining effective intervention is with the child, the characteristics of concern, and the environment.

Reflection During Social-Emotional Intervention

The development and practice of reflective skills affords teachers the opportunity to step back to review the informal data collected as well as plan for the additional data that will need to be collected in order to design the appropriate intervention and/or to contact the appropriate supports to bring in for the next step in intervention.

Reflection Scenario

A new boy has just begun to attend your class. You do not have much information on this child other than learning that the family is new to town, he has no siblings, the parents are both students as well as working as many hours a week as they can. The child is 5 years old, you have no school records, and you are not sure when or if school records will appear. The child does not interact with anyone. He connects with his mother when she brings him to school and picks him up, but he does not appear over-joyed to see her. He goes to her when she comes next to him. He does not run to her when she enters the room. You have not heard him speak to her, to the children in the class or to any adult, including yourself.

Questions for Reflection:

1. What will you do in the child's first two weeks in your class to include the child in the culture and routine of the class?
2. What information do you want to gather?
3. Why is this information important to you?
4. Are there any school personnel you want to have come to observe the child?
5. Are there any physical changes you want to make to the classroom?
6. What do you intend to do with this information once it is collected?

Positive Outcomes: Friendship

After focusing on characteristics of individual children the next step, though this is rarely a linear process, is to identify what we would like to see the child doing. Professionals can think of these as desired outcomes or objectives (Bricker & Squires, 1999). These outcomes or objectives are often based on how children who are demonstrating healthy social-emotional development perform without extra intervention. For example, considerable emphasis in the early childhood years is placed on the making of meaningful friendships. An essential element of meaningful friendships involves the healthy exchange of feelings. A child's ability to make meaningful friendships is often considered an important prerequisite for school readiness and academic success.

Co-occurrence of Social Competence and Academic Success

Children who are socially competent are often more academically successful. Poor social skills are seen as a strong predictor of academic failure. Webster-Stratton and Reid (2004) described a specific curriculum program that teaches skills such as emotional literacy, empathy or perspective taking, friendship, communication skills, anger management, interpersonal problem solving, and how to be successful in school. This training program The Incredible Years Dinosaur Social Skills and problem-solving Child Training Program, a child training curriculum that strengthens children's social, emotional and academic competencies such as understanding and communicating feelings, using effective problem solving strategies, managing anger, practicing friendship and conversational skills, as well as appropriate classroom behaviors. was originally designed to be used as a small-group treatment program for young children who were diagnosed with oppositional defiant and conduct disorders. Prescribed or packaged curriculum may not be appropriate for all classrooms or for all teachers, but some teachers may find such curricula a comfortable place to begin developmentally appropriate programming or intervention in the social emotional area.

Treatment of Autism

Multiple approaches exist for the treatment of autism. Educational treatments often address communication and behavior, and one of the most widely accepted treatments is applied behavior analysis. There are other strategies that have helped some students but are disputed in the field. Some children with autism have been helped by additional educational methods but these have not been validated by large-scale studies. Other treatments for autism include biomedical and dietary approaches. These approaches, too, have proponents and opponents (Rimland & Baker, 1996).

EDUCATIONAL IMPLICATIONS

There are educational implications for children with autism or serious emotional disturbance. All professionals who work with young children will need to carefully consider the many factors that comprise an inclusive educational environment, but when working with young children with autism, this consideration becomes much more critical. It is very important to remember that autism is not a form of serious emotional disturbance even though it affects social interaction. The following variables need to be carefully planned and implemented: the total classroom environment including the amount and use of space, the numbers of children in groups, the teacher to child ratio, supervision both indoors and outdoors, shifts in schedule, level of sound, and level of light.

Significant Environmental Factors

Children who have difficulty controlling their behavior perform optimally when they are supported by environments that are predictable, consistent, and structured supports. A structured environment does not need to be rigid, but it should give children a sense of security by allowing them to anticipate what will be happening. Transitions are often especially challenging for children who have trouble with self-regulation, and there are strategies that can facilitate adjustment during those times of change. The importance of a positive classroom and school climate cannot be overstated. An atmosphere of mutual respect and positive regard sets the tone for positive relationships that are central to healthy emotional development.

Positive Behavioral Supports

Educational programs for children with emotional disturbances need to include attention to providing emotional and behavioral support as well as helping the children master academics, develop social skills, and increase self-awareness, self-control, and self-esteem. There is a large body of research about methods of providing students with positive behavioral support (PBS) in the school environment, so that problem behaviors are minimized and positive, appropriate behaviors are fostered. PBS is a set of research-based strategies used to increase quality of life and decrease problem behavior by teaching new skills and making changes in a child's environment (Sugai & Horner, 2002).

PBS combines valued outcomes, behavioral science, biomedical science, validated procedures, and systems change to enhance quality of life and reduce problem behaviors such as self-injury, aggression, property destruction, pica, defiance, and disruption. The overriding goal of PBS is to enhance quality of life for children and others within social settings such as the home, school, and community settings (Sugai & Horner, 2002).

For a child whose behavior impedes his or her learning, or the learning of his or her peers, the educational team developing the child's Individualized Education Program (IEP) needs to consider strategies to address that behavior, including positive behavioral interventions, strategies, and supports. Children who are eligible for special education services under the category of emotional disturbance may have IEPs that include psychological or counseling services. These are important related services that are available under law and are to be provided by a qualified social worker, psychologist, guidance counselor, or other qualified personnel.

Importance of Family Involvement

There is growing recognition that families of children with challenging behavior need support, respite care, intensive case management, and a collaborative, multi-agency approach to services. Many communities are working toward providing these wrap-around services. A growing number of agencies and organizations are actively involved in establishing support services in the community (Bowman & Moore, 2006). Clarity about roles within a team is essential. When children have seriously challenging behavior as preschoolers, certain behaviors might have been present during the toddler years as well. Because extreme frustration and tantrums are considered normal for toddlers, identification may not occur until children are preschool age.

Communication with families during the assessment of challenging behavior may be especially sensitive, and it is vital to avoid any blame that could contribute to a family's defensiveness. Awareness of and sensitivity to cultural factors are important, especially as professionals consider variations in expectations and social norms. This is true for families whose primary language is other than English as well.

Curriculum Packages

When a teacher uses curriculum that is prescribed and does not take into consideration individual children's behavior and interests, it will be challenging to the teacher as well as to the children in the class, regardless of whether or not they have social and emotional issues. A crucial element to effectively supporting the social-emotional development of young children involves careful consideration of individual patterns of strength, need, and motivation for all children. Professionals should appreciate and celebrate variations and diversity in culture and familial values, priorities, and styles rather than have the expectation that "normal" development is defined as conformity to a uniform set of behaviors and values (Barbarin, 2006).

Considerable research has suggested that of all the conditions associated with eligibility for special services, challenging behavior is often the most difficult. For some this may seem counterintuitive. The appearance of a child arriving in a preschool program with significant physical challenges and the equipment to go along with that challenge may suggest more difficulty. On the other hand, children who have challenging behavior may look "normal." It is not evident from their appearance that difficulties do exist. Paradoxically, others, especially children, may find this lack of apparent difference difficult. It is easy for teachers and other professionals to assume intentionality when children are disruptive and/or acting out.

ADAPTING CURRICULUM: PLAY AND SOCIAL DEVELOPMENT

Examples of Developmentally Appropriate Curriculum

There are many curricular activities that support healthy social and emotional development. These activities range from child-centered sensory opportunities like sand and water play, the use of manipulates like play dough, to socio-dramatic play, like puppet play to active block play. All of these activities may be relevant and meaningful to children with developmental challenges. In some cases, minimal support is needed for these activities. In others, significant supports may be needed. It is the team's responsibility to identify strategies that can be used to increase the likelihood that children with developmental differences may fully participate.

Activities and Embedding Effective Strategies

If a child with emotional challenges who tends to be withdrawn does not initiate playing in the socio-dramatic area with other children, strategies can be embedded into the activity. Props can be added that are especially motivating to this child, and one or two peers who might also participate. Materials for more than one role might increase the likelihood that more than one child will join in. Adults can be supportive, providing assistance as needed, but should avoid being obtrusive, exiting when children's spontaneous interaction with each other takes off.

Engagement

While play is considered a natural medium through which young children learn and develop their social skills, children with social and emotional issues may not develop play behaviors and skills without support and mediation. All young children benefit from encouragement to engage in new activities with different toys or materials, but children with social-emotional issues need more support (McWilliam & Casey, 2008). Children with social issues may need more structured support such as hand-over-hand support in order to get into the play. New things might be scary for children with social issues, and they may be hesitant to try something new for fear of failure, fear of the outcome of the activity, or fear of the permanence of the activity. For example, a child may be fearful of painting due to the requirement of wearing a smock in order to paint. Perhaps the smock is a real barrier and dropping the requirement of wearing the smock may be all that it takes to get the child involved and enjoying the experience.

Modeling

Modeling appropriate play behavior is another intervention that can help a child gain play skills and begin to experience with the joy of play. Not all children know how to play with specific toys or materials, and they may not know how to play at all. A child who is very structured and engages in a considerable amount of repetitive behavior will need guided play experiences in order to learn how to play. This kind of play training requires that an adult spend time with the child attempting to model the play behavior associated with a specific toy or material. An example might be driving a car in a pattern and making car sounds, or cuddling a baby doll and singing to the doll. Other examples might include modeling caring behaviors with stuffed animals and dramatic play with house items.

Encouragement of Social Language

If the child has language, another area to facilitate would be the encouragement of the use of social language. Some children with social issues do not know how to use social language. They may speak, but the language heard is directed toward themselves. A child may say something like "drink" and then attempt to get the drink from the kitchen without understanding that adults in the classroom can facilitate getting the drink if the request is made of them. A child who engages in this kind of behavior needs support for learning to use language outwardly in order to have access to people, places, and things.

Selection of Materials

Toys and other materials for play need to be durable and safe. Some children with social-emotional issues may not take care with materials and toys. They might throw things in the air in a ritualistic manner. They might also rip or tear things. Children who are prone to this kind of behavior would need outlets for the behavior, and would need to have access to items that are more appropriate to ripping, tearing, or knocking over. It is more beneficial to provide a child with a realistic and socially appropriate outlet for a behavior that is likely to be prolonged than it is to create an environment in which the child hears negatives all the time.

Grouping Children Together

Pairing children with social-emotional delay and children without delays together in a role-play/mediated play situation can be very helpful for a child with social-emotional issues. There are many children who prefer the company of children to the company of adults. Some children have the potential to be excellent mediators, role models, or facilitators for their peers. The one caution is to make sure that there are physical and social spaces for the child in need of this intervention.

Clear Limits

Children should not be allowed to destroy other children's work or activities. Often a child will need to be distracted, redirected, or removed from an area. If it is the practice in the classroom to always remove the student from a specific kind of situation, it is more likely that the child will never learn the appropriate behavior or response. In this type of situation, the child would benefit from social scaffolding.

In indoor and outdoor play, teacher should be sure that the child cannot wander off. Actual physical boundaries are not enough to contain a child who has no real concept of getting lost. Children who are engaged in meaningful activity in the classroom will be less likely to wander. Next, the child might move beyond toys and materials to interact with other children and adults; this would be satisfying and productive reason why a child would no longer wander.

Games and activities that require physical participation have potential to engage a child with autism or an emotional disturbance. Games that involve touching or any kind of social interaction can help to make social contact less threatening.

Importance of Scaffolding Social Development

Scaffolding is the difference between what someone does on their own and what someone can do with expert help. Social scaffolding is the provision of social support for a child who is in need of mediation to make progress to the next level of social behavior that would eventually have the child becoming part of the social community. Wood, Bruner, and Ross (1976) introduced the term "scaffolding" to describe the sensitive guidance that is required of adults involved in children's play and learning. Sensory play can be very soothing. This term was also used by Lev Vygotsky (1967). Learning to think about adaptations that can match the child's needs may become a relatively automatic process, with experience. For example, if a child is acting out and not staying within the limits, the teacher should be clear about those limits.

DEVELOPING A REPERTOIRE OF STRATEGIES   When teams are considering possible strategies for a child, the professionals should have a well-developed repertoire of adaptations to choose from. Figure 6.2 is a concise overview of potentially helpful strategies.

WHAT DO YOU THINK?   You have been a teacher of young children for several years. Initially, the children in your classes were children from middle-income families. You then transferred schools and began to teach children from the inner city and began to see an increase in the numbers of children in your classes with delays or some type of disability. As the years go by, you find it challenging to know what to do with the young children who are not developing typically. You are not sure why after years of experience you are encountering these challenges. Shouldn't you be finding teaching to be easier than it was when you first began to teach? You are not sure what to do or with whom to speak about this.

Questions for Reflection:
1. Why do you think this teacher is having doubts about his or her teaching?
2. Where do you think this teacher should begin to seek answers?
3. Do you think the teacher should entertain a change of career?

Structured environment

Predictable schedule and routines

Clear expectations

Clear limits

Clear statement of consequences ("If . . . then")

Support

Encouragement

Opportunities for play and social interaction

Support for conflict resolution

Verbal guidance

Redirection

Replacement of "inappropriate" behavior with more pro-social behavior

Scaffolding

Provision of clear, structured choices

Use of social stories

Support for self-soothing; calming

Support during transitions

Groupings and intentional facilitation of peer interaction

Selection of materials to enhance motivation

Response to children's initiatives and interests

Expansion of children's repertoires (e.g., in play)

Modeling of social language

Support for children's purposeful engagement

Integration of questioning strategies to support engagement

Provision of more structured intervention when needed

Adjustment of environmental factors so the classroom climate is conducive to focus, not overstimulating

FIGURE 6.2 Strategies for Social and Emotional Development

THE IMPORTANCE OF THE MATCH BETWEEN CHARACTERISTICS AND INTERVENTION

This chapter has considered many examples of matching each child's individual needs with strategies that are used. Table 6.4 provides examples of creating matches as we support healthy social and emotional development, along with the rationale for making such decisions.

Teams

Multi-, inter-, and transdisciplinary educational teams, which include parents, must design programs to meet the individual behavioral and academic needs of children identified with challenging behavior. Most children can benefit from supportive treatments provided in regular early childhood classroom programs. For others, at least temporary placements in special classrooms, schools, or institutional programs may be appropriate.

REFLECTION IN ACTION
REFLECTION SCENARIOS

Earlier, Ms. Lightborne reflected on learning to work effectively with Jordan. As time went by, she began to notice that there were specific times during the day when he acted out more than others. Specifically, she began to notice that he often became disorganized and aggressive during transition times. She noted that during any session, there were multiple transitions between activities. Once Jordan became wound up, it took him a long time to unwind. It became clear that the melt- downs Jordan was experiencing during transitions had cumulative negative effects on his behavior and interfered with Jordan's positive engagement in other contexts. Once she recognized this pattern, she was able to intentionally plan to orchestrate more positive transitions, by providing support, structure, and motivation to each transition. This was very effective. Ms. Lightborne kept data on Jordan's successes as well as his difficulties, and this was helpful in documenting strategies that worked.

TABLE 6.4   Matching Children's Characteristics with Intervention

Characteristic	Possible Strategy	Rationale
Aggression Hitting Biting Kicking Pushing Interfering Verbalizing Vocalizing	Clear limits Redirection Physical activity Expression of feelings (anger, etc.) Focus on positives Replace behavior	Aggression can be aggravated by many factors, and children may need very specific, clear, firm guidance to change aggressive patterns
Withdrawal Isolating Separating out Avoiding Disengaging	Engagement of child in activities of personal interest	Children may need support to engage in purposeful ways. Sometimes children withdraw when they are overwhelmed or need time to process
Difficulty expressing feelings Demonstrating blank or flat affect Being physically impulsive	Support and guidance for expression of feelings	Acceptance and expression of feelings, especially fear, anger, sadness and other sometimes distressing feelings may be challenging, and may not occur without support
Difficulty with state/ self-regulation; soothing; calming down Being agitated	Support for calming; soothing; strategies for adjusting	Children with difficulty calming down may need to learn and practice specific strategies

Structured Environments

Special programs usually attempt to provide a structured environment where children experience a high degree of success, rules and routines are predictable, and students are consistently provided with positive feedback for appropriate behavior. Behavior management techniques, which rely on direct measurement and monitoring of behavioral change, such as positive reinforcement, token economies, contracting, and time-out, are commonly used in programs for children with serious emotional disturbance. Other models may be more effective and psychodynamic. Identification of each child's needs and underlying factors contributing to their challenges, helps to determine which approach and strategies are most useful. The assessment and systematic teaching of social skills through modeling, discussion, and rehearsal are frequently used to help children increase control over their behavior and improve their relations with others. In addition, supportive therapies involving music, art, exercise, and relaxation techniques are sometimes implemented for children who would benefit from such strategies.

Devon

Devon is a sweet and sensitive boy who is 3 years, 4 months old. He has recently begun attending a new early childhood program, and had not had much social experience prior to his current preschool setting. His teachers are concerned about his difficulty with behavior, including his challenges relating emotionally to other children. Much of the time he is quiet and reserved, preferring to play by himself with some repetitive use of toys. He has a younger sibling in the same program who is outgoing and able to quickly connect with others, both children and adults. Sometimes Devon has been observed to get very wound up. When this happens, he appears to be out of control, not just to others but also to himself. It appears there may be some biological difficulty with self-soothing and/or calming himself down.

Questions for Reflection:

1. What additional information might be helpful in planning appropriate intervention for Devon?
2. Who might be helpful as you gather that information?
3. What sorts of strategies might be effective to help Devon calm down?
4. How might your team work together to implement and monitor a plan of action that would address Devon's specific challenges?

Positive Outcomes for Devon

While Devon has not yet been officially identified as being eligible for special services, the team has enough concern that there is a mutual agreement to monitor his development, especially in the social and emotional areas, and see how he progresses over time. Some of the strategies the team is using are Tier II strategies. Specifically, they are focusing on providing support to increase Devon's engagement with other children. They are also focusing on providing support to help Devon calm down or de-escalate, when he gets wound up. Even though Devon does not yet have an IEP, the team has written objectives that help guide the team. These include:

> Devon will engage in play with other children, given facilitation as needed, on a daily basis.
>
> Given support as needed, Devon will disengage from activities that are very frustrating to him, long enough to calm down.

These are two examples of objectives.

Strategies that have been especially helpful with Devon have included physical proximity of adults, verbal cues, materials that are motivating, and quiet music in the background when he is very wound up. A predictable schedule is also very helpful. The staff and Devon's parents have been working together to keep a record of how he is doing in school and at home. Meetings have been scheduled on a regular basis to discuss his progress.

Questions for Reflection:

1. How might an intervention strategy be different if a child has a neurologically based difficulty with self-regulation? Please be specific.
2. Identify and list three specific ways in which inappropriate behaviors may be replaced with those that are more appropriate. How would these be helpful?
3. Please identify three factors related to family and/or culture that are relevant to the consideration of healthy social emotional development.
4. What are some of the factors we use to distinguish between characteristics that are challenging, but "normal," and those that need intervention?

Summary

This chapter has discussed the contexts in which social and emotional development occur, some characteristics of conditions, and the process through which professionals consider what would be a good match between a child's characteristics and effective intervention strategies.

This chapter has discussed some of the obstacles inherent in understanding behavioral challenges. Given the importance of the environment, including predictability, structure, and social support, a professional's willingness to consider and implement healthy options can yield very positive results. Ultimately, we want to communicate hope through this process of identifying and implementing effective adaptations. Children with social and emotional challenges often respond very well to effective intervention, and a team commitment to resolving issues together can make a powerful difference in the lives of children.

Key Terms

Positive behavioral supports   Stages of play

Children's Books Addressing Social and Emotional Aspects of Development

ANGER

And My Mean Old Mother Will Be Sorry by Martha G. Alexander

Blackboard Bear by Martha G. Alexander

When Sophie Gets Angry—Really, Really Angry . . . by Molly Bang

Let's Talk About Feeling Angry by Joy Wilt Berry

Smoky Night by Eve Bunting

Dark Day, Light Night by Jan Carr

Larky Mavis by Brock Cole

Carousel by Pat Cummings

It's Hard to Be 5: Learning How to Work My Control Panel by Jamie Lee Curtis

Today I Feel Silly & Other Moods That Make My Day by Jamie Lee Curtis

Llama Llama Mad at Mamma by Anna Dewdney

I Was So Mad by Karen Erickson

Mean Soup by Betsy Everitt

Harriet, You'll Drive Me Wild by Mem Fox

Feeling Angry by Helen Frost

At Daddy's On Saturdays by Linda W. Girard

Lilly's Purple Plastic Purse by Kevin Henkes

Princess Penelope's Parrot by Helen Lester

Alley Oops by Janice Levy

I'll Always Be Your Friend by Sam McBratney

I Was So Mad by Mercer Mayer

The Book of Mean People by Toni Morrison

Smudge's Grumpy Day by Miriam Moss

Bounjour, Butterfly by Jane O'Connor

Goldie Is Mad by Margie Palatini

Very Far Away by Maurice Sendak

Where The Wild Things Are by Maurice Sendak

Caps for Sale by Esphyr Slobodkina

Lila Bloom by Alexander Stadler

Mouse Was Mad by Linda Urban

Sometimes I'm Bombaloo by Rachel Vail

The Quarreling Book by Charlotte Zolotow

EMBARRASSMENT

Shenandoah Noah by Jim Aylesworth

Arthur's Underwear by Marc Brown

Daniel's Duck by Clyde Robert Bulla

A Picnic in October by Eve Bunting

Loudmouth George and the Big Race by Nancy L. Carlson

Great-Uncle Felix by Denys Cazet

Molly's Pilgrim by Barbara Cohen

Donald Says Thumbs Down by Nancy Evans Cooney

My Dad by Niki Daly

Quiet! There's a Canary in the Library by Don Freeman

The Rooftop Mystery by Joan M. Lexau

My Father Always Embarrasses Me by Meir Shalev

ENVY/JEALOUSY

Nobody Asked Me If I Wanted a Baby Sister by Martha G. Alexander

When the New Baby Comes, I'm Moving Out by Martha G. Alexander

Cousins by Elisa Amado

Bear's Bargain by Frank Asch

I Don't Like It! by Ruth Brown

A Surprise for Mitzi Mouse by Kathleen Bullock

I Need a Lunch Box by Jeannette Caines

High-wire Henry by Mary Calhoun

Herbert Binns and the Flying Tricycle by Caroline Castle

Janet's Thingamajigs by Beverly Cleary

The New Baby at Your House by Joanna Cole

Ella and the Naughty Lion by Anne Corrtinger

A Bunny Ride by Ida DeLage

Jealousy by Eva Ericksson

I Wish I Was Sick Too! by Franz Brandenberg

Geraldine's Baby Brother by Holly Keller

Best Friends by Steven Kellog

Alexander and the Wind Up Mouse by Leo Lionni

I'd Rather Have an Iguana by Heidi Stetson Mario

Lottie's New Friend by Petra Mathers

One Frog Too Many by Mercer Mayer

A Visit to Amy-Claire by Claudia Mills

The Luckiest One of All by Bill Peet

Dancing on the Moon by Janice M. Roper

Because You're Lucky by Irene Smalls-Hector

Lyle and the Birthday Party by Bernard Waber

Mabel Ran Away with the Toys by Jan Wahl

Sometimes I'm Jealous by Jane Werner Watson

Fox by Margaret Wild

A Baby Just Like You by Susan Winter

To Hilda for Helping by Margot Zemach

Popcorn Dragon by Jane Thayer

FEAR/COURAGE

I Can Do It Myself by Diane Adams

Mikale of Hawaii by Maya Angelou

Brave Martha by Margot Apple
Pepito the Brave by Scott Beck
Snip Snap! What's That? by Mara Bergman
Too Many Monsters by Eve Bunting
Harriet's Recital by Nancy L. Carlson
There's a Big Beautiful World Out There! by
    Nancy L. Carlson
What's That Noise? by William Carman
Boo! Made You Jump! by Lauren Child
My Brother John by Kristine Church
Good, Says Jerome by Lucille Clifton
Bravery Soup by Maryann Cocca-Leffer
Jim Meets the Thing by Miriam Cohen
Eugene the Brave by Ellen Conford
The Bear Under the Stairs by Helen Cooper
Stop, Drop and Roll by Margery Cuyler
Scared Stiff by Katie Davis
Llama Llama Red Pajama by Anna Dewdney
Go Away, Big Green Monster by Ed Emberley
Harry and the Terrible Whatzit by Dick Cackenbach
Zee Is Not Scared by Michel Gay
Brave Little Raccoon by Erica Wolf
Lights Out by Arthur Geisert
Keep Your Socks on, Albert! by Linda Glaser
A Lion at Bedtime by Debi Gliori
Night Lights by Barbara Diamond Goldin
Dear Bear by Joanna Harrison.
The Storm by Marc Harshman
Fang by Barbara Shook Hazen
The Knight Who Was Afraid of the Dark by Barbara
    Shook Hazen
The Knight Who Was Afraid to Fight by Barbara Shook
    Hazen
Some Things Are Scary by Florence Parry Heide
Big Chickens by Leslie Helakoski
The Very Noisy Night by Diana Hendry
Go Away, Bad Dreams! by Susan Hill
My Own Big Bed by Anna Grossnickle Hines
Bedtime for Frances by Russell Hoban
There's a Monster Under My Bed by James Howe
Penguin Small by Mick Inkpen
Little Rabbit Goes to Sleep by Tony Johnston
Something Might Happen by Helen Lester
The Listening Walk by David Kirk
The Spider's Tea Party by David Kirk
No Such Thing by Jackie French Koller
Noel the Coward by Robert Krauss
Don't Touch My Room by Pat Lakin
Trevor's Wiggly-Wobbly Tooth by Lester I. Laminack
Ben Has Something to Say by Laurie Lears
Something Might Happen by Helen Lester

Froggy Learns to Swim by Jonathan London
First Day by Dandi Daley Mackall
Good Night, Stella by Kate McMullan
Brave Bear by Kathy Mallat
Nathaniel Willy, Scared Silly by Judith Mathews
There's a Nightmare in My Closet by Mercer Mayer
There's an Alligator under My Bed by Mercer Mayer
Jump Up Time by Lynn Joseph
You're the Scaredy Cat by Mercer Mayer
Can't Scare Me! by Melissa Milich
A Big Day for Little Jack by Inga Moore
Rainbow Fish to the Rescue! by Marcus Pfister
Nosey Gilbert by Abigail Pizer
Thunder Cake by Patricia Polacco
Katie Catz Makes a Splash by Anne F. Rockewll
Welcome to Kindergarten by Anne F. Rockewll
The Sneetches, and Other Stories by Dr. Seuss
Brave Irene by William Steig
What's Under My Bed? by James Stevenson
The Owl Who Was Afraid of the Dark by Jill Tomlinson
My Mama Says There Aren't Any Zombies, Ghosts,
    Vampires, Creatures, Demons, Monsters, Fiends,
    Goblins, or Things by Judith Viorst
Can't You Sleep, Little Bear? by Martin Waddle
Let's Go Home, Little Bear? by Martin Waddle
Owl Babies by Martin Waddle
Tom Rabbit by Martin Waddle
Rosie and the Nightmares by Philip Waechter
The Moon in My Room by Ila Wallen
Henry and the Cow Problem by Iona Whishaw
The Little Old Lady Who Was Not Afraid of Anything by
    Linda Williams
Max's Starry Night by Ken Wilson-Max
Give Maggie a Chance by Frieda Wishinsky
Brave Little Raccoon by Erica Wolf

FRIENDS, SHARING, AND COOPERATION

Friend Is Someone Who Likes You by Joan Walsh
    Anglund
Willie's Not the Hugging Kind? by Joyce Durham
    Barrett
One for You and One for Me by Wendy Blaxland
Stone Soup by Marcia Brown
Friends at School by Rochelle Bunnett
Friends at Work and Play by Rochelle Bunnett
Will I Have A Friend? by Miriam Cohen
Best Friends by Miriam Cohen
May I Bring a Friend by Deatrice Schenk DeRegniers
That's What a Friend Is by P. K. Hallinan
Friends by Helme Heine

Alfie Gives A Hand by Shirley Hughes
Friends? by Rachel Isadora
George And Martha One Fine Day by James Marshall
Messy Bessey's Closet by Patricia McKissack and
        Fredrick McKissack
Mirandy and Brother Wind by Patricia C. McKissack
All Fall Down by Helen Oxenbury
The Rainbow Fish by Marcus Pfister
Margaret and Margarita by Lynn Reiser
What if the Zebras Lost Their Stripes by John Reitano
Making Friends by Fred Rodgers
Rose and Dorothy by Roslyn Schwartz
The Giving Tree by Shel Silverstein
Cherries and Cherry Pits by Vera B. Williams

GRIEF/LOSS

The Two of Them by Aliki
The Dead Bird by Margaret Wise Brown
The Memory String by Margaret Wise Brown
Rudi's Pond by Margaret Wise Brown
You Hold Me and I'll Hold You by Jo Carson
Everett Anderson's Goodbye by Lucille Clifton
Nana Upstairs and Nana Downstairs by Tomie
        De Paola
A Dog Like Jack by DyAnne DiSalvo-Ryan
Tough Boris by Mem Fox
Goodbye Mousie by Robie H. Harris
Poppy's Chair by Karen Hesse
Liplap's Wish by Jonathan London
The Tenth Good Thing About Barney by Judith Viorst
I'll Always Love You by Hans Wilhelm
The Old Dog by Charlotte Zolotow

HAPPINESS/JOY

If You're Happy and You Know It! by Jane Cabrera
Life Is Fun by Nancy Carlson
Across the Blue Mountains by Emma Chichester Clark
Happy to You! by Caron Lee Cohen
Mr. Happy by Roger Hargreaves
Photographer Mole by Dennis Haseley
Grandpa Bear's Fantastic Scarf by Gillian Heal
A Good Day by Kevin Henkes
What Comes in Spring? by Barbara Savadge
        Horton
Charlie's Checklist by Rory S. Lerman
Stone Soup retold by Jon J. Muth
The Boy Who Cried Fabulous by
        Lesléa Newman

If You're Happy and You Know It! by
        Jan Ormerod
The Feel Good Book by Todd Parr
The Happy Hedgehog by Marcus Pfister
10 (Ten): A Wonderful Story by
        Vladimir Radunsky
What Sadie Sang by Eve Rice
Spinky Sulks by William Steig
Susan Laughs by Jeanne Willis
Jubal's Wish by Audrey Wood

HATE

Smoky Night by Eve Bunting
We Hate Rain! by James Stevenson.
Lovable Lyle by Bernard Waber
The Hating Book by Charlotte Zolotow

LONELINESS

My Friend Bear by Jez Alborough
We Are Best Friends by Aliki
My Father Is Far Away by Robin Ballard
Gingerbread Friends by Jan Brett
The Happy Lion Roars by Louise Fatio
Say Hello by Jack & Michael Foreman
Hunwick's Egg by Mem Fox
Big Little Elephant by Valeri Gorbachev
Toby and the Snowflakes by Julie Halpern
The Dog Who Belonged to No One by
        Amy Hest
Grandpa's Soup by Eiko Kadono
The Trip by Ezra Keats
The Other Goose by Judith Kerr
The Howling Dog by Tracey Campbell Pearson
The Rainbow Fish by Marcus Pfister
The Loudness of Sam by James Proimos
Oh, the Places You'll Go! by Dr. Seuss.
When I Miss You by Cornelia Spelman
The Small World of Binky Braverman by Rosemary
        Wells
The Lonely Doll by Dare Wright
Janey by Charlotte Zolotow

LOVE/COMPASSION/AFFECTION

Mommy's Best Kisses by Margaret Anastas
Oh My Baby, Little One by Kathi Appelt
I Love You Because You're You by Liza Baker
Why Do You Love Me? by Martin Baynton

The Velveteen Rabbit by Margery
Fuzzy Rabbit by Rosemary Billam
Grandmother and I by Helen Elizabeth Buckley
Everett Anderson's Goodbye by Lucille Clifton
Leon and Albertine by Christine Davenier
You're My Nikki by Phyllis Rose Eisenberg
Ask Mr. Bear by Marjorie Flack
The Hippopotamus Song by Michael Flanders
Koala Lou by Mem Fox
Corduroy by Don Freeman
Even if I did Something Awful by Barbara Shook Hazen
Mama Do You Love Me? by Barbara M. Joose
A Mother for Choco by Keiko Kasza
Little Miss Spider by David Kirk
Mouse in Love by Robert Kraus
Big and Little by Ruth Krauss
Baby Loves by Michael Lawrence
Grandfather's Lovesong by Reeve Lindberg
A Koala for Katie by Jonathan London
What Do You Love? by Jonathan London
Guess How Much I Love You by Sam McBratney
Who Loves Me? by Patricia MacLachlan
Sisters by David M. McPhail
The Teddy Bear by David McPhail
Knots on a Counting Rope by Bill Martin
Two Homes by Claire Masurel
Loving by Ann Morris
Mommy Loves Her Baby; Daddy Loves His Baby by Tara Jayne Morrow
Love You Forever by Robert N. Munsch
Mole and the Baby Bird by Marjorie Newman
I Love You So Much by Carl Norac
I Love You, Bunny Rabbit by Shulamith Levey Oppenheim
Daddy All Day Long by Francesca Rusackas
On Mother's Lap by Ann Herbert Scott
Pierre: A Cautionary Tale in Five Chapters by Maurice Sendak
Tiffky Doofky by William Steig
Elizabeti's Doll by Stephanie Stuve-Bodeen
I love You, Little One by Nancy Tafuri
Do You Know How Much I Love You? by Donna Tedesco
Frog in Love by Max Velthuijs
Love and Kisses by Sarah Wilson
Do You Know What I'll Do? by Charlotte Zolotow
If You Listen by Charlotte Zolotow

Say It! by Charlotte Zolotow
Some Things Go Together by Charlotte Zolotow

SADNESS/DISAPPOINTMENT/HURT

When I'm Sad by Jane Aaron
We Are Best Friends by Aliki
The Hurt by Teddi Dolesky
Flyaway Katie by Polly Dunbar
Glad Monster, Sad Monster: A Book About Feelings by Ed Emberley
No One Is Perfect by Karen Erickson
Yesterday I Had the Blues by Jeron Ashford Frame
The Tangerine Tree by Regina Hanson
Lizzy's Ups and Downs: Not an Ordinary School Day by Jessica Harper
Jamaica's Blue Marker by Juanita Havill
Toot and Puddle: You Are My Sunshine by Holly Hobbie
The Aunt in Our House by Angela Johnson
Why Do You Cry? Not a Sob Story by Kate Klise
Hurt Feelings by Helen Lester
The Mountain That Loved a Bird by Alice McLerran
Michael Rosen's Sad Book by Michael Rosen
Mrs. Biddlebox by Linda Smith
When I Feel Sad by Cornelia Maude Spelman
The Big Little Book of Happy Sadness by Colin Thompson
Misery Moo by Jeanne Willis

GENERAL

Hoot and Holler by Alan Brown
Big Words for little People by Jamie Lee Curtis
Sometimes I Feel Like a Mouse: A Book About Feelings by Jeanne Modesitt
Many Colored Days by Dr. Seuss
Alexander and the Terrible, Horrible, No Good, Very Bad Day by Judith Viorst

CHILDREN WITH EMOTIONAL DISABILITIES

Russell Is Extra Special by C. A. Amenta
Playing by the Rules by Dena Fox Luchsinger
Shelley, the Hyperactive Turtle by Deborah Moss
Blink, Blink, Clop, Clop: Why Do We Do Things We Can't Stop? by E. Katia Moritz and Jennifer Jablonsky
Andy and His Yellow Frisbee by Mary Thompson

Websites

POSITIVE BEHAVIORAL SUPPORT RESOURCES

Center on Positive Behavioral Interventions and Supports
http://www.pbis.org
Journal of Positive Behavior Interventions
http://education.ucsb.edu/autism/jpbi.html

Center for Evidence-Based Practice: Young Children with Challenging Behavior
http://www.challengingbehavior.org

Division for Early Childhood, Council for Exceptional Children
http://www.dec-sped.org

Council for Exceptional Children
http://www.cec.sped.org

Frank Porter Graham Child Development Center
http://www.fpg.unc.edu

The Minnesota Governor's Council on Developmental Disabilities
http://www.mncdd.org

National Information Center for Children & Youth with Disabilities
http://www.nichcy.org

National Institutes of Mental Health
http://www.nimh.gov.org

IDEA Partnerships
http://www.ideapractices.org

References

American Psychiatric Association. (1994). *Diagnostic and statistical manual of mental disorders* (4th ed.). Washington, DC: Author.

Barbarin, O. (2006). ABLE: A system for mental health screening and care for preschool children. In B. Bowman & E. Moore, (Eds.), *School readiness and social-emotional development* (pp. 77–88). Washington, DC: National Black Child Development Institute.

Bergen, D. (2001). *Pretend play and young children's development.* ERIC Digest Pretend Play and Young Children's Development. ERIC Digest. ED458045.

Birch, M. (Ed.). (2008). *Finding hope in despair.* Washington, DC: Zero to Three.

Bowman, B., & Moore, E. (Eds.). (2006). *School readiness and social-emotional development.* Washington, DC: National Black Child Development Institute.

Bretherton, I. (1989). Pretense: The form and function of make-believe play. *Developmental Review, 9,* 383–401.

Bretherton, I., O'Connell, B., Shore, C., & Bates, E. (1984). The effects on contextual variation on symbolic play: Development from 20 to 28 months. In I. Bretherton (Ed.), *Symbolic play and the development of social understanding* (pp. 271–298), New York: Academic Press.

Bricker, D., & Squires, J. (1999). *The ages and stages questionnaires.* Baltimore: Paul H. Brookes.

Bronson, M. B. (2000). *Self-regulation in early childhood: Nature and nurture.* New York: The Guilford Press.

Brown, W., Odom, S., & McConnell, S. (2008). *Social competence of young children.* Baltimore: Paul H. Brookes.

Carr, E. G., Dunlap, G., Horner, R. H., Koegel, R. L., Turnbull, A., Sailor, W., Anderson, J., Albin, R., Koegel, L. K., & Fox, L. (2002). Positive behavior support: Evolution of an applied science. *Journal of Positive Behavior Interventions, 4*(1), 4–16.

Catlett, C., & Winton, P. (2009). Resources within reason. *Young Exceptional Children, 12*(3), 45.

Coplan, R., Gavinski-Molina, M., Lagace-Seguin, D. G., & Wichmann, C. (2001). When girls versus boys play alone: Nonsocial play and adjustment in kindergarten. *Developmental Psychology, 37,* 464–474.

Elias, C., & Berk, L. (2002). Self-regulation in young children: Is there a role for sociodramatic play? *Early Childhood Research Quarterly, 17,* 216–238.

Epstein, A. (2009). *Me, you, us: Social-emotional learning in preschool.* Ypsilanti, MI: High Scope Press/Washington, DC: NAEYC.

Erikson. E. H. (1968). *Childhood and society* (rev. ed.). New York: Norton.

Farran, D. C., & Son-Yarbrough, W. (2001). Title I funded preschools as a developmental context for children's play and verbal behaviors.

Early Childhood Research Quarterly, 16, 245–262.

Fein, G. G. (1981). Pretend play: An integrative review. *Child Development, 52,* 1095–1118.

Fisher, E. P. (1992). The impact of play on development: A meta-analysis. *Play & Culture, 5,* 159–181.

Gartrell, D. (2002). Replacing time-out: Part two— Using guidance to maintain an encouraging classroom. *Young Children, 57*(2), 36–43.

Guralnick, M. J., & Hammond, M. A. (1999). Sequential analysis of the social play of children with mild developmental delays. *Journal of Early Intervention, 22,* 243–256.

Hemmeter, M. L., Fox, L., Jack, S., & Broyles, L. (2007). A program-wide model of positive behavior support in early childhood settings. *Journal of Early Intervention, 29,* 337–355.

Horn, E., & Jones, H. (2006). *Social & emotional monograph.* Missoula, MT: Division of Early Childhood, Council for Exceptional Children.

Hunter, A., & Hemmeter, M. L. (2009). The center on the social and emotional foundations for early learning. *Zero to Three, 29*(3), 5–12.

Jarrold, C., Boucher, J., & Smith, P. K. (1996). Generativity deficits in pretend play in autism. *British Journal of Developmental Psychology, 14,* 275–230.

Kaiser, B., & Rasminsky, J. S. (2003). *Challenging behavior in young children.* Boston: Allyn & Bacon/Pearson Education.

Kinsman, C., & Berk, L. (1979). Joining the block and housekeeping areas: Changes in play and social behavior. *Young Children, 35,* 66–75.

Lillard, A. S. (1998) Wanting to be it: Children's understanding of intentions underlying pretense. *Development, 69,* 981–993.

Linder, T. (1993). *Transdisciplinary play based intervention.* Baltimore: Paul H. Brookes.

Linder, T. (2008). *Transdisciplinary play based intervention.* Baltimore: Paul H. Brookes.

McWilliam, R., & Casey, A. (2008). *Engagement of every child in the preschool classroom.* Baltimore: Paul H. Brookes.

NICHCY (2009). November Newsletter. Washington, DC: National Dissemination Center for Children with Disabilities.

Odom, S. L., McConnell, S. R., & Chandler, L. K. (1993). Acceptability and feasibility of classroom-based social interaction interventions for young children with disabilities. *Exceptional Children, 60,* 226–236.

Parten, M. B. (1932). Social participation among preschool children. *Journal of Abnormal and Social Psychology, 27,* 243–269.

Perry, D., Kaufmann, R., & Knitzer, J. (2007). *Social and emotional health in early childhood.* Baltimore: Brookes.

Pickard Kremenitzer, J., & Miller, R. (2008). Are you a highly qualified, emotionally intelligent early childhood educator? *Young Children, 63,* 106–112.

Riley, D., San Juan, R., Klinkner, J., & Ramminger, A. (2008). *Social and emotional development: Connecting science and practice.* St. Paul, MN: Redleaf Press.

Rimland, B., & Baker, S. M. (1996). Brief report: Alternative approaches to the development of effective treatments for Autism, *Journal of Autism and Developmental Disorders, 26*(2), 237–241.

Rubin, K. H. (1982). Nonsocial-play in preschoolers: Necessary evil? *Child Development, 53,* 651–657.

Rubin, K. H., & Coplan, R. J. (1998). Social and nonsocial play in childhood: An individual differences perspective. In O. N. Saracho & B. Spodek (Eds.), *Multiple perspectives on play in early childhood* (pp. 144–170). Albany, NY: State University of New York Press.

Sandall, S., & Ostrosky, M. (Eds.). (1999). *Practical ideas for addressing challenging behaviors.* Longmont, CO: Sopris West/The Division of Early Childhood, Council for Exceptional Children.

Sawyer, R. K. (1997). *Pretend play as improvisation: Conversation in the preschool classroom* Mahwah, NJ: Lawrence Erlbaum.

Schore, A. (1994). *Affect regulation and the origin of the self.* Hillsdale, NJ: Lawrence Erlbaum.

Shonkoff, J., & Phillips, D. (2001). *From neurons to neighborhoods: The science of early childhood development.* Washington DC: National Academy Press.

Shore, R. (1997), *Rethinking the brain.* New York: Families and Work Institute.

Squires, J., & Bricker, D. (2007). *An activity-based approach to developing young children's social emotional competence.* Baltimore: Paul H. Brookes.

Stanford University Medical Center (2009, October 16). Mechanism of Gene Linked to Autism, Schizophrenia Pinpointed. *ScienceDaily.* Retrieved November 15, 2009, from http://www.sciencedaily.com/releases/2009/10/091012225541.htm

Stormont, M. (2007). *Fostering resilience in young children.* Upper Saddle River, NJ: Merrill/Pearson Education.

Sugai, G., & Horner, R. H. (2002). The evolution of discipline practices: School-wide positive behavior supports. *Child and Family Behavior Therapy, 24,* 23–50.

Tarullo, A. R., Obradovic, J., & Gunnar, M. R. (2009). Self-control and the developing brain. *Zero to Three, 29*(3), 31–37.

Tsao, L. (2002). How much do we know about the importance of play in child development? *Childhood Education, 78,* 230–233.

Van Horn, J., Nourot, P. M., Scales, B., & Alward, K. R. (2007). *Play at the center of the curriculum* (4th ed.). Upper Saddle River, NJ: Merrill/Pearson Education.

Vygotsky, L. (1967). Play and its role in the mental development of the child. *Soviet Psychology, 5,* 6–18. (Original work published in 1933.)

Webster-Stratton, C., & Reid, M. J. (2004). Strengthening social and emotional competence in young children—the foundation for early school readiness and success: Incredible years classroom skills and problem-solving curriculum. *Infants & Young Children, 17*(2), 96–113.

Widerstrom, A. (2005). *Achieving learning goals through play* (2nd ed.). Baltimore: Paul H. Brookes.

Wood, D., Bruner, J., & Ross, G. (1976). The role of tutoring in problem solving. *Journal of Child Psychology and Psychiatry, 17,* 89–100.

Yeargin-Allsopp, M., Rice, C., Karapurkar, T., Doernberg, N., Boyle, C., & Murphy, C. (2003). Prevalence of autism in a US metropolitan area. *The Journal of the American Medical Association, 1289,* 49–55.

Zigler, E., & Styfco, S. (2004). *The Head Start debates.* Baltimore: Paul H. Brookes.

Chapter 7

Circular Adaptations

Language and Literacy

OBJECTIVES

After reading this chapter, students will:

- Have a concept of the scope and content of early language and literacy development;

- Identify factors that may contribute to difficulty in language, communication, and literacy;

- Demonstrate an understanding of the connection between patterns of strength and need, and appropriate strategies in the area of language and literacy;

- Have basic information about a range of possible strategies, including assistive technology and augmentative communication;

- Recognize ways in which an active reflective process may be used to enhance the effectiveness of inclusion during language and literacy activities.

LAYING THE GROUNDWORK

Communication serves many vital functions for people as well as other animals. Basic signal systems are essential for survival and well-being. The ability to engage in reciprocal interaction, whether nonverbal or verbal, is a crucial aspect of relationships and growth. Communication involves outcomes as well as being a means to an end. Communication is a process through which learning may occur. In human societies, communication involves the acquisition of spoken language and, for many, the transition from spoken to written symbol systems, or reading.

The transition from sound production to the association of sounds with shared meaning appears to be a universal process. While there are variations among different cultures, the sequence is remarkably predictable unless there are challenges or difficulties. Ultimately, the core of communication has its center in relationships. Communication depends on reciprocity and mutual response. This is highly evident in the communication of infants whose signals are pure and direct, and designed to make immediate connections. Even with healthy communication between infants and their caregivers, however, there are times when signals may be missed or mixed-up. Babies sometimes give cues that are difficult to interpret, and caregivers may have difficulty responding (Thoman & Browder, 1987).

Overlapping Factors Affecting Communication

Inherent in effective communication is motivation. In healthy development, motivation is integral to the reciprocal process, which begins as part of attachment. Professionals in early childhood education may not have all the information about underlying causes or difficulty with this process, but there is no question that there are overlapping effects of difficulties in different domains. If there are challenges in relationships and social interaction, those issues often affect communication. Conversely, if there are difficulties in communication, those issues affect social interaction. When there are difficulties in the cognitive process, language acquisition can be delayed. Difficulties in language acquisition can affect a child's verbal processing of concepts and demonstration of comprehension. In healthy development, quality interaction is intrinsically rewarding. The reciprocity and mutuality provide momentum in communication and invite responses. In healthy relationships, this interaction usually supports and nurtures communication and language without direct, intentional teaching of skills. Professionals can use the marvelous dynamic that occurs in normal language acquisition as a model for intervention in natural contexts (Weitzman & Greenberg, 2002). When children are having difficulty, strategies can be used to provide support as much as possible through natural interactions. These might include physical proximity, eye contact, nonverbal communication, facial expressions, and tone of voice.

Patterns

It helps to identify and acknowledge several broad patterns regarding language acquisition and competence. Some of the most basic and important include signal production/encoding (sounds, gestures, etc.), signal comprehension/decoding, turn-taking, association of sounds and symbols with meaning, **intent to communicate**, and organization of communication (Ysseldyke & Algozzine, 2006). When difficulties arise, they may be centered on one or more of these basic functions. It is not always easy to assess language, but there are many effective methods, as well as specialists with expertise in those areas. Challenges with speech production, including specific sound production (**phonemes**), articulation, and fluency, would be classified as difficulties with speech as distinct from language. Speech and language therapists (sometimes called speech pathologists) have extensive training and expertise in speech and language (Ysseldyke & Algozzine, 2006).

Assessment of Difficulties in Language

As professionals and parents seek to better understand the complexities of atypical language development, it is essential that they have a clear awareness of the sequence and qualitative factors associated with a "normal" progression of skills. Even within the range of normal **expressive and receptive language** development there is infinite variability in style, rate of growth, and ways of connecting with others. At the same time, in typical development there are patterns that emerge and remarkably predictable benchmarks that occur within a span of time that may vary from child to child, but still be within an expected range. Professionals can use developmental frameworks to better understand exceptional development and to identify desired outcomes during program planning. Table 7.1 provides a concise overview of significant benchmarks in receptive and expressive language.

Characteristics of Challenges in Language and Communication

Children who do not attain benchmarks at a certain age, may demonstrate challenges in language and communication. Given the broad range of normal development, the identification of children who demonstrate a need for intervention is not always easy. Some children may clearly have delays, while others may only have different communicative styles. Table 7.2 provides an overview of some developmental challenges in language and/or communication.

Assessment of Language and/or Communication Delays

During assessment of language and/or communication delays, professionals work together to determine areas of challenge and degree of delay. Because language delays are the most common form of challenge in early childhood (http://www.NICHCY.org),

TABLE 7.1   Did You Know? Developmental Benchmarks in Language and Communication

Crying

Eye-contact

Facial expressions

Gestures

Vocalization and sound production

Babbling

Jargoning and playing with intonation

Reciprocal interaction with expressions, vocalization, etc.

Increased control over sound production

Imitation of sounds

Wide range of sounds

Beginning to focus on more frequently used sounds in specific language (phonemes)

Word approximations

Increased association of sounds with shared meaning (morphemes)

Increased use of gestures and sounds to intentionally express wants and needs

Word approximations shifting toward first words

Single words being used as sentence (holophrases)

Two words combined to form sentences
in which key elements are included, but descriptors, pronouns, etc. are not (telegraphic speech)

Increasing complexity of expressive language structures (use of pronouns, adjectives, etc.)

Increased ability to articulate a range of sounds

Ability to retrieve and organize words to form intelligible statements

Vocabulary

Ability to engage in reciprocal conversations

Ability to decode or read nonverbal cues and sometimes subtle social signals

Second language learners distinguish between contexts and use language as appropriate

---

there are many contributing factors. Credentialed specialists may identify delays based upon specific areas of difficulty. The degree to which a child's development is different from typical development is a determining factor in the types of intervention the child may receive. There are times when children progress along a developmental sequence at a slower rate than other children, but are nonetheless making progress and experiencing success with developmental benchmarks. Comparing a child's age for skill acquisition with the ages when the skills are typically mastered helps to identify eligibility for special services. There are other times when a child's course of development is significantly different from typical patterns, and professionals will select the methods according to those individual needs.

Identification of Patterns

Identifying underlying patterns is often helpful in aligning the intervention with the unique needs of each child. While professionals may not always know why a child is having difficulty with expressive language, it is helpful when we do. For example, if a

TABLE 7.2 Did You Know? Developmental Challenges in Language/Communication

Difficulty communicating through crying, eye-contact, or facial expressions

Lack of or difficulty with gestures, vocalization, sound production, and babbling

Lack of or difficulty with jargoning, playing with intonation, reciprocal interaction with expressions, vocalization, etc.

Lack of or difficulty with increased control over sound production, imitation of sounds, production of a wide range of sounds

Difficulty with focus on more frequently used sounds in specific language (phonemes)

Few or no word approximations or increased association of sounds with shared meaning (morphemes)

Lack of or difficulty with use of gestures and sounds to intentionally express wants and needs

Less evidence of word approximations shifting toward first words

Few or no single words being used as sentence (holophrases)

Difficulty with two words combined to form sentences in which key elements are included, but descriptors, pronouns, etc. are not (telegraphic speech)

Lack of or difficulty with increasing complexity of expressive language structures (use of pronouns, adjectives, etc.)

Difficulty with increased ability to articulate a range of sounds

Difficulty with retrieval and organization of words to form intelligible statements

Difficulty with engagement in reciprocal conversations

Difficulty decoding or reading nonverbal cues and subtle social signals

Difficulty for second language learners distinguishing between contexts and using language as appropriate

Limited vocabulary

---

child was born prematurely, it is possible that language delays may be the result of difficulty with neurological processing. If a child has hearing loss or intermittent fluid in his ears, language delays are more likely to be the result of differences in auditory acuity (Clark, 2006). Sometimes genetic patterns occur in families.

EXAMPLE 1   Lily

A practitioner's reflection can play a positive role as they try to predict future development in children. For example, Lily, who was adopted as an infant, demonstrated characteristics of selective mutism while she was in preschool. The assessment determined that her language was developing well in the familiar context of home, but in the context of school Lily rarely spoke. As she approached the transition to kindergarten, the team working on her assessment determined she met the diagnostic criteria for selective mutism and was officially eligible for special services. The question arose about whether or not to officially enroll Lily in special services, especially since she was approaching a new setting. With active participation on the part of her parents, a decision was made to have her start the new school year without special services, monitor her progress, and provide services if needed. With the transition, Lily essentially started fresh. She had three older brothers in the same school.

(continued)

She did not demonstrate the characteristics of selective mutism in her new school. Therefore, she did not need special services. The reflective process was an essential element during Lily's assessment, and many team members participated in a variety of contexts. Lily's family and their active role were crucial. Through discussions and informal observation, as well as intervention that sought to create more of a bridge between home and school, the process helped decrease the extent to which there may have been real or perceived pressure for this child to speak in school. Ultimately, we may never know exactly why the positive change occurred in Lily's development. It is clear, however, that there was some resolution of the presenting symptoms.

Questions for Reflection:

1. Which environmental factors may have been significant for Lily, in their effects on her performance in different settings?
2. In what ways might the team members adjust their interactions to support Lily?
3. If you were Lily's kindergarten teacher, what might you do to provide support as she joined your class?

REFLECTION AND INTERPRETATION OF DATA

Assessment is far more than scores on standardized tests. This is true for language as well as other domains of development. One example was illustrated in Mark, a boy who was referred for special services when he was three years old because of significant expressive language delays. He had an expressive vocabulary of approximately forty words, which is significantly less than what is considered normal at his age. In other domains, Mark was progressing well in terms of benchmarks. He had well-developed fine and gross motor skills. It was observed, however, that in climbing stairs he consistently led with one foot rather than alternating feet. That may or may not have been a significant detail. Sometimes lack of left-right motor coordination is indicative of lack of left-right integration of the hemispheres in the central nervous system. When his teacher, who had established a warm and trusting relationship with Mark, was evaluating him he saw a picture of a cat, pointed, and gestured eleven with his fingers, first showing all ten, then one more. The teacher responded to his nonverbal signal by saying, "Yes, a cat. Eleven?" He nodded. "You have eleven cats?" He nodded again. The teacher noted this remarkable interaction and later checked with Mark's mother, who confirmed there were eleven cats living in their barn! This is a very significant anecdote. If the teacher had ignored Mark's gestures and followed the script of the assessment instrument rigidly, this very meaningful dimension about Mark would not have been part of the overall picture of his capabilities. It is true that his presenting symptom was a significant language delay. After one year of preschool, however, he was talking in long, very complex sentences, and further evaluation indicated that he was highly gifted and talented, with a measured I.Q. of about 160.

Questions for Reflection:

1. What signals did Mark use to communicate his inner thoughts?
2. If you were his teacher, how might you adjust your style to support him?

Communication can occur in many ways.

OUTCOMES AND OBJECTIVES

Identification of Areas of Concern

Through careful assessment parents and professionals can identify areas of concern and strength. Goals and objectives to address areas of concern can be designed based on what is known about each individual child as well as what is known about benchmarks of typical development. Goals focus on improving the quality and/or quantity of expressive and receptive language. To that end, strategies that support the acquisition of language and communicative competence in many ways can be used.

INTERVENTION

Given the infinite interactive and caregiving styles along with the complexity of linguistic structures, it is quite remarkable that most children acquire language without direct instruction. When children, however, have difficulties with language acquisition and use, intervention is best designed to match the unique individual needs of students.

Among the general population of children there is a range of styles and needs. In addition, among parents and teachers there are also many styles and approaches to caregiving. Some adults are more directive than others. Some are more responsive. When designing individualized programs and intervention for young children, the different styles and personalities of adults are taken into consideration, but the individual needs of children would take priority. If a caregiver is more responsive than directive, but a child needs more direction and explicit communication, it is important that the caregiver develop the ability to adjust his or her interactive style to accommodate the child. If a caregiver is exceptionally verbal, this can provide a wonderfully rich language environment for a child, but unless there is a match with the child's developmental needs by simplifying adult language, the opportunity may not have a positive effect on the child's language acquisition.

For example, if a child is stuck using one word sentences, it will probably be more functional for the teacher and parents to model two-word phrases that maintain the content of the child's intent to communicate, rather than using highly complex sentences that are way beyond what Vygotsky (1978) would call the child's "zone of proximal development."

The central imperative for practitioners is to be able to adjust their interactive styles and levels to meet the individual developmental needs of each child. This must be recognized as part of a high-quality inclusive classroom. Certainly knowledge of curriculum, methods, and child development is necessary, but it is not in itself sufficient to ensure implementation of appropriate strategies. Intervention must be adjusted and calibrated on a child-by-child basis. Children, of course, are full of surprises whether or not they have identified exceptionalities, so a large part of a professional's preparedness is having the ability to adjust as needed. This occurs when professionals have a deep understanding of the basic concepts involved, a comprehensive awareness of options available, and the ability to regroup, as needed. Plans are developed based on what professionals know about each child and what the goals and objectives are for the entire class. Plans can be adjusted as needed, during the application phase.

Setting a Tone for Quality Communication

There are infinite permutations of the variables contributing to effective communication. One factor, however, that may be relatively universal but not always acknowledged, is the significance of the tone set by the professional or parent. This has been characterized in different ways, including "anticipatory set," and wait time, and it can take different forms. It involves creating an atmosphere of mutual regard and respect. The message is conveyed, directly or indirectly, that listening is an important part of communication. The adult may set a positive tone for communication, especially by attending well to what a child is trying to communicate. In typical, healthy development communication's beginnings occur during the rhythms of taking turns when babies are nursing. Linguists have identified the origins of conversation in the simple pausing, sucking, mutual eye-contact, and other actions that occur when infants are being fed and playing an active role in sending signals to their caregivers. Responsive caregivers are drawn into this mutual experience (Brazleton & Cramer, 1990; Snow, 1983).

When babies are being nurtured in healthy relationships, they most often are natural communicators. The transition to toddlerhood is marked by shifts in developmental needs, but when there is a solid, mutual context for communication, the frustration accompanying a child's need to communicate is decreased by the support of the child's relationships. This mutual commitment to communication is helpful to children and caregivers alike (Thoman & Browder, 1987).

Sometimes a central factor in a child's difficulty with language stems from the lack of a strong context for communication. Shared attention, which is a basic element in communication, may not happen without explicit focus on the part of the caregiver. In this multitasking world, it is not uncommon for adults to be attempting to do many things at once. When this pattern is identified, it can be adjusted so that children are receiving full attention.

When adults pay full attention to children, this sets a tone quality communication. It can also be accomplished through tone of voice and pacing. Questioning strategies can be used. There are many specific strategies that can be used to gain and sustain

mutual attention with positive dispositions. This is very effective in preventing challenging and disruptive behavior.

In considering the many ways in which parents and professionals may provide
opportunities to enhance the language development of young children, it is evident
that they are using strategies that are intentional (Epstein, 2007). Methods can be designed and adjusted spanning a broad continuum of options. These methods will
represent intentional application of teaching techniques and approaches. It helps to
have a repertoire of strategies from which to draw when planning intervention.
Table 7.3 provides some strategies for your consideration.

TABLE 7.3   Possible Strategies in Language and Literacy Activities

Condition	Possible Characteristics	Possible Strategies
Autism	Difficulty processing language Very literal	Immediate use of language related to relevant experience Augmentative communication Picture exchange Sign language Social stories™
Blind/visually impaired	Lack of visual acuity	Large print Braille Clear pictures (outlines) Objects; Positioning Big books Textures
Deaf/hearing impaired	Difficulty hearing	Text/print Position Augmentative communication (sign language, total communication)
Developmentally delayed	Delayed performance	Language experience Literacy experiences Much informal interaction
Intellectually disabled/ mentally retarded	Limited vocabulary Difficulty with concepts	Use of objects Much experience with sensory activities and language Explicit connections
Language delayed	Limited expressive language, vocabulary, and syntax	Language experience
Learning disabled	Difficulty with word retrieval Organization	Cues and prompts Help with sequencing
Neurologically impaired	Problems with retrieval and organization	Cues and prompts Pictures
Physically challenged	Problems with physical coordination of language	Use of books with alliteration Repeated sounds
Serious emotional disturbance	Difficulty expressing feelings	Support for social interaction Use of words to express feelings

THE CONTINUUM OF INTERVENTION

There are two broad categories of intervention. One involves carefully planned strategies that are relatively scripted or predictable. If professionals know, for instance, that a child uses word approximations in certain contexts and is able to refine articulation given a language model, they can provide prompts and models when a child uses a word approximation with a request for a clearer statement on the part of the child (Clark, 2006).

In contrast, with the second there are many more spontaneous opportunities for interaction in the context of play and informal engagement. These two broad categories represent different aspects of the continuum of curricular adaptations discussed in Chapter 5. There is a range of adaptations spanning from child-centered activities to more teacher-directed activities, depending on the individual needs of children (Schwartz & Heller Miller, 1997).

Though at times the two categories of intervention overlap, this book will address them in separate sections. The first involves less reflection and more information about specific strategies. The second involves a much deeper level of reflection and the ability to adjust in the course of spontaneous interaction. Both are valuable forms of intervention and may complement each other well when implemented effectively. Intentional teaching (Epstein, 2007) may be used with either approach. Specific objectives that are identified on an individualized education program (IEP) may be integrated or embedded into informal interactions with children. Clearly, this takes a significant level of teacher preparation because it involves spontaneously generalizing specific skills in a wide variety of contexts. This is likely to be somewhat easier for parents, since their primary focus is their child, rather than an entire group.

Child Focused Teacher-Directed Instructional Strategies

Teacher-directed instructional strategies are most often used when children have more significant challenges and are less likely to learn through informal, incidental opportunities. If children are responding well to more informal intervention and interaction, then more structured intervention is not necessary or appropriate. When these consistent, carefully planned interactions are used, practitioners should use them in as natural a way as possible (McCathren & Howard Allor, 2002; McCathren & Watson, 2001).

When children need more focused and directed intervention in order to express themselves, all members of the team should consistently model language. This does not mean that they pretend to be clones of each other. Natural variation in style, intonation, and personality make life interesting. It does mean, however, children who are having trouble processing language benefit from cues and prompts that are consistent and predictable. Figure 7.1 illustrates the importance of clear communication.

Imagine an adult speaking to a child who has been running inside. She says, "You need to stop and think about what you are doing, honey. It is not safe for you to go so fast inside with all the other children in the class. Inside, it is not ok to run!"

But the child hears, "................................run!"

FIGURE 7.1 Matching Language with Children's Processing

TEACHER-DIRECTED/CHILD-FOCUSED INSTRUCTIONAL STRATEGIES

Child A's current level of functioning:

Word approximations; Gestures; pointing

Objective: *Child will use single word phrases to express his or her wants and needs, given prompts and cues, in the context of daily activities at least three times a day.*

Intervention: *During routines and other activities, teacher will prompt Child A with questions, using a consistent sequence and structure.*

Embedded/Integrated into daily activities:

Teacher, at snack: *"What do you want?"*

"Do you want juice or milk?"

"Do you want a cracker or fruit?"

Prompts are offered in a sequential progression. If the child does not respond to the initial question, but looks at the juice, the teacher responds to that cue and says: "Juice? Do you want juice?" If the child is capable of using a word approximation, he or she will be asked to use the sound. If he or she is able to use a word, he or she will be asked to say the word, given a model.

When a child is using total communication, with the sign provided along with the word, the teacher will model this combination of spoken word and sign.

This sequence of questions and prompts can be adjusted to work in many different activities and routines.

As team members plan for more structured child-focused instructional strategies, they should be guided by specifically identified positive outcomes or objectives. These strategies may include highly consistent prompts that are used by all adults who interact with the child. See box "Teacher-Directed/Child-Focused Instructional Strategies". It illustrates child-focused instructional strategies.

Planning for Language Experiences

Early childhood is a time when language acquisition is typically a major progression that can contribute to the early childhood curriculum and recommended practices. Early childhood provides excellent opportunities for interaction. This general climate of communication is fertile ground for children with difficulties in communication to be exposed to and practice language in natural settings (Shickedanz, 2008; Weitzman & Greenberg, 2002). Virtually all of the methods and strategies that are used between caregivers and children in high-quality early childhood programs could be considered beneficial for children who are experiencing difficulty. Sometimes appropriate intervention may involve fairly simple modifications of what is already occurring within a classroom. For example, if a child is having trouble focusing on certain aspects or attributes of language, he or she might be guided toward listening for certain patterns of sounds. A caregiver might reduce the quantity of language shared with the child if he or she appears to be having trouble processing language.

Clear, simple statements may be used instead of long, complex sentences. Modeling can be adjusted so it better matches the child's level of communication, scaffolding just enough to guide them to a higher level.

Facilitation of Informal Interaction in Natural Contexts

Informal conversation and language modeling provide wonderful opportunities for effective language development. This certainly applies to support for communication with children who are having difficulties with language acquisition as well as those who are developing typically. Inclusive classrooms provide rich opportunities for language experiences within natural contexts, especially during small group activities and play, in which the quality of mutual engagement and shared interest stimulate participation (McCathren & Watson, 2001; Weitzman & Greenberg, 2002).

Adults can play a variety of roles and can adjust their scaffolding to the individual needs of children. When children spontaneously interact with each other, an observant and reflective adult may step back and let the momentum of spontaneous interaction between children be the compelling force in conversation. When children need more language modeling and encouragement, an adult may become more actively engaged and may prompt children to increase their participation.

Strategies that are helpful can be used when they are needed rather than in a scripted fashion. A skillful, sensitive teacher will notice and be attuned to many factors in the situation, including the interests of the children and what they find engaging. Instead of speaking for children, adults can pick up on the intent to communicate expressed by children, and provide models for children to use in their own interaction. This can happen during informal play as well as during semi-structured activities. Teachers can encourage children to actively express their wants and needs in a variety of contexts. Sometimes children need support in sustaining back-and-forth interaction, in order to extend their

---

WHAT TEACHERS NEED TO KNOW

Basic understanding of normal receptive and expressive language development, with all its variations, as well as benchmarks

Understanding of second language acquisitions/English language learners

Understanding of different kinds of difficulties with language acquisition and characteristics associated with challenges

How to read nonverbal cues

How to respond to nonverbal cues

How to check in for understanding

How to adjust interaction as needed, depending on a child's interaction and responses

How to reflect on interactions and make decisions regarding reciprocal interaction

How to reflect on interactions and make decisions regarding structure of activities

How to use reflection to adjust the type and degree of scaffolding to match the individual developmental needs of children

conversations. There are many ways to support this reciprocity, including the effective use of questioning, responses to children's statements, and expansion of what children have initiated. It can include the introduction of descriptive words and more complex concepts, so children are elaborating on what they have expressed. Ideally, this type of intervention during conversations and spontaneous interaction is done in ways that do not make children feel self-conscious. Instead, a shared focus regarding the genuine interests and motivations of the child can be intentionally created. See box "What Teachers Need To Know". It provides some perspective on the competencies needed for early childhood teachers as they support healthy language and communication.

IMPORTANCE OF TEAMWORK

Teachers, Parents, Paraprofessionals, and Speech and Language Therapists

Teamwork is central to improving communication. Environments that offer many opportunities for people to make positive connections with each other are vital for developmentally and individually appropriate practices. Children may experience a range of challenges affecting communication. In turn, there is a need for a broad range of strategies to address challenges. Table 7.4 provides an overview of strategies used by teams in addressing specific challenges.

Culturally and Linguistically Diverse Exceptional Learners

Children who represent diverse cultural groups and/or speak a primary language other than English must be considered in the discussion or general patterns and trends. There are, unfortunately, some statistically documented themes and trends that warrant special concern. One is the overrepresentation of children from culturally diverse groups. Another is the false assumption that all children with language difficulties have language delays. Language delays are not the same as second language acquisition. It is crucial that all team members are able to focus on the competencies of children and to provide support for children who are acquiring fluency in English. In addition to the linguistic differences, it is crucial that professionals recognize differences in nonverbal communication, including eye-contact, gestures, and facial expressions. Tone of voice is also significant. Willingness to address these issues as an ongoing process will greatly enhance the ability to effectively support healthy communication within diverse classrooms. Teachers must address the "achievement gap" in order to create successful inclusive classrooms (Barbarin, 2002; Cartledge, Gardner, & Ford, 2009; Gonzalez-Mena, 2008; Horton-Ikard, 2006; Tabors, 2008).

Augmentative and Alternative Communication

There are many strategies and devices used to augment the language and communication of children who may need support. Such methods and devices may be used when children have hearing loss, processing differences, or intellectual disabilities. Some examples of augmentative and alternative communication as well as assistive technology are identified in Figure 7.2.

TABLE 7.4 Strategies and Methods for Intervention for Developmental Challenges in Language/Communication

Developmental Challenge	Method of Intervention
Difficulty communicating through crying; eye-contact; facial expressions	Adjusting cues to better match those of child Providing feedback regarding wants and need. Soothing.
Lack of or difficulty with gestures and vocalization or sound production and babbling	Initiation of sound play, reciprocal games Use of gestures and vocalization with child
Lack of or difficulty with jargoning, playing with intonation, and reciprocal interaction with expressions, vocalization, etc.	Modeling of jargon Playful interaction with jargon Use of music, stories, etc., with vocal intonation
Lack of or difficulty with increased control over sound production, imitation of sounds, production of a wide range of sounds	Many opportunities to focus on sound production
Difficulty with focus on more frequently used sounds in specific language (phonemes)	Use of stories and songs with alliteration (repeated sounds), repetition in mutually meaningful contexts
Few or no word approximations or increased association of sounds with shared meaning (morphemes)	Encouragement of sound and word production embedded in natural interactions
Lack of or difficulty with use of gestures and sounds to intentionally express wants and needs	Purposeful elicitation of reciprocal gestures and sounds to reinforce expression of wants and needs
Difficulty with comprehension-receptive language usually more advanced than expressive	Clarification of language Use of simple phrases, labeling, concrete objects
Less evidence of word approximations shifting toward first words	Carefully planned activities to support the association of sounds with words
Difficulty with two words combined to form sentences in which key elements are included, but descriptors, pronouns, etc. are not (telegraphic speech)	Adult modeling of 2 to 3 word phrases
Difficulty with increasing complexity of expressive language structures (use of pronouns, adjectives, etc.)	Purposeful exposure to increasing complexity
Difficulty with articulation of a range of sounds	Systematic incorporation of opportunities to practice sounds in natural contexts
Difficulty retrieving and organizing words to form intelligible statements	Cues and prompts Predictable language routines
Difficulty engaging in reciprocal conversations	Planned opportunities for reciprocal conversation Use of questioning strategies
Difficulty decoding or reading nonverbal cues and sometimes subtle social signals	Unobtrusive interpretation of nonverbal cues and signals
Difficulty among second language learners distinguishing between contexts and use of language as appropriate	Modeling and support, as needed

Braille

Picture exchange system (PECS)

Total communication/sign language

Social Stories™

Talking computers

Smartboards

Go Talk™

Big Mac™

Switches

FIGURE 7.2   Augmentative and Alternative Communication and Assistive Technology

LINKING LANGUAGE AND LITERACY

Extension of Symbol System

The bridge between language and literacy is crucial to a child's development of fluency in reading. This occurs in many ways, including exposure to children's literature and print-rich environments. When children have early and frequent positive experiences with language and literacy, their incorporation of language structure and systems progresses in natural ways (Hyson, 2008). The natural incorporation of reading into everyday life provides a context for meaningful learning (Schickedanz, 2008). This is very different from fragmented, rote instruction of letters. Adult literacy is an important element in providing quality opportunities for children. When both children and adults appear to have difficulty with literacy, it is a worthwhile priority for programs to focus on family literacy initiatives.

Teachers can facilitate the bridge between the spoken and written word.

Shared Meaning: Building on Children's Interests

The discovery that literacy involves shared meaning is truly an "Aha!" experience for young children. When they can sit with an adult or another child, look at pictures and text, and realize that this is a shared experience, a powerful, natural reinforcing moment occurs. The intrinsic reward is tremendously satisfying. The ongoing process of building on children's interests ensures motivation for engagement.

Association Between Sounds and Written Symbols

A child's understanding of the connection between sounds and letter symbols is central to the acquisition of **phonemic or phonological awareness** (Phillips, Clancy-Mechett, & Lonigan, 2008). One practical ways in which this can occur involves putting labels on objects in the classroom and designing experiences that involve opportunities for children's discovery. Creating a print-rich or **literacy-rich environment** conveys on a daily basis the function of words as meaningful, written symbols. Many methods that are relevant for the support of language development are equally useful to bridge oral and written language. When written language is integrated right from the start, with exposure to books and the integration of text into language generated by children, there is a natural progression toward literacy. Phonological awareness is part of that progression.

USING REFLECTION WHILE FACILITATING COMMUNICATION DEVELOPMENT

Reflection is an integral element in the facilitation of interaction and communication development. In order to effectively adjust strategies for the unique needs of children, caregivers need to have an internal compass telling them what would be considered typical development for each given age. This book has shared a brief overview of developmental benchmarks as well as basic information regarding challenges to communication development. When practitioners know the types of strategies that might be useful then they have a resource base for intervention. Decisions about implementation of strategies, however, are made on a child-by-child basis. There are times when interaction is spontaneous. Sometimes the patterns of spontaneous interaction include communicative patterns that have been established in more structured contexts, but at other times the patterns are less structured.

Personal Inventory

Professionals may use personal inventory intentionally as they integrate reflection into their practice. Professionals should systematically consider factors and elements as they relate to children, so reflection does not lead to reactions and ramblings that may be less relevant to implementation of strategies.

EXAMPLE 2   Amanda

Introduction and Background Information

Amanda is 3. She began having seizures when she was an infant. Her developmental progress had initially been normal, but over time Amanda began to demonstrate delays, especially in the area of expressive language. Over many months, her seizure disorder was monitored and medical tests were conducted to try to determine the cause of the seizures. When she was 17 months old, a magnetic resonance imaging (MRI) indicated a shadow on part of the hippocampus in her brain. She was diagnosed as having a brain tumor. Amanda's parents explored many options for treatment, in addition to the early intervention services she was receiving. They sought out more than one opinion from neurosurgeons, and ultimately decided to have Amanda's surgery done in New York City by a doctor widely respected and recognized for his work with this sort of tumor. The doctor recommended waiting until Amanda was 2 before doing the surgery, to decrease the inherent risk associated with brain surgery.

Identification of Significant Elements

From when Amanda first started having seizures to when she had surgery spanned about 15 months, or more than half her 24 months on earth. During that time, she demonstrated virtually no use of words that would be considered expressive language. She rarely used sounds, though she sometimes produced a squealing exclamation.

Her parents, extended family, and family friends continued to use language with her, while also providing developmentally appropriate activities such as playing in puddles and using paint. While she was engaged in activities, they talked with her narrating and asking questions, all the while providing a language-rich environment. Essentially, they interacted with her as though Amanda were engaging in conversation, without responses from her. This ongoing exposure to conversation was done in the hope that she had receptive language. All of the exposure to language in meaningful contexts provided the opportunity for Amanda to acquire language structures and meaning, even though she was not able to respond at the time.

Significant Element: Lack of Child's Response

Sustaining engagement even for a few minutes can be difficult, evidenced by when one tries to have a conversation but appears to be talking to oneself; the other party does not hear, listen, or respond. To continue to share verbal perspectives without much response for 15 months would be very frustrating.

Using reflection and personal inventory to identify the ways in which this challenge is tremendously important to parents, extended family members, friends, and teachers. Identifying the issue makes it possible to structure contexts so that more than one person can be interacting and providing language exposure without attempting to use a strategy that may seem artificial or contrived.

Another strategy that addresses a lack of response on the part of the child is to observe carefully for any change in expression or disposition, to learn to read the subtle cues that might otherwise be missed. Augmentative communication can be especially helpful when children have very limited expressive language. In Amanda's case, her early intervention team introduced sign language/total communication before she turned 2. Her parents and teachers all consistently used some basic signs with her, and Amanda's response to this form of communication was very positive.

The use of personal inventory and reflection by Amanda's parents and teachers helped them identify together how difficult it was to sustain expressive language without a clear response from Amanda. By identifying this element, they were able to develop creative strategies that allowed them to continue to expose her to rich language opportunities during the 15 months when she was not responsive.

Follow-up

After her surgery, Amanda made excellent progress. Before her hair had grown back, Amanda was using single words. Within a few months, she was putting words together to form sentences. There can be no doubt that the rapid rate of acquisition of expressive language was a direct result not just of the surgery, but of all the language experiences she had participated in during the time she was not able to speak.

ACTIVITIES THAT SUPPORT LANGUAGE AND LITERACY

Overview of Activities with Embedded Strategies

From a developmental perspective, activities should be engaging and meaningful to children. They should involve hands-on sensory experiences. All activities have the potential of providing language-rich experiences. Some are designed with this purpose explicitly in mind. This book will guide you through the active process of creating a plan, considering factors for individual adaptations and strategies, and reflecting on what could have been done differently. Reflection in this context complements formative assessment. In Figure 7.3, a sample activity is presented.

Figure 7.4 is an example of an activity that extends the themes of previous activity.

Team Reflection

LILY   The team has agreed not to put pressure on Lily to speak in school. Her teacher has made a few home visits, and that seems to be helping. Lily's school is in close communication with her home. While Lily did not speak during the home visits, she did appear actively engaged. A decision was made, based on this engagement, to rephrase some questions so nonverbal responses would be built into the activity. For instance, instead of asking if anyone has seen a caterpillar, the speaker could phrase the question to ask for those who have seen a caterpillar to raise their hands.

The team agreed to focus initially on small group activities following the story as a natural opportunity to engage in language. An adult would engage with another child in verbal interaction, while also participating in the topic-related construction of representational art. Communication between home and school has included bringing art and other forms of representation home. In this case, the family had a copy of *The Very Hungry Caterpillar* but if they had not, the school would have sent one home.

The teacher and speech and language therapist discussed tone of voice and language structure. The possibility of using a "Big Mac" at home for Lily to record her answers to questions was considered as an extension of the activity. The decision was made not to create a plan that would demand or require Lily to speak in order to earn a reinforcement. Instead, any intent to communicate was reinforced naturally with a meaningful response.

Much of the reflection regarding intervention for Lily focused on providing an accepting social environment in which she felt she belonged and in which she would be able to learn that she had some control. This positive, supportive environment can be attuned to her unique needs, and simultaneously provide encouragement to communicate, without being overly directive or confrontational. An intentional focus on Lily's interests and motivation provide extra incentive.

Objectives:

Children will listen to the story and answer questions about the caterpillar and what it is eating.

Use vocabulary identifying fruits.

Identify fruits when named.

Describe transformation from caterpillar to butterfly

Standards: NAEYC: 1 and 4   CEC/DEC: 4 & 6

Materials:

Big book—*The Very Hungry Caterpillar* by Eric Carle

Smaller board books available.

Felt board with pieces (caterpillar, fruits)

Initiation:

The teacher waits for children to attend.

Sets tone for positive engagement.

Provides mats for children to sit on.

Repositions children if it appears necessary.

Teacher holds up big book of *The Very Hungry Caterpillar* and asks some questions, engaging students.

Asks sample questions: "Have you ever seen a caterpillar?"

"We're going to find out what this caterpillar likes to eat. What do you think it likes to eat?"

Teacher distributes felt-board pieces so each child has a piece.

Procedure:

Teacher reads story, using engaging intonation and pausing frequently for questions.

Sample Questions:

What do you think the caterpillar is going to eat next?

What do you think happened to the caterpillar?

Closure:

Teacher asks:

"Does anyone remember what the caterpillar ate?"

"Do you remember what happened to the caterpillar?"

(Extension: Children may put felt pieces on board as they respond to questions.)

Transition:

Children are asked to flap their arms like butterflies, and are picked to transition to next activity.

Assessment:

Teacher observation and anecdotal records.

Responses to questions.

FIGURE 7.3   *The Very Hungry Caterpillar* by Eric Carle

Objectives:

Children will decide whether to construct a butterfly or caterpillar.

Children will use fine motor skills to manipulate art materials.

Children will use language (or another communication system) to describe what they are doing.

Standards: NAEYC: 1 and 4

CEC/DEC: 4 & 6

Materials:

For caterpillars—egg cartons cut lengthwise and various decorations to glue on.

For butterflies—paper towels or coffee filters cut into the shape of butterflies, food coloring, squeeze-droppers for different colors.

Procedure:

Teacher introduces the materials and solicits conversation about what caterpillars and butterflies look like.

Vocabulary regarding shape and color will be used. Pictures will be available for prompts, as needed.

This activity is quite open-ended. The primary role of the teacher is to facilitate conversation and provide assistance if needed.

Closure:

As each child finishes, the teacher facilitates conversation about what the butterfly or caterpillar looks like, with child using descriptive words.

FIGURE 7.4 Small Group Activity: Art —Construction of Butterflies or Caterpillars

Lily's Current Level of Performance *Areas of Strength:* At 4 years of age, Lily enjoys art and movement activities very much. She is an emerging reader, with a great interest in the content of what is in books. Her receptive language is excellent. She demonstrates her comprehension through following directions and participating in activities. At home Lily talks, and her use of expressive language structures, syntax, and vocabulary are well within a range expected for children her age.

GOALS AND OBJECTIVES

Goal: *Lily will increase her communication in the context of school.*

Objectives:

1. *Lily will express her wants and needs in school, given cues and prompts as needed, on a daily basis.*
2. *Lily will participate in large and small group activities in school, and engage in interaction with at least one other child, using a mutually agreed upon cuing system on a daily basis, with facilitation as needed.*
3. *Lily will use symbols such as pictures and words to enhance communication within the classroom on a daily basis with facilitation as needed.*

Areas of Concern: The primary area of concern for Lily is her selective mutism outside her home. Initially, this was not officially diagnosed, but after the pattern persisted over time, an official diagnosis was made. Lily uses well-constructed language consistently at home, but not in other places, including school.

Lily's IEP   Since Lily's development in most domains was within a normal range, the goals and objectives in all the domains primarily focused on expressive communication. Below is the goal specifically addressing expressive language.

AMANDA   Team members agreed that Amanda responded to a somewhat more directive approach than Lily. Amanda's parents, who were very specific in their questions, accentuated this. For example, using a two-choice question rather than a totally open-ended question greatly increased the likelihood that Amanda would be able to successfully retrieve an answer. The team agreed that offering some choice was preferable to being totally directive and convergent in questioning style.

It is evident that in most contexts Amanda has difficulty sustaining attention. It is not clear whether this is a function of her neurological risk, secondary to having had a tumor, or if it is another issue. Whatever the contributing factors, it is evident that her ability to communicate, solve problems, and attain her potential are all contingent on her ability to sustain attention.

The team recognized and reflected on this pattern and acknowledged the importance of having strategies that assisted Amanda to first attend, then respond. Together, the team decided not to demand that Amanda look at them as a first step, though sometimes this strategy is used. Instead, they decided to create a shared attention. In the case of *The Very Hungry Caterpillar*, for instance, it was decided that the teacher would make sure Amanda was looking at the book. Positioning seemed to be a very important element, and it was decided through reflection that the teacher would check in with Amanda, asking her if she could see the book well enough. This would serve the dual purpose of making a positive connection with her while also making sure she was ready for the activity. It served the very constructive purpose of preventing more distressed or disruptive behavior that sometimes resulted from Amanda's lack of engagement.

During the small group follow-up activity, the team agreed that this would be an excellent opportunity for interaction using expressive language. The teacher used that time to intentionally facilitate active conversation between Amanda and another child, while also reinforcing vocabulary from the book and phonological awareness. Text was generated as part of the art activity, and this was good for supporting Amanda's sound production and phonological awareness.

Amanda's Current Level of Performance   *Areas of Strength:* Amanda has excellent comprehension and has been making very good progress in acquiring expressive language since the surgery to remove the brain tumor on her hippocampus. The richness of her language experience appears to have been very helpful in supporting her comprehension. She is motivated and enjoys participating in sensory activities.

Areas of Concern: Amanda continues to have expressive language delays secondary to a tumor on her hippocampus for the first 2 years of her life. She continues to need support to focus on a shared topic and to sustain engagement. Directions need to be very clear and simple, with follow-up monitoring of her engagement.

Encouragement helps her when she gets frustrated. Amanda currently needs prompting to use expressive language with her peers. She is provided with opportunities to do this spontaneously.

Amanda's IEP

GOALS AND OBJECTIVES

Goal: *Amanda will increase expressive language.*

Objectives:

1. *Amanda will use 3 word sentences when asked questions, at least 3 times a day, 5 days in a row.*
2. *Amanda will spontaneously use expressive language with her peers at least 1 time per day, 3 days out of 5.*

Discussion

Through considering the characteristic patterns of strengths and needs for individual children and how they may be matched with strategies for adapting activities, reflection can be used to adjust conditions to more effectively ensure that each child is able to fully participate and accomplish their realistic objectives. Examples have been shared that illustrate the different approaches or continuum of option that may be used, determined by the child's needs. When children respond well to less directive approaches, those are the strategies that are used. In contrast, when they appear to need more focused intervention, such strategies are integrated into the activities. Thus, the tiered approach to intervention is addressed in all activities.

Summary

This chapter has identified the basic features of language acquisition and the transition to early literacy. This chapter has considered challenges that may occur for children in the process of acquiring language, and how approaches may be adjusted to more effectively match children's developmental needs.

Specific strategies have been shared, along with the consideration of factors that can increase the quality of the match between the strategies and the children's needs. Factors related to linguistic and cultural diversity have been addressed.

Key Terms

Expressive and receptive communication

Intent to communicate

Literacy- rich environment

Phoneme

Phonemic awareness

Phonological awareness

Children's Books Related to Disabilities

Attention-Deficit Disorder

Quinn, P. (1991). *Putting on the brakes: A child's guide to understanding and gaining control over attention deficit hyperactivity disorder (ADHD)*. New York: Magination Press. (Ages 4–7)

Cerebral Palsy

Gould, M. (1991). *Golden daffodils*. Newport Beach, CA: Allied Crafts. (Grades 4 and up)

Holcomb, N. (1989). *Patrick and Emma Lou*. Hollidaysburg, PA: Jason & Nordic Publishers. (Ages 3–8)

Deafness

Hodges, C. (in press). *When I grow up*. Hollidaysburg, PA: Jason & Nordic Publishers. (Ages 4–9)

St. George, J. (1992). *Dear Dr. Bell—Your friend, Helen Keller*. New York: Putnam.

Down Syndrome

Becker, S. (1991). *Buddy's shadow*. Hollidaysburg PA: Jason & Nordic Publishers. (Ages 3–8)

Holcomb, N. (1992). *How about a hug?* Hollidaysburg, PA: Jason & Nordic Publishers. (Ages 3–8).

Kneeland, L. (1989). *Cookie*. Hollidaysburg, PA: Jason & Nordic Publishers. (Ages 3–8)

Rabe, B. (1988). *Where's chimpy*. Morton Grove, IL, Albert Whitman & Company.

Learning Disabilities

Gehret, J. (1992). *Learning and the don't-give-up kid* (2nd ed.). Fairport, NY: Verbal Images Press. (Ages 6–10)

Other Disabilities

Holcomb, N. (1990). *Sarah's surprise*. Exton, PA: Jason and Nordic Publishers. (About a 5-year-old girl who cannot talk but who uses a picture board and then an augmentative communication device to communicate)

Peckinpah, S. L. (1991). *Rosey ... the imperfect angel*. Woodland Hills, CA: Scholars Press. (About an angel with a cleft palate)

Pirner, C. W. (1991). *Even little kids get diabetes*. Morton Grove, IL: Albert Whitman. Scott, S. (1992). *Not better ... not worse ... just different*. Amherst, MA: Human Resource Development Press. (A book to teach children ages 5 to 10 to be kind to one another)

Thompson, M. (1992). *My brother Matthew*. Rockville, MD: Woodbine House. (A sibling's story about living with a brother with disabilities)

Websites

American Speech and Hearing Association
http://www.asha.org

Augmentative and Alternative Communication Intervention
http://www.aacintervention.com/

National Dissemination Center for Children and Youth with Disabilities
http://www.nichcy.org

References

Barbarin, O. (2002). The black-white achievement gap in early reading skills: Familial and socio-cultural context. In B. Bowman (Ed.), *Love to read* (pp. 1–16). Washington, DC: National Black Child Development Institute, Inc.

Beukelman, D., & Mirenda, P. (2005). *Augmentative and alternative communication* (3rd ed.). Baltimore: Paul H. Brookes.

Bowman, B. (Ed.). (2002). *Love to read*. Washington, DC: National Black Child Development, Inc.

Brazelton, T. B. & Cramer, B. (1990). *The earliest relationship*. Reading, MA: Addison-Wesley.

Cartledge, G., Gardner, R., & Ford, D. (2009). *Diverse learners with exceptionalities*. Upper Saddle River, NJ: Merrill/Pearson Education.

Clark, M. (2006). *A practical guide to interaction with children who have a hearing loss.* San Diego, CA: Plural Press.

DiCarlo, C., Banajee, M., & Buras Stricklin, S. (2000). Embedding augmentative communication within early childhood classrooms. *Young Exceptional Children. 3*(2), 18–27.

Dunn, L., & Dunn, L., (2000). *Peabody picture vocabulary test–Revised.* Palo Alto, CA: American Guidance Service.

Epstein, A. (2007). *The intentional teacher.* Washington, DC: National Association for the Education of Young Children.

Genishi, C., & Haas Dyson, A. (2009). *Children, language, and literacy: Diverse learners in diverse times.* New York: Teacher's College Press.

Gonzalez-Mena, J. (2008). *Diversity in early care and education.* New York: McGraw-Hill/National Association for the Education of Young Children.

Horton-Ikard, R. (2006). The influence of culture, class, and linguistic diversity on early language development. *Zero to Three, 27*(1), 6–12.

Hyson, M. (2008). *Enthusiastic and engaged learners.* New York: Teachers College Press.

Marvin, C. A., & Ogden, N. (2002). A home literacy inventory: Assessing young children's context for emergent literacy. *Young Exceptional Children, 5*(2), 2–10.

McCathren, R., & Howard Allor, J. (2002). Using storybooks with preschool children: Enhancing language and emergent literacy. *Young Exceptional Children, 5*(4), 3–10.

McCathren, R., & Watson, A. (2001). Facilitating the development of intentional communication. In M. Ostrosky & S. Sandall (Eds.), *Teaching strategies: What to do to support young children's development* (pp. 25–36). Denver CO: Sopris West/Division of Early Childhood.

Nelson, L., & Johnston, S. (2002). Children with cochlear implants in the inclusive early childhood classroom. *Young Exceptional Children, 7*(1), 2–10.

Ordonez-Jasis, R., & Ortiz, R. (2007). Reading their worlds: Working with diverse families to enhance children's early literacy development. In D. Koralek (Ed.), *Spotlight on young children and families* (pp. 44–49). Washington, DC: National Association for the Education of Young Children.

Peterson, D. S., Taylor, B. M., Burnham, B., & Schock, R. (2009). Reflective coaching: A missing piece. *The Reading Teacher, 62,* 500–509.

Phillips, B., Clancy-Menchetti, J., & Lonigan, C. (2008). Successful phonological awareness instruction with preschool children. *Topics in Early Childhood Special Education, 28*(1), 3–17.

Schickedanz, J. (1999). *Much more than just ABC's.* Washington, DC: National Association for the Education of Young Children.

Schickedanz, J. A. (2008). *Increasing the power of instruction.* Washington, DC: National Association for the Education of Young Children.

Schwartz, S., & Heller Miller, J. (1996). *The new language of toys.* Bethesda, MD: Woodbine House.

Snow, C. E. (1983). Literacy and language: Relationships during the preschool years. *Harvard Educational Review, 53*(2), 165–189.

Tabors, P. (2008). *One child, two languages* (2nd ed.). Baltimore: Paul H. Brookes.

Thoman, E., & Browder, S. (1987). *Born dancing.* New York: Harper & Row.

Vygotsky, L. (1978). *Mind in society.* (Trans. M. Cole). Cambridge, MA: Harvard University Press.

Wietzman, E., & Greenberg, J. (2002). *Learning language and loving it* (2nd ed.). Toronto, Ontario, Canada: Hanen Press.

Ysseldyke, J., & Algozzine, B. (2006). *Teaching students with communication disorders: A practical guide for every teacher.* Thousand Oaks, CA: Corwin Press.

Chapter 8

The Arts, Music, and Movement

OBJECTIVES

After reading this chapter, students will:

- Have a concept of the scope and content of **the arts** as a vital component of curriculum for young children, including those with disabilities;

- Identify factors that may contribute to difficulty of children with challenges in participation in the arts;

- Demonstrate an understanding of the value of the arts for learning and appropriate strategies in the area of the arts;

- Have basic information about a range of possible strategies;

- Recognize ways in which an active reflective process may be used to enhance the effectiveness of inclusion during arts activities.

INTRODUCTION TO THE ARTS: SCOPE AND CONTENT

Children learn through play. Children's arts skills and knowledge develop through play as well. The arts serve as a vehicle for important learning for children with and without disabilities. Through the arts, children actively participate in their own learning. The arts nurture the imagination and creative spirit of all children. Sensory awareness (sight, sound, touch, smell, taste) is the foundation for all imaginative activity and creative expression. Historically, children with developmental challenges were often "mainstreamed" into special art activities. While this certainly served some function, it was not always an opportunity for deep and meaningful learning.

Art is important for young children with and without disabilities because of the process of creating rather than the end result. Through children's involvement in the arts, they develop independence, self-esteem, and self-expression. The arts connect all areas of learning and are fundamental to all children's development and education. The arts enable all children to discover more about who they are and gain insight into their own culture and the cultures around them. The arts for young children include visual art, music, creative movement, and dramatic play.

The arts are a natural part of children's early childhood experience. Children love using their bodies and materials to design, create, and explore. These experiences, however, are more than just fun. They are enriched activities that bring together learning in all of the content areas. The arts enhance vocabulary and concept development. They provide children with opportunities to move, listen, scrutinize, discover, create, and engage in activities that are not as exacting as many other areas of curriculum. Teachers who use the arts and the multiple intelligence theory attain desirable outcomes (Gardner, 2006). Using these strategies, more children will be reached, and they will be able to display their understanding—and their problem areas—in ways that are comfortable for them and accessible to others (Pearson, 1998).

Theoretical Perspectives

In 1990, Barbara Bowman delivered an address to the International Conference on Early Childhood Creative Arts. She spoke about the six reasons she believes the arts are especially suited as curriculum for young children:

1. The arts encourage sensory perception. Bowman stated that cognitive development in young children depends on using their senses to learn about the world, and the arts are a wonderful way of stimulating sensual awareness and appreciation. Visual, auditory, kinesthetic, and tactile qualities are inherent in the arts, and children can learn through the arts to use their perceptions to form the basis for more learning.

2. The arts provide opportunities for children to learn to represent and symbolize experience. Through art, reality can be shaped to serve the ego, thus providing the individual with the opportunity for self-healing and self-development. The individual is afforded the opportunity to explore and master emotional, social, cognitive, and physical experience. Bowman compared the arts to play because it offers the chance to release feelings, to remember the past in order to master it, and to try out alternative solutions to problems. It integrates the affective and cognitive components of the human mind.

3. The arts provide opportunities for children to make things happen, to do things that are valued by other people, to create, and to build. All children need to feel that they can affect people and things. This is very empowering. Bowman states that the arts are especially valuable for children who find it difficult to compete with other children or to learn as much or in the same way as other children. These children may fail in other activities. Children who learn differently than most may have fewer opportunities with which to be judged competent. Success in the arts can spill over into other aspects of the life of a child.

4. Participation in the arts can foster a sense of community. Being part of a group involved in an arts activity may include joining in singing, or just being where the singing is happening. Drawing part of a group picture or moving to the beat of a drum as part of a whole group provides a sense of accomplishment for the individual child. Though the child may not be particularly skilled in the specific art area, the child will feel empowered by the experience and appreciate the social experience.

5. Academic skills learned in the context of the arts may form the motivation necessary for further school learning. Children who are not traditional learners often find it challenging to fit into the structure of the expected ways of learning. The arts can be that pathway to more appropriate learning opportunities for many children.

6. The arts expand our world. Viewing art from different cultures and places around the world, listening to and making music from other cultures, and moving to different rhythms and sounds help children to understand more about the world (Bowman, 1990).

Benchmarks

There are various sets of benchmarks that pertain to the arts. Below are the benchmarks that are more global and refer to arts education in general. The following sections contain benchmarks for different areas of the arts.

NATIONAL STANDARDS FOR ARTS EDUCATION The **National Standards** for Arts Education outline what every K–12 student should know and be able to do in the arts. The Consortium of National Arts Education Associations developed the standards through a grant administered by The National Association for Music Education (MENC,

1994). Keeping in mind that these standards do not specifically address preschool age children, the National Standards for Arts Education does provide the cultural context for the importance of the arts and the parameters for the integration of the arts into classrooms, which enables all children to share the same opportunities, regardless of their abilities. The narrative of the standards provides critical information pertaining to the arts. Important to understanding the context of the arts across cultures and time is the following statement:

DISCOVERING WHO WE ARE

The arts have been part of us from the very beginning. Since nomadic peoples first sang and danced for their ancestors, since hunters first painted their quarry on the walls of caves, since parents first acted out the stories of heroes for their children, the arts have described, defined, and deepened human experience. All peoples, everywhere, have an abiding need for meaning—to connect time and space, experience and event, body and spirit, intellect, and emotion. People create art to make these connections, to express the otherwise inexpressible. A society and a people without the arts are unimaginable, as breathing would be without air. Such a society and people could not long survive.

The arts are one of humanity's deepest rivers of continuity. They connect each new generation to those who have gone before, equipping the newcomers in their own pursuit of the abiding questions: Who am I? What must I do? Where am I going? At the same time, the arts are often an impetus for change, challenging old perspectives from fresh angles of vision, or offering original interpretations of familiar ideas. The arts disciplines provide their own ways of thinking, habits of mind as rich and different from each other as botany is different from philosophy. At another level, the arts are society's gift to itself, linking hope to memory, inspiring courage, enriching our celebrations, and making our tragedies bearable. The arts are also a unique source of enjoyment and delight, providing the "Aha!" of discovery when we see ourselves in a new way, grasp a deeper insight, or find our imaginations refreshed. The arts have been a preoccupation of every generation precisely because they bring us face to face with ourselves, and with what we sense lies beyond ourselves. (The National Standards for Arts Education. Section 1, 1994).

The Importance of the Arts to Life and Learning

If arts education is to serve its proper function, each student must develop an understanding of such questions as these: What are the arts? How do artists work, and what tools do they use? How do traditional, popular, and classical art forms influence one another? Why are the arts important to my society and me? As students seek the answers to these questions, they develop an understanding of each arts discipline and the knowledge and skills that enliven it. The content and the interrelatedness of the standards go a long way toward producing such understanding. The concept of meeting the standards, however, cannot—and should not— imply that every student will acquire a common set of artistic values. Students are ultimately responsible for their own values. The standards provide a positive and substantive framework for those who teach young people how valuable the arts are to them as persons and as participants in a shared culture. (The National Standards for Arts Education. Section 2, 1994).

The affirmations below describe the values that can inform what happens when the standards, children, and teachers come together. These expectations draw connections among the arts, the lives of students, and the world at large:

- The arts have both intrinsic and instrumental value; they have worth in and of themselves and can also be used to achieve a multitude of purposes (e.g., to present issues and ideas, to teach, persuade, entertain, design, plan, and beautify).
- The arts play a valued role in creating cultures and building civilizations. Although each arts discipline makes its unique contributions to culture, society, and the lives of individuals, their connections to each other enable the arts disciplines to produce more than one of them could produce alone.
- The arts are a way of knowing. Students grow in their ability to apprehend their world as they learn the arts. As students create dances, music, theatrical productions, and visual artworks, they learn how to express themselves and how to communicate with others.
- The arts have value and significance for daily life. They provide personal fulfillment, whether in vocational settings, avocational pursuits, or leisure.
- Lifelong participation in the arts is a valuable part of a fully lived life and should be cultivated.
- Appreciating the arts means being able to understand the interactions among the various professions and roles involved in creating, performing, studying, teaching, presenting, and supporting the arts, and in appreciating their interdependent nature.
- Awakening to folk arts and their influence on other arts deepens respect for one's own and for others' communities.
- Openness, respect for work, and contemplation when participating in the arts as an observer or audience member are personal attitudes that enhance enjoyment and ought to be developed.
- The arts are indispensable to freedom of inquiry and expression.
- Because the arts offer the continuing challenge of situations in which there is no standard or approved answer, those who study the arts become acquainted with many perspectives on the meaning of "value."
- The modes of thinking and methods of the arts disciplines can be used to illuminate situations in other disciplines that require creative solutions.
- Attributes such as self-discipline, a collaborative spirit, and perseverance, which are so necessary to the arts, can transfer to the rest of life.
- The arts provide forms of nonverbal communication that can strengthen the presentation of ideas and emotions.
- Each person has a responsibility for advancing civilization itself. The arts encourage taking this responsibility and provide skills and perspectives for doing so. (The National Standards for Arts Education. Section 2, 1994).

DEVELOPMENTAL ASPECTS IN ALL ARTS AREAS

Understanding Each Individual Area of the Arts

It is important to have an understanding of each area of the arts in order to help build arts opportunities for children with and without disabilities. Some teachers are not skilled, proficient, or comfortable engaging in the arts because of a lack of their own positive experiences. Teachers should cultivate the ability to see the depth and breadth of what can be done with young children in the visual arts, dance, music, and drama.

National Standards for Arts Education, 1994

Developed by the Consortium of National Arts Education Associations (under the guidance of the National Committee for Standards in the Arts), the National Standards for Arts Education is a document that outlines basic arts learning outcomes integral to the comprehensive K–12 education of every American student. The Consortium published the **National Standards** in 1994 through a grant administered by MENC, the National Association for Music Education. While the standards address the whole scope of K–12 education, the focus presented here will be on grades K–4 and where appropriate, the years prior to kindergarten.

The National Standards for the Arts were published in 1994 after much deliberation and consultation between all of the arts education organizations. These standards begin by outlining the importance of arts education for all children. The importance of the arts is stated as follows:

> Knowing and practicing the arts disciplines are fundamental to the healthy development of children's minds and spirits. That is why, in any civilization—ours included—the arts are inseparable from the very meaning of the term "education." We know from long experience that no one can claim to be truly educated who lacks basic knowledge and skills in the arts. There are many reasons for this assertion:
>
> The arts are worth studying simply because of what they are. Their impact cannot be denied. Throughout history, all the arts have served to connect our imaginations with the deepest questions of human existence: Who am I? What must I do? Where am I going? Studying responses to those questions through time and across cultures—as well as acquiring the tools and knowledge to create one's own responses—is essential not only to understanding life but to living it fully. The arts are used to achieve a multitude of human purposes: to present issues and ideas, to teach or persuade, to entertain, to decorate or please. Becoming literate in the arts helps students understand and do these things better. The arts are integral to every person's daily life. Our personal, social, economic and cultural environments are shaped by the arts at every turn—from the design of the child's breakfast placemat, to the songs on the commuter's car radio, to the family's nighttime TV drama, to the teenager's Saturday dance, to the enduring influences of the classics.
>
> The arts offer unique sources of enjoyment and refreshment for the imagination. They explore relationships between ideas and objects and serve as links between thought and action. Their continuing gift is to help us see and grasp life in new ways.
>
> There is ample evidence that the arts help students develop the attitudes, characteristics, and intellectual skills required to participate effectively in today's society and economy. The arts teach self-discipline, reinforce

self-esteem, and foster the thinking skills and creativity so valued in the workplace. They teach the importance of teamwork and cooperation. They demonstrate the direct connection between study, hard work, and high levels of achievement. (The National Standards for Arts Education, 1994).

THE BENEFITS OF ARTS EDUCATION

According to the National Standards group:

> Arts education benefits the *student* because it cultivates the whole child, gradually building many kinds of literacy while developing intuition, reasoning, imagination, and dexterity into unique forms of expression and communication. This process requires not merely an active mind but a trained one. An education in the arts benefits *society* because students of the arts gain powerful tools for understanding human experiences, both past and present. They learn to respect the often very different ways others have of thinking, working, and expressing themselves. They learn to make decisions in situations where there are no standard answers. By studying the arts, students stimulate their natural **creativity** and learn to develop it to meet the needs of a complex and competitive society. And, as study and competence in the arts reinforce one other, the joy of learning becomes real, tangible, and powerful. (The National Stands for Arts Education, 1994).

The Arts and Other Core Subjects

The standards address competence in the arts disciplines, but that competence provides a firm foundation for connecting arts-related concepts and facts across the art forms, and then to sciences and humanities. For example, the intellectual methods of the arts are precisely those used to transform scientific disciplines and discoveries into everyday technology.

Embedding Competencies Within Activities

There are many ways in which skills and competencies can be integrated into daily classroom activities. When child-focused activities are intentionally integrated into routines and schedules, children have multiple contexts in which to practice and develop important skills as well as sensibilities. Table 8.1 offers an overview of how strategies and skills can be integrated into varied activities to support positive child outcomes. The roles of the adults will vary depending on the needs of each child and the degree of difficulty of the activity.

Characteristics of Challenge Within the Arts

When students engage in art, they bring their capabilities, their prior knowledge of the arts such as familiarity with the art form, their own culture, and their willingness to become involved and sometimes take a risk. If an individual has a disability that is manifested physically, modifications to materials and equipment can be made to support the individual to be able to have a positive experience in that area of the arts.

TABLE 8.1   Positive Child Outcomes in the Arts and Movement

Outcome	Modification	Curricular Opportunity
Explore a variety of textures	Available support; hand-over-hand	Collage, finger paint, dough, etc.
Participate in fine motor activities	Nonslip surfaces	Table-top activities; construction materials (blocks, Legos, etc.)
Use a variety of media for symbolic representation	Available materials; variety of materials (special grippers for crayons, etc.)	Visual art activities; writing; drawing, etc.
Use a variety of media to explore colors and forms	Materials of different textures and colors	Table-top activities with paper, other materials
Participate in fine and gross motor activities	Scaffolding, as needed; physical support as needed	Movement activities

ADAPTATIONS

The arts provide benefits as well as present challenges to children whose physical disabilities prevent them from interacting with their environment in the same way as other children. Both low-tech and high-tech options can help all children participate in the arts. Low-tech options, such as foam grippers for markers, extensions for brushes, and slant boards for positioning paper, give children with physical disabilities greater independence when engaged in visual arts activity. Velcro can secure materials, switches can activate music, and various arts forms can be combined to enhance the experience for children and to motivate them to engage in activities that they have not experienced before. High-tech options may include computers with specific software programs, and adaptive peripherals bring arts experiences within the reach of any child (Hutinger, Betz, Bosworth, Potter, & Schneider, 1997).

ADAPTATIONS IN VISUAL ARTS

Size of Child

Physical equipment can create a barrier for a child who has a physical disability. When a child cannot reach an easel, modifications can be made, so that the child is able to be close to the easel. Sometimes, the barrier deters the child from experiencing art activities, and only requires a modification as simple as a platform for the child to stand on to reach the easel. The child may need the easel's surface and paint well lowered, so he or she can sit at the easel to paint. This makes the easel accessible for a child with physical disabilities. The child may need a higher or lower chair to be able to reach the table, or the child may need to stand in order to be able to participate in the art experience. When a child cannot hold on to the paintbrush, a lighter brush may make it easier for the child to paint. If the lighter brush does not make painting accessible, the child may be able to work with a brush with an adaptive device designed specifically for the size of the child's hand. This device may be something as simple as a small sponge ball with a slit in the center into which the brush handle fits. The sponge ball is then placed in the child's closed fist. The child may then be able to use paints with or without gentle adult support. The adult facilitating the activity may find it necessary to lend support

Participation in a variety of art activities is valuable.

by lifting the child's elbow. If the child is in a wheelchair or other adaptive chair, the professionals may provide a foam wedge to support the child's elbow so, he or she may to be able to reach the paper on the easel. This is a simple modification. The gratification experienced by the child with special needs who is able to paint at the easel just like the other children is well worth the effort necessary to make the modifications.

A child in an adaptive seat with a tray may need to have the art activity brought to the tray instead of attempting to move the child up to the table. If the child can be easily moved close to the table, the surface for painting, drawing, or creating a collage may need to be taped to an inclined surface such as a triangular hollow block or wooden wedge, so that the child can have access to it. If collage materials are cut into very small pieces, the child with physical disabilities may simply need materials that are larger or thicker in order to be able to pick them up by him or herself. The materials for the collage may also be selected to provide a variety of textures.

Visual Impairments

Children with mild to moderate visual impairments often require few modifications. For a child with minor impairments, allowing him or her to work on a surface that brings the art materials closer affords the child an opportunity to engage in the same activities as the other children. It may also be necessary to have the child work on a white or black background for contrast. It is important for the child to work in a well-lit room to maximize the child's vision. This child may initially need larger tools and surfaces to work with. Once the child is familiar with materials, tools, and surfaces, there are usually few modifications necessary.

Children with visual impairments often enjoy the whole body experience of art activities, which by nature are very sensory. A vision specialist, physical therapist, or occupational therapist can offer suggestions for other modifications when necessary. Each child presents unique challenges to professionals working with the child. Teamwork makes the work much easier and the outcome more positive for the child.

These accommodations are not detrimental to the program or the environment, and none of these modifications disturb other children. These accommodations demonstrate a willingness to provide a developmentally appropriate environment based on the knowledge and understanding of what makes an environment and a program accessible and appropriate for children.

Social-Emotional or Behavior Disorders

Children who display behaviors that are challenging to peers and/or adults sometimes stay away from art activities. Often, these children do not engage in new activities because they are unsure of what to do. They do not yet understand the nature of the open-endedness of art activities. Children with social-emotional or behavior disorders should be provided with opportunities for quite a while before they are encouraged to attempt to try something themselves. Professionals should allow them the time and space they need in order to feel comfortable. Sometimes, a child with behavior problems will need support in the area of impulse control. Although art activities are ideal for helping such a child to move toward more control, initially there may be many messes before the child begins to develop mastery over materials and tools. A child who exhibits a profile of social immaturity will certainly benefit from art activities. Art activities are motivating, rewarding, and promote socialization through the sharing of materials and the commentary on each other's artwork. Both teachers and peers may be involved in the social growth that can take place through engagement in art activities. Teachers observing children with behavior problems will be able to document growth through the children's products and the growth children make over time as they attain more self-esteem and gain more control over his or her environment.

Learning Challenges and Intellectual Disabilities

When a child is not able to learn at a rate similar to other children of the same chronological age because of a delay or a learning deficit caused by physical, visual, or other reasons, professionals might modify the activity to enable the child to participate. Teachers may state instructions or procedures in a very simple manner, demonstrate techniques necessary to participate in the activity, or assist the student to enable him or her to totally participate. Experimenting without pressure to produce a specific product allows children to develop their own style, to take risks, and to take their time (Barbour, 1990). Development takes time and a variety of experiences. It is wise to avoid making assumptions about what children are and are not able to do. Professionals should provide the same rich experiences to all children, which, when coupled with support and encouragement, will maximize the child's potential.

Language and Communication Deficits

There are many reasons why children have delayed language development or experience communication problems. Art is of great importance in promoting growth in the deficit areas. As a means of nonverbal expression, art may become the vehicle for initiating communication with peers and adults. Engaging in art activities allows a child the opportunity to hear the language of the other children as well as the language of the teacher offering materials, asking questions, and responding to questions posed by the children. By being part of the group in a safe, physical sense, a child with language and/or communication deficits will be encouraged to begin to speak.

ADAPTATIONS IN MUSIC AND MOVEMENT

In the area of music, **adaptations** for children might involve modified instruments and physical adaptations to enable a child to participate in much the same way as the other children will participate. The type of music will also need to be considered to match any sensory issues a child may have.

Teachers should design a program for music and movement that considers the range of children's special needs. As each of the other areas of curriculum must be planned to meet the needs of individual children as well as to be integrated into the lesson's theme, music and movement must be planned for in a similar way. Teachers must be prepared to make modifications to some materials or activities or possibly design alternative activities for children with special needs. General modifications will be listed by nature of what makes the experience initially inaccessible to a child.

Size of Child and Physical Disability of Child

PHYSICAL EQUIPMENT CREATES A BARRIER   Music activity is something in which all children are able to participate whether with their voices or with their bodies. A child with severe physical disabilities may not be verbal but may be vocal and able to use that vocal ability to respond to the music he or she hears. Children with physical disabilities and limited or no communication ability are able to demonstrate recognition of music heard previously through eye contact, a smile, or a nod. This demonstrates that while the physical child may be disabled, the music child is not disabled. This concept has been reported and discussed in music therapy literature by authors such as Nordoff and Robbins (1970, 1977, 1983). They contend that musical involvement by children with severe physical disabilities is one way to assess the intelligence of the child. Music activity that responds to the uniqueness of each child provides stimulation and satisfaction for the child and provides information about the child's untapped potential. Making music with typical rhythm instruments may not be available to a child with physical disabilities, but switch-operated instruments may be appropriate substitutes. Teachers and therapists need to work together to brainstorm possible adaptations that allow for the inclusion of the child in a variety of musical activities. Being in the midst of music can have therapeutic value for a child with physical disabilities. Music with the right rhythm and tone has the potential to energize or relax a child.

A petite, almost 3-year-old child with physical disabilities finds music very calming. Her mother learned the value of music for this child early in the child's life and is rarely without a portable cassette player for the child to use when she becomes anxious. New social situations produce a certain level of anxiety for this child, and she typically asks for her music. Now that the child is to be included in a preschool program, the teachers will need to figure out a way to provide this support for the child without it attracting too much attention or distracting the other children. After observing the child in the new environment for a few days, the teachers may meet to brainstorm how to handle any necessary transition of the music support.

Children with physical disabilities who use adaptive devices may pose circumstances that require creative planning for movement activities. When planning movement activities, teachers should keep in mind that children with physical disabilities are not always totally disabled. The child may be able to move a limb, fingers, or his or her head and neck. This allows the child to engage in certain activities with no modifications necessary. The child with a physical disability might need to engage in some movement activities from a wheelchair. Once space is organized so that all children have the room they need in order to do the activity, all may participate. If locomotion is part of the activity, the child using a wheelchair may need a peer or adult to move the wheelchair around. An example of this may be an activity in which the children to move around the room like birds. The child in a wheelchair with limb mobility can either move around the room with assistance (if the child cannot manage the chair independently) or be a stationary bird flapping its wings. Even if a teacher has considerable experience working with children with physical disabilities, it is always wise to consult with specialists who work with a particular child and with the family to describe the kinds of activities you are planning to make sure they are appropriate for the child. Because working with specialists is a critical component of planning for any child with special needs, the specialist will prove to be an asset to your planning process. If the planned activity involves the use of scarves and the child uses a wheelchair and cannot hold onto items, the scarf may be tied onto the child's arm. If the child uses a walker, using scarves in a movement activity requiring children to move around the room will not be feasible. It would be appropriate for that child to use the scarf while sitting down. This way, the child can reap the benefit of the upper torso movement even though the element of locomotion is eliminated from the activity. Teachers should plan adaptations to encourage the child with physical disabilities to participate in some way, on some level, in every activity. The child will then feel like a part of the activity, even though he or she may not be doing exactly the same thing the other children are doing. Teachers need to take time to reflect and look at the environment to explore the possibilities. The child's peer group can also be enlisted to come up with new ideas for the child or new ways of facilitating inclusion in movement activities.

Visual Impairments

Children with visual impairments can certainly participate in music activities. Regardless of how severe the visual deficit, the child can hear and feel the music and respond to it with voice or body. In a situation where instruments are being presented to or used by the children, a child with visual impairments may need to get as close to the instruments as possible. This child may initially need some guidance from an adult to learn how to use the instrument without damaging it. This will also help the child to engage in the activity in a safe manner. Children with visual impairments enjoy the stimulation of music activities. Very often, children with visual impairments are rhythmic and respond to music in a very relaxed manner. In movement activities, a child with visual impairments may need to hold the hands of an adult or another child in order to feel safe in an activity that requires locomotion in an open space. If the child feels comfortable in the space, it is possible that no modification is necessary. Some children with visual impairments do not cross boundaries. This means that they do not cross thresholds, walk through doorways, or step onto a slightly different level surface unless someone they trust assists them. Once they have mastered this task, they will be comfortable crossing thresholds by themselves. When planning a movement activity, if a child with visual impairment is in the classroom, the teacher should take care to minimize the barriers (different surfaces) that the children cross during the activity, until the child with visual impairment is acclimated to the environment.

Social-Emotional or Behavior Disorders

Music has a calming effect on many children. Children with social-emotional or behavior disorders of an acting-out nature may find that music calms them down. Once calmed down, they can then engage in the other activities provided. A child who is withdrawn may be very inactive. Music that serves to calm children down may be inappropriate to use with this child. This child may need music of a more energizing nature. In selecting music for background listening, it is important to take stock of the types of children in the group at the time. An overly active child certainly does not need buzzing music. This might further energize the child beyond the point of manageable behavior. The child who may be afraid of failure and stays away from activities that are personally intimidating may find that listening to or playing music is not at all demanding. If the child does not want to sing or move, just being part of the group can give the child a sense of accomplishment and belonging. In time, the child may engage in hand motions for songs or appear to mouth words but not offer to sing. Each child should be able to respond at his or her own level, within a framework that is personally rewarding. The child with social-emotional problems may find a release of emotion through music. Once the child begins to actively participate in music activity, these activities may become the core of the socialization process and help to bridge school to home.

This may be the same pattern for movement activities as well. The similarity makes perfect sense because the music and movement are closely related. Teachers may find, however, that it takes longer for the child with social-emotional challenges to find a comfort level with movement activities where children are paired. Teachers should look for joy and an increasing interest in music participation instead of perfection. A child who has acting-out behavior and few coping skills needs to participate in activities that do not look for exacting responses. A child with this presenting profile may be apprehensive at first and cautious about participation because music is not something in which the child has had a lot of experience. Over time and maybe with careful observation from a distance, the child may move closer to the activity and begin to reap the benefits of joining in. With movement activities, the same caution that keeps the child away will probably prevail. The goal for movement activities for the child with social-emotional challenges is for him or her to experience the joy of movement and the sense of accomplishment that comes from having control over one's body in space. Dance therapy uses dance movements as a means of nonverbal communication, emotional release of hostile and tender feelings, physical relaxation, and increased self–awareness (Toombs, 1968). Many over-controlled children who perform well in academic areas reveal their loss of spontaneity and developing inability to express emotion by their inhibited response to dance. Teachers can use dance as a means of assessing children. Espenak (1981) observed that certain moods or attitudes are expressed through characteristic postures used in dance: dejected attitude, evident by slumped shoulders, the head on the chest, and fumbling steps; retiring attitude, in which the child's shoulders are drawn and his or her head is lowered; heightened tension where the shoulders are lifted to the ears, the child's head is in the neck, elbows are tense, and the hands nervous; and aggressive attitude where the child has a strutting chest, a swagger, and an accent on his or her heels. While early childhood teachers may not feel comfortable making assessments based on these movement types, it provides examples of how a child's movements might be more telling than previously imagined.

Assessment based upon movement could help teachers look beyond the more traditional means of assessment and use the natural behaviors of children, which can help teachers better understand children's behaviors. A socially immature child may just need more time before venturing to try some music activities. Often, this pattern is how the socially immature child approaches all activity areas. Since some music activities can be implemented sitting on the floor rather than being out in the middle of open space, the child may feel more secure, which can afford the child the opportunity to participate more readily than he or she might in a movement exploration activity. Because the child may not feel ready to hold someone else's hand or be in close proximity to another child, the teacher must be careful to plan appropriate activities that would facilitate the inclusion of this child.

Learning Challenges and Intellectual Disabilities

Music needs little introduction in order for children to participate. Very few modifications are necessary to include the child with learning impairments. The child may need encouragement and an adult nearby to facilitate participation, but because there is little that needs to be learned about the process, music is a natural activity. If the child has trouble remembering words of songs, humming along is appropriate. If the child expresses an interest in working on remembering songs, special practice sessions might be arranged so that the child has time to build skill prior to joining in the activity the next time. The teacher initially may want to sit near the child during music in order to provide the best model for the child. The language of an adult has greater clarity than that of the peer group regardless of how skilled with language the peer group language is. The teacher should not sit near the child for the whole year, however, because the child may develop the feeling that teacher proximity is necessary for successful participation. Children need to become independent of teachers during the course of the year. Teachers need to facilitate the process of building independence.

In movement activities, children with learning challenges may need a teacher or a peer to assist with directionality and to model appropriate movement for the child with learning challenges to imitate. Rather than have the child collide with the peer group because he or she is going in one direction and the group is going in another, a little facilitation goes a long way. The child may also need reassurance to be able to work in the middle of open space. Working with a partner may work well for this type of child. The child will probably not be intimidated by another child and will learn the joy of participation and gain a sense of mastery over his or her body. Table 8.2 provides an overview of possible strategies matched with challenges.

TABLE 8.2 Possible Adaptation Strategies for Movement, Music, and Arts Activities

Characteristics	Strategies	Possible Outcomes
Physical challenges	Positioning	Participation; coordination
	Adaptive equipment: walkers, wheelchairs, special seats	Accessibility Mobility Independence
Sensory Processing Difficulties	Different textured sensory materials	Full engagement in activity
Fine motor challenges	Adaptive equipment: Scissors, paintbrushes, crayons, markers, etc.	Coordination Increased independence
Gross motor challenges	Physical space accessible	Enhanced mobility
Motor challenges Sensory impairments	Musical instruments of varying sizes and weights	Involvement Participation
Physical and behavioral challenges	Work-space trays with rims	Clear, safe boundaries
Physical and/or communication challenges	Assistive technology as appropriate	Enhanced communication
Autism	Social stories^{TM}	Theory of mind Awareness of activity
Physical challenges	Easels Slantboards	Increased coordination

INNOVATIVE PRACTICES FOR YOUNG CHILDREN WITH AND WITHOUT DISABILITIES

The ArtExpress Model

The ArtExpress model (1997) is an example of an innovative program based on the NAEYC developmentally appropriate guidelines. While developing the model, the ArtsExpress project staff worked with and collected data from 16 early childhood classrooms, over 370 children with mild, moderate, and multiple disabilities and their families. Activities and materials were field-tested, evaluated, revised, and adapted. The outcome was a set of guidelines and suggested experiences, not a set curriculum. This flexibility is a critical component of any arts experience for young children with and without disabilities. Children are primed for different experiences at different times. This is due to their own abilities, their prior experiences, and the energy they have to expend towards engaging in something that is new for them.

The primary goal of the 3-year Expressive Arts Outreach (EAO) project in the College of Education and Human Services at Western Illinois University was to integrate and replicate the Expressive Arts (EA) model, which is based on developmentally appropriate experiences in the expressive arts and has an emphasis on visual arts, into early childhood programs for children ages 3 to 8 with a wide range of disabilities. The second goal was to enhance the knowledge and skills of families, professional staff, and early childhood decision makers, so they can effectively use developmentally appropriate art activities for young children and adaptations for children with severe disabilities. The third goal was to serve as a national resource and information exchange for art-related materials and products for young children with disabilities. Objectives included awareness activities; replication; product development, revision, and dissemination; training and consultation; assistance to Empowerment Zones, Enterprise Communities, and states; and participation in local, regional, and national cooperative activities.

Twenty-one sites replicated the EA model between October 1, 1997, and September 30, 2000. The sites contained a total of 60 classrooms served by 38 teachers and 60 support staff. Four sites housed self-contained special education classrooms serving children with multiple and severe disabilities. Five sites had self-contained special education classrooms serving children with mild to moderate disabilities. Five sites had inclusion classrooms serving children at risk and children with disabilities. Five sites had classrooms serving children at-risk (two pre-K and three Head Start). Two sites served infants and toddlers, one was a center-based program, and the other was a home-based program. Over the 3 years, the project affected 1,176 children. Data were collected on 277 children who had disabilities or were at risk. Project findings point to positive benefits for teachers, children, and families. Replication site staff showed gains in implementing art activities and making adaptations for children with disabilities. They increased their skill in planning appropriate child-directed activities in drawing, painting, and creating three-dimensional projects for children demonstrating different developmental levels. All children, whether their disability was mild, moderate, or severe, participated in developmentally appropriate expressive arts activities and projects without the need for adult-directed activities, making images that grew increasingly more complex.

Children's communication skills, social abilities, problem-solving skills, expressive abilities, and motor abilities improved as a result of their participation in expressive arts. Family surveys indicated satisfaction with the project, benefits to their children, and increased participation in expressive art activities with their children at home. Products resulting from the project include print materials, such as the revised *ArtExpress* curriculum, *Summer Family and Child Art Activity Booklet*, the *ArtExpress Adaptive Resource Packet*, and a monthly newsletter. The project maintained web sites at www.mprojects.wiu.edu and www.wiu.edu/thecenter/art. Video products include *The Expressive Arts Project: A Case Study Approach* and *Celebrate Children's Learning Through the Expressive Arts.* Over the 3-year period, project staff conducted 34 workshops and conference presentations attended by over 2,060 early childhood educators, therapists, paraprofessionals, and family members. (Hutinger, Potter, Schneider, Guzman & Johanson, 2002).

The Early Childhood-Healthy Foundations Initiative

The Early Childhood-Healthy Foundations initiative began in 1992 through the Very Special Arts program in Wisconsin. It uses the arts as a tool to better prepare children with disabilities and those at risk to succeed when they enter typical school environments and to train early childhood educators to use the arts to foster literacy and to support physical, social, and emotional growth and encourage the role of parents in providing optimal growth and development for their children. This work is done through the exploration of four art mediums (movement, music, drama, or visual arts). This arts-in-education program provides a framework for creating comprehensive learning experiences, evaluating, and improving conditions for children with disabilities, ages birth to 6 (VSA arts of Wisconsin).

Evidence-Based Practices

Early childhood educators have long recognized the importance of creative activities and are passionate about promoting children's creativity. Because of their acknowledged role in enhancing children's intellectual, social and emotional development, most early childhood curricula have a strong focus on creative experiences—especially in music, movement and visual arts.

Recently, the longstanding focus on creative activities has received a resounding endorsement from neuroscientists working in the brain research area who say that neural pathways in the brain are formed and shaped by early experiences (Shonkoff & Phillips, 2000). In the first 3 to 4 years in particular, rich experiences are necessary to build the brain's neuro-circuitry, which then influences development, general well-being, and later academic performance in school. The growing knowledge of how children's brains develop has helped refocus and energize community and government interest in strengthening and expanding early childhood programs. Current initiatives, such as the Australia's Stronger Families, Stronger Communities program, build on compelling evidence that early developmental outcomes are linked to later well-being.

In light of evidence about the importance of early experience, children's active engagement in singing, music and movement, storytelling, and art and craft activities is especially significant. All new and sustained experiences help create unique brain connections that have short and long-term impacts on developmental pathways. As the current National Enquiry into Literacy draws to a close, attention is focused on the best ways to develop literacy and ensure that every child is a reader. This report undoubtedly will highlight the key role of rich, early language and literacy experiences for young children. In preschool and childcare, the core of these experiences is frequently arts-based with children painting, drawing, singing, dancing, and storytelling at the heart of good early literacy programs. Ensuring that these traditional early childhood activities, complemented by newer digital experiences, will translate into strong early literacy skills requires thoughtful planning and pedagogies that grow out of targeted initial training and professional development (Elliott, 2005).

CREATIVITY—WHAT IS IT AND HOW DOES IT RELATE TO THE YOUNG CHILD WITH AND WITHOUT SPECIAL NEEDS?

Thinking about creativity and the process through which one exercises creativity raises many questions. A very important question to consider when working with young children is whether one is born with creative abilities or whether one learns and acquires them over time?

What enhances the development of creativity? The variables to consider include the following:

- Personality
- Intelligence and knowledge
- Experience
- Thinking styles
- Motivation and commitment
- Environmental support

As one can see, there are several key variables that contribute to the development of creativity. There is no science or formula that exists to cause one child to be more creative than another; but a melding of several variables contribute to the potential for creativity.

The beauty of creativity for children with special needs is that the very nature of creativity is not exacting. Creative outlets balance out the exact nature of math, science, and many areas within language arts. In the visual arts, movement/dance, and some aspects of music and drama, there is no exact response being sought. In the early stages of artistic development, the process is more important than the product. The arts are very meaningful for children with and without disabilities because they provide open-ended possibilities through the creation of a nonjudgmental environment.

Approaching the Teaching of the Arts: The Role of the Teacher

A teacher of young children can take on many different roles while working within the various areas of the arts. The teacher may be a facilitator who makes suggestions about the kind of activity to be undertaken, but the teacher may also choose not to give any specific instruction associated with the activity, so he or she is not too directive. The teacher may also add new materials to the activity, whether art, music and movement, or drama. Again, the teacher does not direct the way the materials are to be used other than to be sure that they will be used in a safe manner. The teacher may extend or enhance the children's experiences by introducing a new way of using a tool or of accomplishing the same action—painting, moving, carrying out a role, etc. The teacher may prompt new experiences by posing problem-solving questions that spark new activities. The teacher may also provide opportunities for children to integrate various arts into their activity and not just isolate arts experiences.

There are many ways that teachers can encourage children to be involved in the arts, so that they can reap different benefits. The arts can be a pathway to developing a child's area of need.

Children's involvement in the arts comes from experience. Experience with materials and activities as well as exposure to the arts, provides young children with the background to explore on their own. Some instruction is part of arts education, but exploration is a very big part of the whole arts experience. Young children are expected to learn a considerable amount of information in exacting areas, such as language, language arts, math, and science. The deep value of the arts is that the child is encouraged to explore and develop interests and skills, but exacting outcomes are not required. The child can produce products and have experiences that are unique to the child. The arts are very accepting and very encouraging of development in other domains.

Child-Centered Arts and Teacher-Directed Activities

There is certainly a time and place for teacher-directed activities (or projects and performances, etc.). Child-centered arts provide children with the opportunity for self-expression. Projects or performances are more public and structured. The Project Approach to arts education is different. The Project Approach refers to a set of teaching strategies, which enable teachers to guide children through in-depth studies of real world topics. The Project Approach is not unstructured; there is a complex, but flexible framework with features that characterize the teaching-learning interaction. When

Adults can scaffold activities with young children.

teachers implement the Project Approach successfully, children can be highly motivated, feel actively involved in their own learning, and produce work of a high quality
(Katz, 1989). Figure 8.1 provides an example of an adapted child-centered activity.

With regard to the Project Approach and standards in early childhood education,
Katz (2007) presents the case for providing experiences for children that support their
quest for understanding. This is in contrast with the idea of delivering educational end
products or outcomes. She cites as examples of standards of experience for the child,
among them to be intellectually engaged and absorbed, to be intellectually challenged, to
be involved in sustained investigations, to have confidence in his or her questions, and to
feel that he or she belongs to a group of peers.

Materials:	Assorted collage materials in containers on table (*varied textures*) Assorted cutting utensils; variety of scissors (*adaptive scissors*) Assorted paper for background (*high contrast available);* Assorted adhesives (*glue sticks, white glue, tape*)
Introduction:	Teacher verbally introduces center (*sets clear limits proactively*); Discusses choices for children; Demonstrates choosing material and pasting it on paper, without directing children's choices
Procedure:	Adult remains at or near center, available to help as needed; Up to four children may select this activity at one time; Teacher may facilitate verbal interaction and guidance without directing activity (*engages with children to sustain participation, as necessary*)
	If child generates language about creation, adult may ask child if he or she wants his or her ideas and words written down.
	Teacher does not ask the child *what* he or she has made, but may ask the child to share perspectives. (*"Would you like to tell me about it?"*)

FIGURE 8.1 Sample Child-Centered Activity

Objectives of Arts Activities for Children with and Without Disabilities

A quality arts program can begin prior to the preschool years and continue throughout the school years. The arts program during the early childhood period should provide for the developmental needs of young children regardless of their age, rate of development, or nature of disability. These needs focus on the language, perceptual, emotional, aesthetic, and creative areas and can best be fostered through visual and tactile perceptual experiences, the production of artistic works, opportunities for the aesthetic judgment and the valuing of the arts, and discussions and activities focusing on the heritage of various arts forms (Arts Education Partnership, 1998; Herberholz & Hanson, 1995). In order to accomplish these goals within the area of visual and productive art, Heberholz and Hanson (1995) suggest that teachers provide experiences in the following:

- examining intensively both natural and human-made objects from many sources and through a variety of means
- expressing individual ideas and feelings through the use of a variety of art media suited to the manipulative abilities and expressive needs of the child
- experimenting with art materials and processes to determine their effectiveness in achieving personal expressive form
- working with tools appropriate to the child's abilities, in order to develop manipulative skills needed for satisfying aesthetic expression
- organizing, evaluating, and reorganizing work–in-process to gain an understanding of the formal structuring of line, form, color, and texture in space
- looking at, reading about, and discussing works of art including painting, sculpture, constructions, architecture, industrial, and handcrafted products using a variety of educational media and community resources (Herberholz & Hanson, 1995).

During the early years of development, children with and without disabilities encounter many experiences that require them to learn exact information. Art is a unique area because the art children create is purely their own expression. There is really no right or wrong. An adult cannot say that the painting or drawing needs to be done over again because when a child declares the work to be complete, it is complete. It is important to allow children to talk about their art experiences. Teachers should not merely ask children to say what they have just made, but rather should invite them to talk about their process, or their feelings experienced while creating their art. When teachers do this, they send a message to children that the process of the art experience is as valuable as the product produced. Teachers can validate the child's participation and show that they value the child. The product on the piece of paper is not critical. Kuschner (1989) shares the viewpoints of several professionals in early childhood (Klein, Kantor & Fernie, 1988; Spodek, 1986; Suransky, 1982) who point out that the manner in which a child comes to believe what is important comes from the value messages delivered by adults. If adults want to cultivate a child's interest in art activity, they must promote the child's interest in that art activity with language and behavior that indicates support.

REFLECTION AND THE ARTS

Teachers can learn so much from observing a child creating a work of art. One may assess a child based on the use of space, selection of color, control of paint or other media, or articulation about the creation. Just observing the child in the process of

REFLECTION IN ACTION

MS. LIGHTBORNE

Initially Ms. Lightborne was a little reluctant to put out "messy" materials when Jordan was at the center. His behavior was impulsive and explosive enough at times that she was concerned he might throw paint at another child or across the room. Eventually, when she realized what she was worried about, she made an intentional decision to try providing this opportunity, creating a safe context for Jordan's exploration. He was immediately responsive to this opportunity to express himself, and art activities soon became among his favorites. Figure 8.2 provides a graphic representation of Ms. Lightborne's decision making.

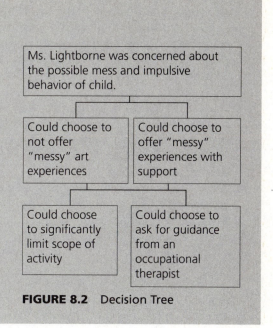

FIGURE 8.2 Decision Tree

creation gives the opportunity to see whether the child is somewhat impulsive or more reflective. The teacher's observation may yield information concerning a child's comfort level, spontaneity, independence, and/or previous experience with art materials. When teachers listen to what a child has to say about the process he or she used to create the work of art, it adds insight into the language and conceptual development of the child. It may also help teachers learn how the child feels about him or herself and how comfortable the child is with sharing experiences. One must be careful about reading into what a child creates or says about what has been created. When pressed to tell something about a creation a child who has not had any particular idea in mind when creating might feel as though the teacher is expecting a story, so the child produces a story. Teachers need to be careful about planting these kinds of expectations. Children should be enjoying the experience, building a framework of knowledge and discovery, and looking forward to other such experiences.

USE OF THE REFLECTIVE PROCESS TO ENHANCE THE EFFECTIVENESS OF INCLUSION DURING ARTS ACTIVITIES

If there is no real right or wrong relative in producing arts activities then what role does reflection play? When a teacher engages in reflection during and after an arts activity, the teacher should be thinking about the following:

- Did the children willingly engage in the activity? The reflective teacher will note the approach the child used in coming into the activity.

- Was my objective for the activity met? Reflection will assist the teacher in determining whether the objective for the activity was appropriate, and whether the activity was developmentally appropriate, when he or she takes into consideration the abilities and disabilities of the children in the class. Sometimes during the planning process, teachers cannot know the answers to these questions up front. Observing and reflecting during and after children engage in the experience will help the teacher to refine future planning to maximize the experience children will have.
- What did I learn about the class as a whole as a result of having introduced the activity? The reflective teacher might learn that the class is calmer and more productive if provided with some type of arts activity each day. The teacher might identify the most productive time period of the day to engage in arts to maximize learning and participation.
- What did I learn about the skills, interests, and challenges of individual children in the class? The teacher might learn that a child that he or she thought was very shy and quiet is not at all shy and quiet when given an opportunity to sing, make music, or dance. The teacher might also learn that a simple rule such as requiring a child to wear a smock in order to paint actually prevents the child from engaging in a painting activity.
- What did I learn about myself as a result of implementing this activity? What might a teacher learn about him or herself through observing and participating in arts activity? A reflective teacher might begin to see areas of learning that he or she needs to undertake. A teacher might also learn that engaging in arts activities has calming effects for him or herself that renew the energy that is much needed to move positively through the day in an early childhood classroom.

Engaging in arts activities with the children in the class should enable teachers to observe aspects of a child's skill repertoire that they might be unable to observe through the more cognitive/academic areas. Teachers might be able to glimpse different aspects of children's development than they are able to observe through other activities and lessons. A child that appears to have a very short attention span may engage in painting or working with clay for an extended period of time. The sensory components of arts activities afford all children the added value of relaxation and engagement at their own level. The reflective teacher will make note of the change in the activity level of a child and consider ways to use this assessment of the child to plan for future arts activities as well as for all other aspects of the environment. Because the prevailing focus is on closing the achievement gap, others may question the value of young children spending time on arts experiences. The reflective teacher will be able to show the ways in which the arts enhance learning and behavior as well as interest in school.

EXAMPLE 1   Cassandra

Cassandra was a very quiet and seemingly shy child. It was sometimes challenging for teachers to assess her skills because she was so hesitant to try things. One day a classroom teacher planned a movement activity that used a variety of music.

Cassandra initially just hugged the wall, did not make eye contact, and acted like her "typical" self. When Cassandra heard Caribbean island music, it was as if the teachers were looking at a whole different child. Cassandra's face and whole body lit up! She began to move her body beautifully, and she participated enthusiastically in the movement activity. When the teachers told her mother (who was also a quiet person) and a comment was made that Cassandra and her mother must dance a lot at home, her mother indicated that she never had music on at home or in the car, and that they never danced together! The teachers wondered—where did the positive response come from?

Questions for Reflection:

1. What was the dynamic going on in this situation?
2. As a teacher what can you take from this new development to apply to other areas to help the child to grow and develop?
3. Is there anything that you might want or need to learn about in order to better help this child?

EXAMPLE 2   Andrew

Andrew was a 3-year-old boy who was extremely verbal, not so skilled motorically, and cautious about doing anything he considered messy. He was also hesitant to join group time. Andrew did however engage in serious dramatic play. When he began preschool, his mother was pregnant with a second child. Each day Andrew played in dramatic play with babies in the housekeeping area. During his play, the teachers observed him putting the doll in the refrigerator or in the stove. As he played out his story, the baby was always getting hurt and would need to be rescued and to see the doctor. The teachers pondered the situation.

Questions for Reflection:

1. Is there anything to be concerned about?
2. What might you want to pay attention to with this child?
3. Is there anything you want to say to the family? Are there questions you have for them?
4. Is there anything you should do in terms of intervention?

EXAMPLE 3   James

James was afraid of failure, so he exhibited opposition to activities with which he had no previous experience. He stayed away from art activities for this reason. He also attempted to intimidate other children who wished to participate in art activities by telling them that painting is for sissies. It was important for him to see that men can be artists too. The teachers placed pictures of male artists around the art area and also introduced prints of the work done by famous male artists. After some initial indifference to these exhibits, James was seen to show interest in them when he thought there was nobody watching him. After some time, James began to use art materials. His drawings and paintings often were negative in nature, but his involvement in the art area did allow him to express himself and begin to relax. He also began to relax in his peer interactions while engaged in art activities.

Questions for Reflection:
1. Did the teachers appropriately implement the intervention?
2. What do you think prompted the "art is for sissies" concept held by James?

Summary

Including the arts in the curriculum for young children with and without disabilities provides opportunities for growth and development for children and their teachers. The arts may serve as a teaching and learning vehicle as well as a diagnostic tool through which one may learn about the potential and intelligence of a child. The joy of creating alone or together with peers and teachers may help a child to see his or her own potential. The possibilities are endless. As a teacher, you will always need to learn and grow. Embracing the arts is one way to enjoy that journey even more!

Key Terms

Adaptation
Creativity

National Standards
The arts

Websites

Every Child Magazine
http://www.earlychildhoodaustralia.org.au/every_child_magazine/every_child_index/new_evidence_linking_the_arts_and_learning_in_early_childhood.html

National Standards on the Arts
http://www.ed.gov/pubs/ArtsStandards.html

Very Special Arts (VSA Arts)
http://www.vsawis.org

Art Education Sites

The Nonverbal Dictionary of Gestures, Signs, and Body Language Cues
http://members.aol.com/nonverbal2/diction1.ht

Arts Education Partnership
http://aep-arts.org

Visual Thinking Strategies (VTS)
http://www.vue.org

Learning Disabilities Online
http://www.ldonline.org

Art Image Sites

The Natural Child Project
http://www.naturalchild.com/gallery

The George Lucas Foundation
http://www.edutopia.com

The John F. Kennedy Center for the Performing Arts
http://www.artsedge.kennedy-center.org

The Getty Center for Education in the Arts
http://www.getty.edu/education

The Artchive: Juxtapositions
http://www.artchive.com/juxt/juxt.html

Art in a Click—Commercial art prints
http://www.artinaclick.com

National Art Education Association
http://www.naea-reston.org

New York Foundation for the Arts
http://www.nyfa.org/

Personal gallery of Landscape painter Brent Melander
http://www.northlight.com/brent

Master Prints—Commercial art gallery
http://www.masterprints.com

ArtDaily—An art newspaper on the Net
http://artdaily.com

Visit Claude Monet's house and garden
http://www.giverny.org/gardens

Exploring Leonardo da Vinci
http://www.mos.org/sln/Leonardo/LeoHomePage.html

Children and Family Sites

Kidzart—Displays children's art and encourages art in Education
http://www.kidzart.org/

Crayola—Art lesson plans and activities
http://www.crayola.com

Kid's Space—Art for kids and by kids
http://www.kids-space.org

The Children's Museum of Houston
http://www.rice.edu/cmh

The Children's Museum of Indianapolis
http://www.childrensmuseum.org/

ArtEdventures
http://www.alifetimeofcolor.com/

Kid's Zone—African American cultural site
http://www.afroam.org/children/children.html

Family Fun
http://www.familyfun.com

The National Gallery of Art, Washington, DC
http://www.nga.gov/kids

The Educator's Reference Desk
http://ericir.syr.edu/

The Core Knowledge Foundation
http://www.coreknowledge.org

Tantalizing Tessellations
http://mathcentral.uregina.ca/RR/database/RR.09.96/archamb1.html

The Museum of Modern Art's (MoMA) Visual Thinking Curriculum Project
http://www.pz.harvard.edu/Research/MoMA.htm

Tessellations
http://forum.swarthmore.edu/sum95/suzanne/links.html

Art Junction
http://www.arts.ufl.edu/art/rt_room/index.html

National Association for the Education of Young Children
http://www.naeyc.org

Museums and Art Galleries

Guggenheim Museum, New York
http://www.guggenheim.org/

Metropolitan Museum of Art, New York
http://www.metmuseum.org/Index.html

Emory University's Carlos Museum, Atlanta
http://www.cc.emory.edu/CARLOS

Art Education of New Jersey, Atlantic City, New Jersey
http://www.aenj.org

Akron Art Museum, Akron, Ohio
http://www.akronartmuseum.org

The Harmon Museum
http://www.npg.si.edu/exh/harmon/index.htm

Takase Studios—Fine Japanese calligraphy
http://www.takase.com

Smithsonian Museum, Washington, DC
http://www.si.edu/

National Portrait Gallery, Washington, DC
http://www.npg.si.edu

The Oriental Institute, University of Chicago
http://oi.uchicago.edu/

The National Gallery of Art, Washington, DC
http://www.nga.gov

Shelton Memorial Art Gallery and Sculpture Garden
http://sheldon.unl.edu/HTML/ARTIST/Walker_K/SSII.html

Art in Context—The Art of Faith Ringgold
http://www.artincontext.org/artist/r/faith_ringgold/

The Fine Arts Museums of San Francisco
http://www.thinker.org

Asian Arts Gallery
http://www.asianart.com/hotlist.html

Music Sites

National Association for Music Education; Early Childhood Network; National Pre-K Standards in Music Education
http://www.menc.org

Wolf Trap Education Institute for Early Learning Through the Arts
http://www.wolftrap.org

Kid Rhino Music Store
http://www.kidrhino.com/kids25.html

Online Resource Page by Wolf Trap
http://www.artsplay.org

Teacher Resource Sites

Art activities for preschool children
http://artforkids.about.com

Art materials resource
http://www.artistresource.org/market.htm

Learning intervention resources
http://www.donjohnston.com

Computer resources
http://www.warehouse.com/ed

Scholastic
http://www.scholastic.com/

Early Childhood
http://www.earlychildhood.com

Eric Carle Web site
http://www.eric-carle.com/

Kodak lesson plan Web site
http://www.kodak.com/cluster/global/en/consumer/education/lessonPlans/lessonPlan083.shtml

The Artcyclopedia
http://artcyclopedia.com

Visual Arts resource
http://arttalk.com

Special education resource
http://seriweb.com

Search engine for the arts
http://dir.yahoo.com/Arts/Education/K_12

Preschool education resources
http://www.preschooleducation.com

HILL's Special Edulinks
http://www.boulderactivist.org/edulinks

Creative Communicating
http://www.creative-comm.com

Kinder Art Activities
http://www.kinderart.com/lessons.htm

Scholastic online with Faith Ringgold
http://teacher.scholastic.com/authorsandbooks/authors/ringgold/bio.htm

Bright Ring
http://brightring.com

Study Web
http://www.studyweb.com/teach/tocart.htm

World Wide Arts Resources
http://wwar.com

References

Arts Education Partnership. (1998). *Young children and the arts: Making creative connections.* Arts Education Partnership.

Barbour, N. (1990). Whose creation is it anyway? *Childhood Education, 66,* 130–131.

Bowman, B. (1990, December). *The arts and development.* Paper presented at the International Conference on Early Childhood Creative Arts, Los Angeles.

Elliott, A. (2005). New evidence of linking the arts and learning in early childhood. *Every Child, 11,* Early Childhood Australia, Inc.

Espenak, L. and Koch, N. (1981). An interview with Liljan Espenak. *American Journal of Dance Therapy, 4(2),* 4–20.

Gardner, H. (2006). *Multiple Intelligences: New horizons in theory and practice.* New York: Basic Books.

Herberholz, B., & Hanson, L. (1995). *Early childhood art* (5th ed.). Dubuque, IA: Wm. C. Brown.

Hutinger, P. L., Betz, A., Bosworth, J., Potter, J., & Schneider, C. (1997). *ArtsExpress: A curriculum for young children with disabilities.* Retrieved from ERIC Document Reproduction Service No. ED433653 (Educational Resources Information Center) database.

Hutinger, P. L., Potter, J., Schneider, C., Guzman, M., & Johanson, J. (2002). *Expressive arts outreach project 1997–2000: A final report* (Project No. H024D70014). Washington, DC: U.S. Department of Education Office of Special

Education and Rehabilitative Services, Office of Special Education, Research and Innovation to Improve Services and Results for Children with Disabilities. Retrieved March 2007 from ERIC database.

Katz, L. G., & Chard, S. C. (1989). *Engaging children's minds: The project approach.* Norwood, NJ: Ablex.

Katz, L. G. (2007). Viewpoint: Standards of experience. *Young Children, 62,* 94–95.

Klein, E., Kantor, R., & Fernie, D. (1988). What do young children know about school? *Young Children, 43,* 32–39.

Kuschner, D. (1989). Put your name on your painting, but the blocks go back on the shelves. *Young Children, 45,* 49–56.

Lowenfeld, V., & Brittain, W. L. (1987). *Creative and mental growth.* New York: Macmillan.

Lubawy, J. (2009), *Visions of creativity in early childhood: Connecting theory, practice, and reflections.* Castle Hill, New South Wales, Australia: Pademelon Press.

Music Educators National Conference (MENC). (1994). National Standards for Arts Education. Reston, VA: National Association for Music Education.

Nordoff, P., & Robbins, C. (1970). *Therapy in music for handicapped children.* London: Gollancz.

Nordoff, P., & Robbins, C. (1977). Creative music therapy: Individualized treatment for the handicapped child. New York: John Day.

Nordoff, P., & Robbins, C. (1983). Music therapy in special education. St. Louis, MO: MMB Music.

Pearson, B. (1998). Three positive ways to apply multiple intelligences theory in schools. *ArtLinks.* Retrieved April, 2007 from http://www.barbarapearson.com/p-mi-apply.html

Schirrmacher, R., & Fox, J. E. (2009). *Art and creative development for young children.* New York: Thomson Delmar Learning.

Shonkoff, J. P., & Philips, D. A. (Eds.). (2000). *From neurons to neighborhoods: The science of early childhood development.* Washington, DC: National Academic Press.

Spodek, B. (1986). Development, values, and knowledge in the kindergarten curriculum. In B. Spodek (Ed.), *Kindergarten: Exploring the knowledge base, expanding the curriculum* (pp. 32–47). New York: Teachers College Press, Columbia University.

Suransky, V. (1982). *The erosion of childhood.* Chicago: University of Chicago Press.

Smith, S. (2001). *The power of the arts: Creative strategies for teaching exceptional learners.* Baltimore: Paul H. Brookes.

The National Standards for Arts Education (1994). The National Association for Music Education. http://www.menc.org/resources/

Toombs, M. (1968). Dance therapy. In E. Gaston (Ed.), *Music in therapy.* New York: Macmillan.

Very Special Arts of Wisconsin. (1992). Early Childhood-Healthy Foundations Initiative. Wisconsin: VSA Arts of Wisconsin Early Childhood.

Chapter 9

Solving Problems in Everyday Life

Math, Science, and Beyond

OBJECTIVES

After reading this chapter, students will:

- Demonstrate an understanding of various theories of cognitive development and problem solving;

- Identify ways in which cognition can be assessed for the purpose of making curricular adaptations;

- Identify ways in which certain conditions affect cognition;

- Have a concept of how adaptations can be made for a variety of developmental challenges in math and science activities;

- Reflect on the ways in which strategies may be embedded into problem-solving activities;

- Associate identified patterns of strength and weakness with possible strategies for adaptation with differentiated instruction;

- Demonstrate the ability to integrate/embed math and science concepts into the **activities of daily living.**

OVERVIEW OF THEORETICAL PERSPECTIVES

Problem solving and cognition form the core of learning for people of all ages. Research strongly supports the importance of the early years of life as formative. The experiences in the first years of a child's life can create a profound difference in how the child approaches the world, for better or worse. This is true for behavior and what the child does. It is also true on a biological level in terms of how each child's brain is developing. The brain, also called the central nervous system (CNS), has the potential to be affected by each child's experiences; it is crucial, and the interaction between early childhood educators and young children and their families can make a tremendous difference in the lives of children.

Early childhood programs should convey excitement about learning to all children. Early childhood programs should be places where daily discoveries are made, celebrated, and documented. This culture of enjoyment might be considered by the "big" world to be simple pleasures. There are many wonderful curricular models and approaches to creating environments in which children may thrive in their thinking as well as their social well-being (Katz & Chard, 2000; Chalufour & Worth, 2003).

Creating environments where children thrive is at the heart of early childhood education. Early childhood educators must start with early childhood programs at their best, with a clear, fresh understanding about the vitality of practices that fully engage children and excite them in their own learning process. Professionals cannot afford to take this for granted. The best strategies and adaptations have little effect in classrooms that are not attuned to the needs and interests of all the children.

This chapter expands the understanding of solving problems and cognition, especially with respect to daily activities. This book will not assert that one area is necessarily more important than the others. Within an integrated curriculum model, there is considerable interrelatedness between areas. As professionals focus on this very important domain of development, they should acknowledge the different perspectives regarding cognition.

TABLE 9.1   Did You Know? Theoretical Perspectives: Key Constructs Related to Young Children with Exceptionalities

Theorist	Theory	Elements
Jean Piaget	Constructivist	Stages Sensorimotor activities and concepts such as cause and effect, means–end, conservation, etc.
Maria Montessori	Constructivist	Sensory materials Self-correcting materials Activities of daily living
Lev Vygotsky	Constructivist	Scaffolding **Zone of proximal development**
Howard Gardner	**Multiple intelligences**	Different kinds of intelligence
B. F. Skinner	Learning theory	Stimulus, Response, Reinforcement
George Miller	Information processing theory	Repetition, long- and short-term memory, retrieval
Benjamin Bloom	Bloom's taxonomy	Different levels of learning

Table 9.1 provides an overview of different theoretical models.

The first perspective, well represented by theorists such as Lev Vygotsky (1978), Jean Piaget (1952), Maria Montessori (1912/1964), and Howard Gardner (2000) and methods such as the Reggio Emilia approach (Wein, 2008), guides us toward developmentally appropriate practices (Gardner, 2000 ; Wein, 2008). When professionals plan curricula and environments that demonstrate the wealth of all that has been learned about how children grow and develop, there is no question that recommended practices would exemplify constructivist theory (Hyson, 2008).

The notion that children can construct their own knowledge is very powerful. The teacher's role is to provide **scaffolding**, support, and guidance as needed. This role is flexible enough to accommodate different learning styles as well as abilities (Hyun, 2006). Constructivist perspectives consider cognition to be a rich process through which children come to a deeper understanding of concepts by participating in meaningful and engaging sensory activities (Schickedanz, 2008).

Other views of cognition focus primarily on rote memory and retrieval of facts and information, as measured by certain tests and certain kinds of performance. The information processing theory (Miller, 1956) provides a framework of cognition that is componential, much like a computer, in which there is input, output, memory, and recall or retrieval. The effective functioning of these processes depends on each component working well. A person must be able to receive information, store it, and retrieve it when needed, and use it in conjunction with other stored information to reach solutions. All of these processes happen in a remarkably automatic way in normal development.

The Environment

There are many variations of developmentally appropriate practices in early childhood environments that are conducive to learning and healthy development. Each classroom will be distinctive in its own way, and all classrooms should not be rigidly uniform. At the same time, it is evident that there are common elements that provide support, cohesion, and focus within the environment. These include lighting, acoustics, layout of furniture, and size of room (Clifford & Harms ; Watson & McCathren, 2009). It is clear that among the overall population of young children, there are considerable differences in their need for structure, their tolerance for distraction, and how they relate to clutter. Equally, there are individual differences between teachers and parents regarding these important elements. This book's approach to problem solving and cognition includes some explicit discussion of key elements as well as personal styles.

Activities of Daily Living and Adaptive Skills

Realistically, professionals will continue to use methods that provide children with opportunities to practice their new-found skills. These opportunities can be provided in meaningful, hands-on ways that are integrated into daily activities. In real life, rote recall is less valuable than the ability to recall relevant information in meaningful contexts.

Increasingly, the focus in special education has been on the acquisition of functional skills or **activities of daily living** (ADL). When teams consider the children's current levels of performance in the cognitive realm, they need to be aware of what will be useful to each individual and how to provide supports that will help every child to more effectively cope with daily life (Montessori, 1912/1964).

Functional Experience

ADJUSTING WHAT ONE DOES TO MAKE IT WORK A major indicator of functional intelligence is the ability to adjust strategies based on outcomes and what is happening. This is true for young children. Young children solve many problems that arise in their lives on a daily basis, but this problem solving is often intuitive or impulsively accomplished. It is also true for parents and practitioners. In the heat of the moment, adults sometimes act first and think later. Ongoing observation and assessment make it possible to regroup, reflect, and reconsider approaches. Learning how to learn from experience is central to one's process. The recognition of key elements is integral to the ongoing process of adaptation.

Identification of crucial factors is part of being able to more explicitly and intentionally make choices about how support is provided . Inevitably, making mistakes is part of the learning process for children. The professional should respond to mistakes, provide guidance, and support the creation of a warm, nurturing, and safe place for children to take initiative, build trust, and try new ventures. Adults are often able to think something through before making a mistake, but there are times when they also need to be willing to reconsider what they are doing and be open to constructive feedback.

Generalization of Skills

It may be easier for children to learn discrete concepts and skills using highly structured teacher-directed, child-focused activities, but those skills may have little functional value unless they are generalized to real-life situations. For children who may need more direction and explicit instruction to get them started, follow-up activities provide a crucial link to what will hopefully become meaningful, useful skills. For example, identification of a color out of context may be measurable and relatively easy to document, but asking for the red cup or red crayon is functional. Being able to point to the picture of the big apple compared to the little apple in a highly structured context is a measurable skill. Being able to ask for the big apple at snack time serves an important function. Discrete skills can be reinforced with positive feedback. Functional skills can be reinforced with natural reinforcers that are intrinsically part of a context or situation. If a child wants to play with others, being able to do so is naturally reinforcing.

Meaningful Activities

A key feature of developmentally appropriate activities is that they are meaningful for children. A child with characteristics of autism might ritualistically piece together manipulatives, but when the child holds up his or her construction to show someone and says, "Ladder," there is a demonstration of meaning beyond a perseverative (repetitive) manipulation of objects. It is effective when team members notice and respond to the interests and initiatives of each child, infusing those activities with relevant meaning (Hyson, 2008).

The concept of seriation, for instance, may be more effectively addressed in a cooking activity that involves sequential steps than in flash cards that employ rote learning of a sequence. In cooking, the sequence of steps is determined by intrinsic meaning. The egg has to be cracked before it is put into the batter. The box has to be opened before it is emptied into the bowl. What comes first, next, and last is determined by a meaningful context and can be understood by children as they engage in motivating, hands-on activities.

MALLEABILITY OF INTELLIGENCE

Effects of Environment and Experience

The biological effects of quality experience on the development of the CNS has been well documented (Bailey & Bruer, 2001; Farran, 2001; Shonkoff & Phillips, 2000; Zigler & Styfco, 2004). The opportunities professionals provide for children can actually make a difference in the biological basis of their cognitive development on a cellular level.

Positive and Negative Change

The complex interaction of environment and experience can have both negative and positive effects on brain development. If children are born with biological risk, such as prematurity, they can make significant progress given appropriate opportunities. If they are born apparently without biological risk, the effects of negative environmental factors, such as exposure to lead and/or malnutrition, can contribute to cognitive difficulties because of central nervous system challenges.

Achievement Gap

The achievement gap has been well documented (Farran, 2005) and has been a major concern in education (Shonkoff & Phillips, 2000). Disparity between the performances of children in different communities must be carefully interpreted so assumptions are not made about inherent abilities or lack thereof. Data analysis indicates that children who live in areas where concentrations of poverty are higher generally have lower performance than children who live in higher wage-earning communities.

TABLE 9.2 Ways to Support Inquiry and Engagement in Classrooms

Method	Rationale
Exciting materials	Range of materials to address many developmental levels.
Variety of activities to support concept development through experiential learning	Opportunities for engagement and experience especially important for children who may have had limited opportunities.
Responsiveness to children's ideas and interests	Meaningful learning more likely to occur when the motivations of children are addressed.
Integration of experiences through verbal narration, literacy, etc.	Verbal narration at an appropriate level supports concept development.
Documentation and use of technology such as digital photography	Social stories can be integrated into activities, along with concept development.
Content that is interesting and relevant, such as changing weather, seasons, "green" environments	When the content is of high interest to children, they are much more likely to be involved.
Plentiful sensory activities that support concepts also addressed in other ways	Multisensory activities add multiple dimensions to experience. For some children, this may be especially crucial.

Professionals need to consider the environmental conditions and risk factors in which children are growing up (Bronfenbrenner, 1979; Zigler & Styfco, 2004). To assess children's performance without consideration of the context in which they are growing up may lead to perpetuation of serious misunderstandings. Table 9.2 provides some perspectives on environmental factors that support healthy development of cognition.

Reflecting on Contexts in Which Children Live

In reflection on a child's performance, teachers should consider the contexts in which he or she is living, including risk factors and protective factors. In assessment and intervention, professionals can intercept such disparities between aptitude and performance. They may significantly reduce the achievement gap that is so frequently found, especially in environments where there is poverty and the associated lack of opportunity. Such risk factors are well documented in the research (Farran, 2001; Zigler & Styfco, 2004). Through effective assessment and reflection, professionals can identify factors that may be contributing to challenges in development and can distinguish them from developmental disabilities that have a more biological basis. When appropriate standards have been set that do not lower expectations for children growing up in poverty, teachers can align these standards with a system-wide commitment to support students in their optimal outcomes. Organizations such as the Children's Defense Fund (Wright Edelman, 1992) have long advocated for supports and services for children to decrease the negative effects of poverty and risk on children who were born into challenging circumstances. Rather than note the predictable negative effects of multiple risk factors on development and lower their expectations of students growing up with such risk, teachers should acknowledge the risk and create ways in which those factors can be alleviated (Farran, 2001).

Economic Factors and Distribution of Poverty

As teachers reflect upon the cognitive development of young children, the economic disparity in the backgrounds of children becomes clear. Some children grow up in contexts in which they have many resources and supports and others in situations where their families and communities are challenged. When multiple risk factors are present in the early lives of children, those risks impact the likelihood of positive outcomes. Poverty is a significant predictor of developmental difficulty. When children are living in poverty, it does not mean they will always have problems with development, but it increases the likelihood that they will have challenges. Statistically, poverty is predictive of difficulty with development. Unfortunately, poverty is a disproportionate factor for families from culturally diverse groups in the United States. Culture is not a risk factor; poverty is a risk factor. It is imperative that teachers compensate for environments affected by poverty by providing rich and appropriate experiences for all young children.

CONDITIONS AFFECTING COGNITIVE PERFORMANCE

Children with Intellectual Disabilities/Mental Retardation

One category of disability that affects cognitive performance is intellectual disabilities, also known as mental retardation. Some conditions, such as Down syndrome, are relatively well known. Other conditions, such as alcohol-related birth defects, may be common but less understood. When children have conditions that affect their appearance, it may be a natural progression for others to make appropriate accommodations. There are times, however, when children look "normal" but have cognitive differences. Sometimes these differences include intellectual disabilities.

Intellectual disabilities involve reduced ability and capacity. See box "Definition of Intellectual Disability" for concise definition of intellectual disability.

Avoidance of Stereotypes

An example of a stereotype of a condition would be the notion that people with Down syndrome are very sociable and friendly. While this may be characteristic of many people with Down syndrome, these individuals also have a range of emotions, including sadness and anger. They often value independence. Thus, it is important that team

---

DEFINITION OF INTELLECTUAL DISABILITY

"An intellectual disability is a disability characterized by significant limitations both in intellectual functioning and in adaptive behavior, which covers many everyday social and practical skills. This disability originates before age 18. American Association on Intellectual and Developmental Disabilities (AAIDD) http://www.aaidd.org/content_100/cf,?navID=21 (retrieved on 11/25/09)

members are aware of stereotypes and careful not to inadvertently perpetuate such misconceptions in the assessment of young children. Professionals who are willing to scan their own beliefs and views can increase their understanding of multicultural perspectives. Such scanning and willingness to reflect on assumptions are very helpful in continuing to reduce bias.

Children with intellectual disabilities may enjoy challenging cognitive activities and the satisfaction that comes with a job well done. They can participate in daily activities and make valuable contributions within the classroom community such as helping set up for snack and joining with the group in all the routines that are part of each day. Predictability within the schedule and routines contributes to children learning to anticipate what will be happening next. It helps in the adjustment to inclusive classrooms.

Children with Learning Disabilities

Learning disabilities are disorders of processing that affect achievement in children who have average or above-average intelligence. In school-age children, a learning disability may manifest as a difficulty with reading or math. With younger children, it might manifest as language delays or difficulty with organizing experience or sustaining engagement. See box "Definition of Learning Disabilities" for concise definition of learning disabilities.

Children with Gifts and Talents

Children with gifts and talents are often undiagnosed when they are very young. They may be exceptionally motivated and enthusiastic regarding learning and engagement. They may also, however, be withdrawn and less involved in social learning experience. They might be frustrated when asked to wait for others and may always be eager to respond to questions. It is important that early learning environments be challenging to a whole range of developmental abilities.

Children may have learning disabilities as well as gifts and talents (Renzulli & Reis, 2004). This may be difficult to recognize in young children prior to formal evaluation. The presenting characteristics may involve inconsistency in behavior and performance in everyday activities. Unfortunately, it is easy to misunderstand or misinterpret a child's

---

DEFINITION OF LEARNING DISABILITIES

"The term learning disability *means a disorder in one or more of the basic psychological processes involved in understanding or in using language, spoken or written, that may manifest itself in an imperfect ability to listen, think, speak, read, write, spell, or do mathematical calculations including conditions such as perceptual disabilities, brain injury, minimal brain dysfunction, dyslexia, and developmental aphasia.*

Disorders not included. The term does not include learning problems that are primarily the result of visual, hearing, or motor disabilities, of mental retardation, of emotional disturbance, or of environmental, cultural, or economic disadvantage." (Individuals with Disabilities Education Act. Section 300.7(c)(10) of 34 CFR Parts 300 and 303). Learning disabilities are no longer identified using a model requiring a documented severe discrepancy between aptitude and performance.

Motivating child-centered activities can support the acquisition of concepts.

inconsistent behavior and performance. Sometimes adults may assume a child is intentionally not performing, based on the documentation of performance in other contexts.

As professionals consider the potential need for adaptations in various domains, it is important to consider the specific skills, knowledge, and concepts children may attain. These provide a developmental framework as well as a useful guide to identify appropriate goals and objectives for each child. Table 9.3 explicitly lists certain cognitive processes and how they contribute to solving problems from the perspective of the information-processing model. The functions are identified in the second column.

Table 9.4 provides an overview of some positive outcomes including the constructivist model of cognitive development. While most children attain these benchmarks without explicit intervention, sometimes children have difficulty with one or more of these functions. In the instance of a child who is eligible for special services, he or she may have individualized education goals and/or objectives addressing the areas of

TABLE 9.3   Positive Outcomes: Information Processing Model

Function	Children's Outcomes
Memory Short-term Long-term Retrieval	Ability to retain and recall relevant information and process information
Sequencing	Ability to organize activities and symbols in meaningful sequences
Sustaining attention	Ability to stay focused on an activity long enough to develop concept
Perceptual–motor coordination	Ability to intentionally manipulate objects and/or symbols in meaningful ways
Auditory processing	Ability to listen and process information and follow directions
Sensory integration	Ability to organize sensory experience to enhance concept development

TABLE 9.4   Significant Cognitive Benchmarks in the Constructivist Model

Benchmark or Concept	Example or Context
Cause and effect	Participation in daily activities.
	When an action contributes to another action or event, cause and effect occurs.
Object permanence	Separation from significant others.
	Games (e.g., "Peek-a-boo")
Transformation	Cooking: Ingredients are combined to yield a different result.
Means-to-end	Children ask for and receive. Children may use a tool or utensil to accomplish something else.
Use of words: Vocabulary	Express wants and needs verbally. Use words to describe and solve problems.Use words to interact with other people.
Curiosity about environment	Explore and discover; activities.
	Active engagement in inquiry.
Problem-solving abilities Numeracy	Application of numeracy skills in a variety of contexts. (Figure out how many napkins eight children need.)
Classification skills	Application of classification skills in classroom activities. (Put different blocks on shelf.)
Concept of colors	Colors are present in all aspects of the environment.
Concept of size	Concepts of size may be generalized to every aspect of environment and are important in mathematical foundations.
Concept of patterns	All sorts of patterns in environment yield meaningful concepts regarding sequencing, math, and literacy.
Nonverbal problem solving	Children may shift their strategies when attempting to solve a problem with manipulatives.

difficulty. Using educational goals and objectives is helpful in strategic planning for the adaptation of activities because it provides a sense of direction for accomplishment.

FORMATIVE ASSESSMENT OF COGNITION

Beyond Intelligence Quotient

Assessing cognition and concept development has changed significantly since the publication of the first tests of intelligence quotient (IQ). When the construct of IQ was first formulated, it was pioneering it became evident, however, that some were over-influenced by children's test scores, and at times inadvertently adjusted their own behavior toward the student based on reported IQ scores. One classic study by Rosenthal and Jacobson (1968) indicated that teachers' expectations of children were affected by the information they had been given. The outcomes for children correlated more closely with the misinformation given to their teachers than to their actual IQ scores.

In addition to ways in which expectations may be affected, some misunderstandings about competence can be perpetuated through an overemphasis on short-term memory rather than on concept development. There are many theories of cognitive development that both complement and contradict each other. The constructivist theory, which posits that children learn through active engagement and hands-on activities with materials, is widely accepted among early childhood educators. Piaget, Vygotsky, Montessori, Gardner, and many others are well established in the field of early childhood education. Teachers need to have well-integrated understandings of the many aspects of cognition and be able to consider multiple possibilities during the assessment of young children's development. If children understand concepts, teachers should document understanding. If children are having trouble with processing, teachers need to be as specific as possible about the ways in which children are having difficulty. This is complicated by the fact that certain errors in cognition are normal for children at certain ages. If professionals and parents fully understand these patterns of normal development, they are more likely to be able to determine the ways in which children are outside that range of typical development.

Factors such as "executive function" or conscious control and the ability to organize multiple dimensions of a problem-solving process are crucial aspects of cognitive processes. Awareness of various dynamics can make a major difference in understanding young children. A teacher's well-integrated concept of cognition will contribute to the validity of the assessment being performed.

Data-Driven Decision Making: Recognition and Response

Documentation regarding each child's current level of performance can be used to inform practice. This is called response to intervention or recognition and response (Buysse & Wesley, 2006). In the domain of cognition, this usually involves extensive observation and learning about what the child knows and how the child learns. Teachers should consider the varied patterns and levels of performance in order to increase the ability to effectively match the child's needs with the intervention, without creating learned helplessness or reducing autonomy.

REFLECTION IN ACTION
MS. LIGHTBORNE

Years ago, Ms. Lightborne attended professional development sessions to enhance the ways in which she addressed math and science. She successfully integrated many materials and activities into her classroom environment and curriculum. This was exceptionally rewarding, and it was very satisfying to appreciate the children's engagement. When asked to include a child with intellectual disabilities into her class, she was willing but unsure of how the child would participate in activities involving higher-order thinking. She found the child flitted from one center to another and had trouble becoming involved with some of the more complex activities. The child was also easily frustrated. After significant reflection, Ms. Lightborne acknowledged that her professional commitment to enhanced opportunities for math, science, and problem solving contributed to her reluctance to simplify the environment. Ultimately, she decided to rotate the abundant materials, so there was less potential for overstimulation. She also adjusted the objectives for the child so that he could effectively participate socially. Sensory involvement was very motivating for him, and the concepts were adjusted to this child's developmental level.

TABLE 9.5 The Potential Effect of Various Conditions on Cognitive Performance	
Condition	**Possible Characteristics**
Autism	Difficulty moving beyond ritualistic perseveration
Serious emotional disturbance Behavioral challenges	Difficulty sustaining engagement, relating to other children during activities
	Distorted thinking, need for "reality checks," obsessive thoughts, avoidance
Blind/visually impaired	Difficulty picking up on visual cues
	Difficulty with conceptually connecting different aspects of complex challenges
	Need for more objects rather than just pictures.
Deaf/hearing impaired	Difficulty with auditory cues and verbal directions
Physical challenges: gross motor, fine motor, and sensory	Difficulty with sensory experience, motor activity, and coordination
Language delays	Difficulty processing verbal narration and directions
	Difficulty expressing their thoughts
Anxiety	Preoccupation
	Difficulty focusing
	Scattered thinking
Neurological impairment	Difficulty sustaining engagement, easily distracted, and disorganized
	Difficulty stopping a train of thought (perseveration)

Table 9.5 summarizes some of the issues one may encounter while assessing a young child. Awareness of the potential characteristics and patterns that might interfere with cognitive performance will help to frame the information that a child produces for the person carrying out any kind of assessment, formal or informal.

LEARNING ABOUT AND REFLECTING ON INFORMATION CHILDREN PROVIDE

A set of examples follows that can help introduce the reader to different children and situations that represent everyday kinds of scenarios. These vignettes provide opportunities for reflection on possible solutions.

EXAMPLE 1   Jared

Jared was 4 years old and attending an inclusive early childhood program when he was referred for a full-scale assessment at a children's hospital. He had characteristics of autism and epilepsy. While he was in the hospital, one of the tests for epilepsy involved a study of brain waves, an electroencephalogram (EEG), after sleep deprivation. The following day, one of several professionals tried to assess his performance on a cognitive task using a standardized instrument. Jared was so tired that he fell asleep. Had the psychologist been fully informed of the sequence of the other assessments being performed, Jared's lack of attention and performance on a cognitive task would have been interpreted very differently. Unfortunately, a very low score was recorded.

In a familiar context, the same child commented to his teacher as they walked past a poster, "Oh, look! Three dogs!" This anecdotal documentation provided valuable information about Jared's cognitive and linguistic abilities. The inconsistency of his performance was certainly worth noting. When a child performs very inconsistently, the question is not just which performances, the high or the low, are more accurate. The more relevant issue relates to clarifying and identifying those factors that most affect performance and designing curricular adaptations that address those variables.

Questions for Reflection:

1. How would you integrate the information from at least two assessment methods to provide a clear and accurate perspective on Jared's development?
2. Based on the information provided, how would you describe Jared's current level of performance?

EXAMPLE 2   Beth

When Beth was 5, she went from being a typical kindergarten student to a child with major health concerns. One day, while playing in the playground, she fell off a see-saw and had her first tonic-clonic seizure.

Questions for Reflection:

1. What might you expect to need to think about and do in the classroom to work effectively with Beth from now on?
2. Based on the little information provided, what would you expect Beth to be like now?

FOLLOW-UP INFORMATION   After many months and many medical tests, it was determined that Beth had a rare disease called Rasmussen's encephalitis. It had affected one hemisphere of her brain and was causing up to one hundred seizures a day. Beth went to Johns Hopkins Medical Center in Baltimore, Maryland, where she had surgery to remove half of her brain. This hemispherectomy was at the time a relatively newly mastered procedure. Beth was young enough to be able to recover remarkably well, with her right hemisphere taking over many of the functions previously accomplished with her left hemisphere. She received special services for her difficulty with language and literacy but was fully included in general classrooms and made remarkable progress.

EXAMPLE 3   Sung Bin

Sung Bin was adopted when he was 5. At the time of his adoption, his communication was mostly nonverbal. Because his country of birth was Korea, the challenge of learning English was one of many he encountered. His nonverbal communication in the form of gestures was further complicated by the fact that he had athetoid cerebral palsy, which made it difficult for him to use gestures intentionally because of involuntary movement patterns.

At age 5, however, Sung Bin was already a remarkably determined child who demonstrated a keen aptitude in unique ways. He remembered people. He engaged in play when positioned appropriately in the play area. He participated fully in classroom routines and activities. His abilities were evident in his engagement, his motivation, and his participation.

Questions for Reflection:

1. If Sung Bin joined your school after being adopted, how might you learn more about his cognitive abilities while also making him feel welcome in your class?
2. If Sung Bin were a student in your class, what might you do to support his cognitive growth and development?

EXAMPLE 4   Mark: Reflection and Interpretation of Data

The assessment of cognitive abilities involves far more than scores on standardized tests. This was illustrated in Chapter 7, in the example of Mark, who was referred for special services when he was 3 years old because of significant expressive language delays. In other domains, however, Mark was progressing very well in terms of benchmarks. When he was being evaluated by his teacher, with whom he had a warm and trusting relationship, he saw a picture of a cat, pointed, and gestured 11 with his fingers by first showing all ten, then one more. The teacher responded to his nonverbal signal by saying, "Yes, a cat. Eleven?" He nodded. "You have 11 cats?" He nodded again. The teacher noted this remarkable interaction and later checked with Mark's mother, who confirmed there were 11 cats living in their barn!

The teacher did not ignore the child's gestures. While Mark had language delays, he was also communicating in other ways, and he was able to convey his cognitive abilities in these ways. After one year of preschool he was talking in long, complex sentences, and further evaluation indicated that he was gifted and talented, with an IQ of 155. It is not clear why he had language delays, but it was important that his teacher did not lower her expectations of his ability based on those delays.

Questions for Reflection:

1. What signals did Mark use to communicate his inner thoughts?
2. If you were his teacher, how might you adjust your style to support him?

THREE SNAPSHOTS

VIGNETTE   Jayden

Jayden is a very energetic boy. He demonstrates an interest in many activities, but in natural settings he is often observed to dart from one activity to another rather than sustaining engagement. During formal assessment, he rarely sustains attention for more than a few minutes, and the results reported are indicative of this difficulty with sustained attention.

Questions for Reflection:

1. How might you adjust the assessment process to better document Jayden's abilities?
2. What measures might you use to make sure the assessment is thorough and representative of Jayden's development?

VIGNETTE   Joshua

Joshua is trying to complete a puzzle and he makes the same mistake several times in a row, without altering his strategy, finally using force to just try to shove the piece in. His teacher documented what she had observed regarding his problem-solving skills.

Questions for Reflection:

1. What thoughts do you have concerning materials that can be prepared or used with Joshua?
2. What can you suggest to the teacher to help her to mediate the situation of Joshua being "stuck" on his strategy to complete the puzzle?

VIGNETTE   Jessica

Jessica is having difficulty completing a puzzle but tries a variety of strategies along the way. There is some evidence that she has broader problem-solving skills. Her teacher and parent have observed, reflected on, and documented her difficulties as well as her strengths. They can use the information to better understand and scaffold Jessica's process. Sometimes providing some verbal guidance helps. If someone intervenes before she has had an opportunity to demonstrate her own process, the assessment of the actual dynamic of her learning strategies may be obscured. Thus, teachers may choose not to intervene with a child until they have determined how a child performs on his or her own.

Questions for Reflection:

Reading about Joshua and Jessica presents you with some information about two children experiencing challenges related to completing puzzles.

1. What are the differences between the two children and the learning strategies they employ?
2. What, if any, other differences can be seen in these vignettes?

PLANNING LEARNING EXPERIENCES

Creating developmentally appropriate learning experiences for young children with and without disabilities requires attention to many details: content standards, appropriate materials, environmental arrangements, and the individual children and their learning needs.

In the areas of math and science, content standards like the ones that follow (CT State Department of Education Math Standards—Pre-K and K) are stated to help focus the teacher on developmentally appropriate curriculum and learning opportunities for children.

Review the standards and then think about classroom scenarios in which these standards might be addressed. As you consider this task, think about whether the learning scenarios would be created through special lesson plans or whether opportunities would present during the course of an average day at school. Table 9.6 presents math standards from a state in the northeast United States.

TABLE 9.6   Connecticut State Department of Education Math Standards

Students Should...	Pre-K	Kindergarten
1.1 Understand and describe patterns and functional relationships.	a. Sort and classify objects by an attribute. b. Describe and extend patterns using the attributes of various objects.	a. Sort and classify objects using attributes. b. Identify a pattern and describe the rule using the physical attributes or position of objects in a sequence.
1.2 Represent and analyze quantitative relationships in a variety of ways.		
1.3 Use operations, properties and algebraic symbols to determine equivalence and solve problems.		
2.1 Understand that a variety of numerical representations can be used to describe quantitative relationships.	a. Use numbers to count, order, and compare. b. Share equal parts of a whole object.	a. Use numbers to count, order, compare, label, locate, and measure. b. Share equal parts of an object. c. Share a set of objects that is divided into groups with equal amounts.
2.2 Use numbers and their properties to compute flexibly and fluently and to reasonably estimate measures and quantities.	c. Count, adding one more to the previous amount.	a. Count, adding one more to the previous number and group and count by ones and tens.
3.1 Use properties and characteristics of two- and three-dimensional shapes and geometric theorems to describe relationships, communicate ideas and solve problems.	a. Identify and sort shapes and solids by physical characteristics.	a. Identify and sort shapes and solids by physical characteristics.
3.2 Use spatial reasoning, location, and geometric relationships to solve problems.	a. Use positional language to describe location, direction, and position of objects.	a. Use positional language to describe location, direction, and position of objects.
3.3 Develop and apply units, systems, formulas, and appropriate tools to estimate and measure.	a. Sequence events during a limited time period. b. Use nonstandard units to estimate measures of length, area, and capacity.	a. Use calendars and clocks to measure and record time. b. Use nonstandard units to estimate measures of length, area, temperature, weight, and capacity.

4.1 Collect, organize, and display data using appropriate statistical and graphical methods.	a. Make comparisons from information displayed in real graphs.	a. Visualize information and make comparisons about information displayed in real and picture graphs.
4.2 Analyze data sets to form hypotheses and make predictions.		a. Extend different types of patterns and make predictions.
4.3 Understand and apply basic concepts of probability.	a. Determine when events are likely to happen again.	a. Observe the frequency of real-world events and identify the likelihood of future events.

State Framework	Grade-Level Expectations

Properties of Matter

K.1—Objects have properties that can be observed and used to describe similarities and differences.

K.1.a. Some properties can be observed with the senses, and others can be discovered by using simple tools or tests.	1. Match each of the five senses with its associated body part and the kind of information it perceives. 2. Make scientific observations using the five senses, and distinguish between an object's observable properties and its name or its uses. 3. Classify organisms or objects by one and two observable properties, and explain the rule used for sorting (e.g., size, color, shape, texture, or flexibility). 4. Use simple tools and nonstandard units to estimate and measure properties such as heaviness, magnetic attraction and float/sink. 5. Compare the observable properties of different materials from which objects are made (e.g., wood, plastic, metal, cloth, and paper). 6. Count, order, and sort objects by their observable properties.

Heredity and Evolution

K.2—Many different kinds of living things inhabit the Earth.

K.2.a. Living things have certain characteristics that distinguish them from nonliving things, including growth, movement, reproduction, and response to stimuli.	1. Use the senses to make observations of characteristics and behaviors of living and nonliving things. 2. Infer from observations that living things need air, food, water, shelter, and space to stay alive. 3. Compare and contrast living things, which grow and can make a new living thing like itself, with nonliving things, which do not grow or reproduce. 4. Give examples of living things and nonliving things. 5. Make observations and distinguish between the characteristics of plants and animals. 6. Match parents with their offspring (both plants and animals) to show that offspring are similar, but not identical, to their parents and to one another.

Energy in the Earth's Systems

K.3—Weather conditions vary daily and seasonally.

K.3.a. Daily and seasonal weather conditions affect what we do, what we wear, and how we feel.	1. Use the senses and simple measuring tools to estimate and record weather data and represent it in bar graphs. 2. Analyze weather data collected over time (during the day, from day to day, and from season to season) to identify patterns and make predictions. 3. Observe, compare and contrast cloud shapes, sizes and colors, and relate the appearance of clouds to fair weather or precipitation. 4. Summarize ways that weather influences humans, other animals, and plants. 5. Make judgments about appropriate clothing and activities based on weather conditions.

Science and Technology in Society

K.4—Some objects are natural, while others have been designed and made by people to improve the quality of life.

This content standard is an application of the concepts in content standard K.1 and should be integrated into the same unit.

K.4.a. Humans select both natural and man-made materials to build shelters based on local climate conditions, properties of the materials, and their availability in the environment.	1. Conduct simple tests to determine properties that make different materials useful for making roofs, windows, walls and floors (e.g., waterproof, transparent, strong). 2. Seek information in books, magazines, and pictures that describes materials used to build shelters by people in different regions of the world. 3. Compare and contrast the materials used by humans and animals to build shelters.

From: Connecticut State Department of Education http://www.sde.ct.gov/sde/site/default.asp retrieved on 11/24/09

Children learn about math and science through motivating activities like cooking.

Math and Science Activities

Small Group Activity

Cooking—Apple Muffins

Pre-K or Kindergarten

Objectives:	Children will participate in the process of making apple muffins.
	Children will demonstrate an understanding of concept of quantity by measuring ingredients.
	Children will use vocabulary such as "half," "quarter," "chop," "stir," "mix."
	Children will engage in conversation about where apples come from (as an extension of field trip.)
Materials:	Apples (from previous field trip)
	Ingredients (may vary depending on food allergies): eggs, flour, butter, salt, muffin tins, mixing bowls, mixing spoons, measuring spoons, and measuring cups
Initiation:	Teacher introduces activity and asks questions—"What do we need to do?" etc.
Procedure:	Sequence of steps, children combining ingredients and stirring. Discussion regarding changes in consistency of dough, etc.
Closure:	Questioning strategies to review sequence of what had been done.

Questions for Reflection:	According to the charts containing math and science standards above, what standards might be addressed through this activity with the objectives as stated?

Think about children with differing disabilities, and identify possible modifications to this activity so that these children may participate in and learn from the activity.

FIGURE 9.1   Differentiated Instruction

What follows is a selection of activity and lesson plans designed for this age group. Taking the time to analyze and discuss these ideas allows for an opportunity to think about meeting the needs of individual children in the classroom, regardless of the level of ability. Several of these are examples of integrated curriculum. This context is focusing explicitly on math and science but also acknowledges how language and motor skills are addressed. Figure 9.1 provides an example of an activity plan.

SUPPORT FOR POSITIVE OUTCOMES

Many strategies may be helpful in supporting positive cognitive outcomes for children with various forms of challenges. Some of these may also be helpful in other domains. Figure 9.2 provides an overview of specific strategies that may be helpful and the rationale for making a selection.

Related Activities

One very effective way to enhance understanding and reinforce concepts is to design activities that relate to each other. Creating common themes increases the likelihood

Strategies	Rationale
Environment—predictable, structured, and organized	Environments that are structured in meaningful ways provide support and guidance to children by creating a context in which children can safely and meaningfully be engaged.
Time—More or less, predictable schedule, routines	When children are slower, they may need more time. When they have trouble sustaining attention, they may need less time.
Materials	Manipulatives and objects may help children understand concepts. Realistic objects may help children who have difficulty with symbolic function.
Provision of assistance and scaffolding (could include task analysis and reverse chaining)	A continuum of support based on individual children's characteristics ensures that there is a good match between the assistance and what is actually needed.
Verbal narration and guidance	Talking through a process assists children in developing mental concepts.
Questioning strategies	Focused questions help engage children and guide them through inquiry.
Peer-mediated strategies	Peers can serve as positive models as well as increase motivation to children with developmental challenges.
Multi-level activities	When activities are designed in ways that appeal to a range of developmental levels, they are relevant to all children.
Adjustment of objectives and differentiation	If original objectives for an activity are not a good match for all children, modified objectives can be used.
"Chunking" complex activities into more manageable units	A task may be overwhelming to a child when considered as a whole. Working on smaller aspects of a project without losing sight of the big picture can make it more possible for all children to participate and complete.

FIGURE 9.2   What Works: Possible Strategies

that children will develop comprehensive concepts and deeper levels of understanding. Figure 9.3 provides a potential follow-up activity regarding cooking. It should be evident that certain concepts can be extended through this activity.

Questions for Reflection:

1. According to the charts containing math and science standards above, what standards might be addressed through this activity with the objectives as stated? Are there any other areas of content standards that might be addressed through this activity?
2. Is this an activity that can accommodate all children regardless of ability? If modifications need to be made, what might they be?

Small Group Activity

Cookbook

Pre-K or Kindergarten

Objectives: Children will use words and pictures to describe the process of making apple muffins.

Children will articulate sequence of steps using words such as "first," "next," "last."

Children will use illustrations and letter/word symbols as part of their cookbooks.

Materials: Should this be Paper for writing and drawing utensils.

Initiation: Teacher will guide introductory discussion.

Teacher shares directions regarding children's opportunity to create their own books.

Review of sequence of activities (field trip, making muffins, eating muffins, etc.)

Procedure: Children will create their own books, given materials and scaffolding from teacher. Support will vary depending on individual needs.

Closure: Teachers and children will "read" books together.

Assessment: Teacher observation and anecdotal notes; work samples.

FIGURE 9.3 Differentiated Instruction

Figure 9.4 shows a more in-depth lesson plan that makes reference to the Connecticut State Department of Education Preschool Frameworks that are organized into developmental domains rather than content areas. Figure 9.4 is an example of an activity plan with differentiated instruction.

REFLECTION

Creating classrooms that are conducive to high-quality concept development involves a focus on the structure of classrooms and the process through which teachers scaffold children's experiences. Small group activities need to be appreciated and encouraged. Teachers should consider a range of factors in their reflection regarding cognitive development. They need to consider how children are thinking about their experiences and need to engage them in meaningful discussions that will help them formulate concepts based on what they are doing. When teachers reflect, they may be more likely to guide children to wonder about what is happening.

Teachers can address some of the problems of struggling learners, as well as normal differences in skill levels and developmental levels, through the use of adaptations or accommodations (Ebeling, Deschenes, & Sprague, 1994), many of which can be incorporated into regular classroom instruction. Activities that provide opportunities for children to use a variety of learning styles can increase the likelihood that more children will understand the new concept or skill being presented. Here are some approaches based on Howard Gardner's theory of multiple intelligences that complement different strengths:

Spatial: Using visual clues

Linguistic: Reading word problems

Student Teacher: Alyssa Civiello

Grade Level: Preschool

Date of lesson: 3/12/10

Institution: Chapel Elementary School

Length of lesson: 50 minutes

Content Standards: Identify one or two primary local, state, **or** national curricular standards that this lesson is designed to help students attain. How will the learning tasks lead students to attain the identified standards?

CT SDE Preschool Framework, COG 5: Compares and orders events and objects. Children will make simple comparisons.

CT SDE Preschool Framework, COG 8: Uses complex sentences and vocabulary to describe ideas and experiences.

Learner Background: Describe the students' prior knowledge or skill related to the learning objective(s) and the content of this lesson, using data from pre-assessment as appropriate. How did the students' previous performance in this content area or skill impact your planning for this lesson?

Students have ordered by size previously during the school year.

Students have obtained varying levels of performance in ordering by size.

Student Learning Objective(s): Identify specific and measurable learning objectives for this lesson.

Children accurately arrange three to five objects in order by size.

Children understand and verbally make comparisons.

Children use complex sentences and vocabulary to describe ideas and experiences.

Assessment: How will you ask students to demonstrate mastery of the student learning objective(s)? Attach a copy of any assessment materials you will use, along with assessment criteria.

Students will individually order group of objects from the largest to smallest.

Students will verbally compare group of objects.

Teacher will use observational data collection and anecdotal records for assessment.

Materials/Resources: List the materials you will use in each learning activity, including any technological resources.

Set of three, four, and five magnetic objects, graduated in size

Magnetic white board

Rectangular board

Five graduated geometric shapes

Graded challenges

Rectangular board showing outlines of geometric shapes in graduated sizes, five identical graduated shapes

Tray, divided into five sections

Set of five objects, graduated sizes

Learning Activities:

Identify the instructional grouping (whole class, small groups, pairs, individuals) you will use in each lesson segment, and approximate time frames for each.

FIGURE 9.4

Initiation: Briefly describe how you will initiate the lesson. (Set expectations for learning; articulate to learners what they will be doing and learning in this lesson, how they will demonstrate learning, and why this is important.)

Read book, *Sizes*, with large group

*Position A. in close proximity during group activity.

*Provide A. with object to hold during group activity.

Discuss ordering by size.

Model ordering by size from the largest to smallest using magnetic white board and set of magnetic shapes/animals

*Maintain eye contact.

*Use gentle touch to allow A. to reconnect, refocus.

Guided Practice—Ask for volunteers to demonstrate ordering by size.

Check for understanding.

*Get A.'s attention before asking question.

> **Ask questions:**
> **Which shape/object is the largest?**
> **Which shape/object is the smallest?**

Introduce center materials.

*Provide A. with clear rules and expectations for group/center activities.

Model ordering using rectangular board/tray.

Facilitate participation in teacher-led group activity.

*Keep directed activity periods short.

Initiation—10 minutes.

Lesson Development: Describe how you will develop the lesson, what you will do to model or guide practice, and the learning activities students will be engaged in order to gain the key knowledge and skills identified in the student learning objective(s).

*Pair A. with pro-social, motivated peer during center activity.

*Provide A. with clear rules and expectations for group/center activities.

Request children to begin with the most simple skill (ordering five geometric objects from the largest to smallest).

Implement graded challenges if necessary.

By ordering objects by size, children will learn to compare objects.

Questions:

> **I wonder if now you are able to order from the smallest to largest.**
> **Which object is the largest/smallest?**
> **Which object is larger than _____?**
> **Which object is smaller than _____?**

Observe children's ordering.

Assess mastery of learning objectives using anecdotal records.

Closure: Briefly describe how you will close the lesson and help students understand the purpose of the lesson. (Interact with learners to elicit evidence of student understanding of purpose(s) for learning and mastery of objectives.)

FIGURE 9.4 *(Continued)*

Back to large group

*Position A. in close proximity during group activity.

Request three to five students to serve as models.

*Maintain eye contact.

*Use gentle touch to allow A. to reconnect and refocus.

Request group to order three to five students from the largest to smallest.

*Get A.'s attention before asking question.

Ask children, "I wonder if we could order now from smallest to largest?"

*Connect group/center activities to A's areas of interest.

Use complex sentences to express comparison (e.g., _____ is the largest; _____ is larger than _____ ; _____ is smaller than _____ .)

*Keep directed activity periods short.

Closure—10 minutes

<u>**Individuals Needing Differentiated Instruction:**</u> Describe one to three students with learning differences. These students may be special or general education students and need not be the same students for each lesson. Students may represent a range of ability and/or achievement levels, including students with IEPs, gifted and talented students, struggling learners, and English language learners.

Note: Differentiated instruction may not be necessary in every lesson. However, over the course of the student teaching placement, it is expected that each student teacher will demonstrate the ability to differentiate instruction in order to meet the needs of students with learning differences.

Which students do you anticipate may struggle with the content/learning objectives of this lesson?

Student name	Evidence that the student needs differentiated instruction	How will you differentiate instruction **in this lesson** to support student learning?
A.	1. Difficulty sustaining focus 2. Difficulty listening 3. Difficulty completing tasks 4. Easily bored	Position A. in close proximity during group activity. Get A.'s attention before asking question. Maintain eye contact. Use gentle touch to allow A. to reconnect and refocus. Provide A. with object to hold during group activity. Pair A. with pro-social, motivated peer during center activity. Connect group/center activities to A's areas of interest. Provide A. with clear rules and expectations for group/center activities. Keep directed activity periods short.

FIGURE 9.4 *(Continued)*

Logical-mathematical: Creating and solving equations

Kinesthetic: Exploring tactile models

Musical: Creating auditory patterns

Interpersonal: Sharing strategies

Intrapersonal: Journal writing (King & Parker, 2001)

The need to develop and implement reflective skills in your classroom will always remain a critical variable in your teaching practice. Here is a way to jumpstart your thinking so that you will be able to help yourself to develop answers to your questions about your own practice as well as questions about individual children in your classroom:

Personal Inventory

- How do you support children's cognitive development?
- What sorts of questions do you use?
- Please provide examples.
- How do you encourage children to wonder about what is happening?
- When children are expressing frustration regarding a cognitive process, what do you do? How do you scaffold?

Questions for Reflection:

1. How can the teacher use "discussion and activities that encourage analysis and reasoning"?
2. How can the teacher "provide opportunities for students to be creative and/or generate their own ideas and products"?
3. How can the teacher "consistently link concepts and activities to one another and to previous learning"?
4. How can the teacher "consistently relate concepts to the students' actual lives"?

Source: From: Pianta, LaParo & Hamre (2008). Classroom Assessment Scoring System. pp. 67–68

Summary

This chapter has reviewed some key issues as they relate to math, science, and problem-solving activities for young children. Examples have been shared that illustrate how complex issues may be addressed to develop and implement strategies for children with a variety of challenges affecting cognition and how those may be integrated into developmentally appropriate activities.

Key Terms

Activities of daily living (ADL)
Multiple intelligence theory

Scaffolding

Zone of proximal development

Children's Books

CURIOSITY

Polly Hopper's Pouch by Louise Bonnett-Rampersaud
Red, Red, Red by Valeri Gorbach

A Penguin Story by Antionette Portis
Curious George: Are You Curious? by H. A. Ray

Web sites

National Council of Teachers of Mathematics
http://standards.nctm.org/
"The Pizza Project" (To address learning standards)
http://www.journal.naeyc.org/btj/200301/
PizzaProjectStandardsChart.pdf

Online Math Resources
http://www.journal.naeyc.org/btj/200301/
onlinemath.asp

References

Bloom, B. et al (1956). *Taxonomy of educational objectives.* Boston: Allyn & Bacon.

Bronfenbrenner, U. (1979). *The ecology of human development.* Cambridge, MA: Harvard University Press.

Cartledge, G., Gardner, R., & Ford, D. Y. (2009). *Diverse learners with exceptionalities.* Upper Saddle River, NJ: Merrill/Pearson Education.

Chaille, C. (2008). *Constructivism across the curriculum in early childhood classrooms.* Boston: Allyn & Bacon/Pearson Education.

Chalufour, I. & Worth, K. (2003. *Discovering nature together.* St. Paul, MN: Redleaf Press.

Charlesworth, R. & Lind, K. (1995). *Math and science for young children* (2nd ed.). Albany, New York: Delmar.

Clements, D. H., Sarama, J., & DiBiase, A. (Eds.). (2004). *Engaging young children in mathematics: Standards for early childhood mathematics education.*

Copley, J. (2000). *The young child and mathematics.* Washington, DC: National Council of Teachers of Mathematics/National Association for the Education of Young Children.

Division for Early Childhood, Council for Exceptional Children. (2007). *Promoting positive outcomes for children with disabilities: Recommendations for curriculum, assessment, and program evaluation.* Missoula, MT: Author.

Ebeling, D. G., Deschenes, C., & Sprague, J. (1994). *Adapting curriculum and instruction in inclusive classrooms: Staff development kit.* Bloomington, IN: Institute for the Study of Developmental Disabilities.

Eliason, C., & Jenkins, L. (2008). *A practical guide to early childhood curriculum.* Upper Saddle River, NJ: Merrill/Pearson Education.

Epstein, A. S. (2007). *The intentional teacher.* Washington, DC: National Association for the Education of Young Children.

Farran, D. (2001). Critical periods and early intervention. In D. Bailey, J. Bruer, F. Symons, & J. Lichtman (Eds.), *Critical thinking about critical periods* (pp. 233–266). Baltimore: Paul H. Brookes.

Gardner, H. (2000). *The disciplined mind.* New York: Penguin Books.

Greenes, C. E., Ginsburg, H. P., & Balfanz, R. (2004). Big math for little kids. *Early Childhood Research Quarterly, 19,* 159–166.

Grisham-Brown, J., Hemmeter, M. L., & Pretti-Frontzcak, K. (2005). *Blended practices for teaching young children in inclusive settings.* Baltimore: Paul H. Brookes.

Harris, K., & Gleim, L. (2008). The light fantastic: Making learning visible for all children through the project approach. *Young Exceptional Children, 11*(3), 27–40.

Henderson, A., Gerson, S., & Woodard, A. (2008). The birth of social intelligence. *Zero to Three, 28*(5), 13–20.

Hyson, M. (Ed.). (2003). *Preparing early childhood professionals: NAEYC's standards for programs.*

Washington, DC: National Association for the Education of Young Children.

Hyson, M. (2008). *Enthusiastic and engaged learners.* New York: Teacher's College Press/National Association for the Education of Young Children.

Hyun, E. (2006). *Teachable moments: Re-conceptualizing curricula understandings.* New York: Peter Lang Publishing Co.

Katz, L. & Chard, S. (2000). *Engaging children's minds.* New York: Ablex Publishing.

King, M., & Parker, C. (2001). *A galaxy of mathematics strategies and accommodations.* city, FL: University of Florida Instructional Technology Resource Center. Retrieved from www.itrc.ucf.edu/other/fdlrs2001/workshops/math/ppt/mathintro.pdf.

Milbourne, S. A., & Campbell, P. H. (2007). *CARA's Kit: Creating adaptations for routines and activities.* Philadelphia: Child and Family Studies Research Programs, Thomas Jefferson University.

Miller, G. A. (1956). The magical number seven, plus or minus two: Some limits on our capacity for processing information. *Psychological Review, 63,* 81–97.

Montessori, M. (1912/1964). *The Montessori method.* New York: Schocken Books.

National Council of Teachers of Mathematics. (2006). *Curriculum focal points for prekindergarten through grade 8 mathematics: A quest for coherence.* Washington, DC: NCTM (National Council of Teachers of Mathematics).

Notari-Syverson, A., & Sadler, F. (2008). Math is for everyone: Strategies for supporting early mathematical competencies in young children. *Young Exceptional Children, 11*(3), 2–16.

Piaget, J. (1952). *The origins of intelligence.* New York: International University Press.

Pianta, R., LaParo, K., & Hamre, B. (2008). *Classroom assessment scoring system.* Baltimore: Paul H. Brookes.

Pretti-Frontzcak, K., & Bricker, D. (2004). *An activity based approach to early intervention* (3rd ed.). Baltimore: Paul H. Brookes.

Renzulli, J., & Reis, S. (Eds.). (2004). *Identification of students for gifted and talented programs.* Corwin Press.

Rosen, D., & Hoffman, J. (2009). Integrating concrete and virtual manipulatives in early childhood mathematics. *Young Children, 64*(3), 26–33.

Schickedanz, J. (2008). *Increasing the power of instruction.* Washington, DC: National Association for the Education of Young Children.

Shonkoff, J., & Phillips, D. (2000). *From neurons to neighborhoods.* Washington, DC: National Academy Press.

Shore, R. (1997). *Rethinking the brain.* New York: Families and Work Institute.

Skinner, B. F. (1948). *Walden two.* New York: MacMillan.

Stormont, M. (2007). *Fostering resilience in young children at risk for failure.* Upper Saddle River, NJ: Merrill/Pearson Education.

Vygotsky, L. (1978). *Mind in society* (M. Cole, Trans.). Cambridge, MA: Harvard University Press.

Watson, A. & McCathren, R. (2009). Including children with special needs: Are you and your early childhood program ready? *Young Children. 64*(2), 20–26.

Wein, C. (Ed.). (2008). *Emergent curriculum in the primary classroom: Interpreting the Reggio Emilia approach in the schools.* New York: Teachers College Press.

West, M. (2007). Problem solving: A sensible approach to children's science and social studies learning and beyond. *Young Children, 62*(5), 34–41.

Wright Edelman, M. (1992). *The measure of our success.* Boston: Beacon Press.

Zigler, E., & Styfco, S. J. (2004). *The Head Start debates.* Baltimore: Paul H. Brookes.

Resources

National Council of Teachers of Mathematics (NCTM)

Principles for School Mathematics

Equity:

Excellence in mathematics education requires equally high expectations and strong support for all students.

Curriculum:

A curriculum is more than a collection of activities; it must be coherent, focused on important mathematics, and well articulated across the grades.

Teaching:

Effective mathematics teaching requires understanding of what students know and need to learn and then challenging and supporting them to learn it well.

Learning:

Students must learn mathematics with understanding, actively building new knowledge from experience and prior knowledge.

Assessment:

Assessment should support the learning of important mathematics and furnish useful information to both teachers and students.

Technology:

Technology is essential to teaching and learning mathematics; it influences the mathematics that is taught and enhances students' learning.

Within the classroom:

Strategies:

To achieve high-quality mathematics education for 3- to 6-year-old children, teachers and other key professionals should enhance children's natural interest in mathematics and their disposition to use it to make sense of their physical and social worlds.

Build on children's experience and knowledge, including their family, linguistic, cultural, and community backgrounds; their individual approaches to learning; and their informal knowledge.

Base mathematics curriculum and teaching practices on knowledge of young children's cognitive, linguistic, physical, and social-emotional development.

Use curriculum and teaching practices that strengthen children's problem-solving and reasoning processes as well as representing, communicating, and connecting mathematical ideas.

Ensure that the curriculum is coherent and compatible with known relationships and sequences of important mathematical ideas.

Provide for children's deep and sustained interaction with key mathematical ideas.

Integrate mathematics with other activities and other activities with mathematics.

Provide ample time, materials, and teacher support for children to engage in play, a context in which they explore and manipulate mathematical ideas with keen interest.

Actively introduce mathematical concepts, methods, and language through a range of appropriate experiences and teaching strategies.

Support children's learning by thoughtfully and continually assessing all children's mathematical knowledge, skills, and strategies.

From National Council of Teachers of Mathematics. http://standards.nctm.org/retrieved on 11/25/09

Chapter 10

Professionalism

Becoming a Lifelong Learner and Organizing Community Resources

OBJECTIVES

After reading this chapter, students will:

- Reflect on the value of lifelong learning;
- Identify key features of professionalism, as they relate to standards and inclusive practices;
- Integrate concepts regarding the value of reflection into their own professional development;
- Build confidence through constructive reflection;
- Increase resourcefulness by identifying community resources that are helpful in sustaining professionalism through ongoing professional development; and
- Actively engage in an inventory of professional skills.

LIFELONG LEARNING

Why Is a Commitment to Lifelong Learning Important in the Field of Education?

Lifelong learning is truly a worldview, and is applicable to all areas of specialization. The field of early childhood special education with a focus on inclusion is in the midst of a major paradigm shift that involves attitudes, governance, and systems management, as well as daily practices in classrooms (Sandall, Hemmeter, Smith, & McLean, 2005). As with transformations regarding civil rights, the actual changes may take many years, given the extent to which discrimination and exclusion were previously established practices.

Decision to Change

The decision to change may be considered the first step on the course of a lifelong journey. Approaching the end of this book, it is evident that the reflective process will be ongoing as you continue your professional development. Thus, in the final discussions of professionalism, it is understood that this is a means to an end, as well as an outcome.

Why Is Commitment to Lifelong Learning Especially Important in the Field of Inclusive Early Childhood Special Education?

Lifelong learning is especially important in the field of early childhood special education because there are many changes every year regarding laws, best practice, and policies. In addition, there are advances in research that may be related to many types of complex conditions, which increases the understanding of many syndromes. Its relevance to a final chapter relates to the commitment to ongoing professional development.

Questions for Reflection:

1. Through your reflection, please note any aspects of working with families that may present challenges to you regarding belief systems or lifestyle. What strategies and resources might you use to address these issues?
2. How will you monitor your own progress as you work with families and children?
3. What record-keeping strategies will be especially useful to you?

4. How will you express your empathy and support to families?
5. What roles have you played in teams?
6. Please describe your interactive style as it relates to the commitment to ongoing professional development.

No matter how much any individual knows at a given time about early childhood special education, new changes will be emerging that require professionals to be willing to increase their knowledge base. Thus, there is a need to apply skills to continue to gain and use new information as it emerges (Buysse & Wesley, 2006).

Structures for Change

When professionals focus on inclusion, a commitment to lifelong learning is also a commitment to change. It is a dedication to identifying recommended practices with adjustments as necessary and appropriate. This also implies a willingness to create and use structures for change (Catlett, 2009; Guralnick, 2001). Such structures may involve regularly scheduled reviews of progress as well as renewal of perspectives regarding outcomes. Attaining and sustaining a vision of shared goals, what teachers value, and how they are proceeding, is part of any process of change. At the start, teachers focus on developing a collective sense of direction. As teachers proceed, they collaborate and mutually make sure all are staying on course. Inherent in this process is the confidence and courage to be honest about what teachers may need to improve.

PROFESSIONALISM

With the increasing acceptance of young children with disabilities into inclusive classrooms, major professional organizations are redefining professionalism based on the need to address a full range of developmental ability. For example, the National Association for the Education of Young Children (NAEYC) identifies addressing atypical development as a core criteria for teachers' and assistant teachers' standards of competence (Copple & Bredekamp, 2009; Hyson, 2003). The Division of Early Childhood, Council for Exceptional Children (DEC/CEC) identifies an understanding of the continuum of development as an essential standard, as well as an ability to implement developmentally appropriate practices (Sandall et al., 2005). Organizations routinely refer to providing appropriate services for *all* children. This means that professionalism includes broadening one's expertise so it is not specific to typical or atypical development. It encompasses the full range of both. As progress is made toward more inclusive systems, leaders in early childhood and special education continue to work together to define and clarify shared responsibilities as well as priorities (Copple & Bredekamp, 2008, 2009). The joint position statement on inclusion published by NAEYC and DEC can be a guide (2009).

Knowledge and Skills

The term "professionalism" evokes a certain generic meaning, across different areas of specialization. Certainly part of the connotation includes quality, regardless of area of focus. Yet there are ways in which there may be specific traits of professionalism associated with certain types of work. In early childhood, professionalism includes being child and family centered, implementing developmentally appropriate activities, and incorporating anti-bias curriculum for a multicultural world (Derman-Sparks, 1989; Derman-Sparks & Edwards-Olsen, 2010; Trawick-Smith, 2008). All of these would also be true for early childhood special education (Chandler & Loncola 2008). There are, however, additional qualities that are essential to professionalism in inclusive early childhood special education (Stayton, Miller, & Dinnebeil, 2003). Such attributes include respect for confidentiality, excellent communication skills, knowledge of the laws, knowledge of protocol and systems, accountability, and knowledge about children's conditions.

Professional Judgment and Problem Solving

Important qualities also include positive dispositions, efficient organization, and an ability to keep up with paperwork. This book has primarily focused on the practical application of specific intervention strategies and the process through which professionals use their judgment and problem-solving skills constructively and collectively to make positive decisions related to curriculum and programs for young children with disabilities. It is acknowledged that while teachers have an abundant repertoire of effective strategies available to them, their knowledge and skills will no doubt continue to be enhanced, given inevitable future change and progress.

Continuing Change

One example of a specific area that will certainly change is assistive technology. Professionals need to be prepared to continue to develop knowledge and skills as time goes by. This is true for many other areas as well, such as the laws and regulations affecting systems (Turnbull, Turnbull, & Wehmeyer, 2007).

Professional Dispositions

In early childhood special education, dispositions include receptivity to listening to others' perspectives, being nonjudgmental, and being exceptionally caring. Dispositions include acceptance of individual differences, even when those differences involve disabilities. Willingness to be responsible, an ability to address difficult situations without being defensive or embarrassed, and expressing support for children and families, are all qualities that manifest professionalism (Jalongo & Isenberg, 2008). It is especially important that teachers of young children with challenges not take it personally when children are experiencing difficulty such as disruptive behavior.

Generalization and Individualization

Professionals working with young children who have disabilities must be able to apply general principles and also adjust their styles to the individual needs of each child. They must be able to persist in efforts, demonstrating a faith in each child's ability to learn, even when children's progress may be slower than most, or when their ways of learning differ significantly from those that are generally expected. When all teachers are prepared to teach all children, this ability to adjust teaching strategies in the context of teamwork is an indicator of professionalism.

Indicators and Marking Progress

Teachers frequently state that seeing a child's progress is one of the greatest motivators. Certainly this is true. When teaching young children with disabilities, however, teachers may need to try several evidence-based strategies before they find those which are most effective (Buysse & Wesley, 2006; La Rocque & Darling, 2008; McWilliam & Casey, 2008). As professionals, teachers must not be dependent on the easy success of children for their own sense of confidence. They must be prepared to be devoted to young children, even when children find everyday accomplishments more difficult. When a strategy is working, teachers must acknowledge the success. Sometimes this also takes the form of authentic celebration and positive feedback to the child.

Dispositions and Reading Cues

Dispositions and attitudes play a paramount role in effective inclusion. If teachers implement all the best techniques and methods without a high level of acceptance and belief in the capability of children, their efforts will be sabotaged by the implicit messages communicated in a myriad of nonverbal. cues or signals, ranging from tone of voice to lack of physical proximity. The use of video for guided reflection can be very helpful in providing perspectives on dispositions. Sometimes if a teacher is tentative he or she may not realize the effects of inadvertent nonverbal cues until they can observe themselves, and reflect on their own performance (Pianta, La Paro, & Hamre, (2007).

Acknowledgment of Issues

In most situations if there is an issue with an early childhood educator's disposition a good place to begin change is by "owning" the issue. It is unlikely that malice is involved, but there are times when professionals have not wholeheartedly accepted the concept of inclusion as a viable option, and/or have not fully acknowledged their own ability to implement the methods associated with the integration of children with a range of developmental challenges in their own classroom. All teachers may benefit from constructive feedback from someone who has observed them in action. This could come from a peer or a supervisor. Reflective supervision is now well-established in the field of early childhood and special education (Caruso & Fawcett, 1999; Eggbeer, Mann, & Seibel, 2007). It helps to work as part of a healthy, cooperative team so if teachers are missing an attribute in their own reflection, they are open to someone else pointing it out. For instance, when a person frequently says, "You guys," they may be attempting to establish rapport or may not even realize they are saying it. Likewise, it is possible to say, "Good job!" hundreds of times in a day without being aware of the semiautomatic form of feedback. Constructive feedback from others can help integrate perspectives into one's own reflection.

Commitment to Problem Solving for Differentiated Instruction

Teachers of children with exceptionalities view their role in terms of figuring out how to reach children who learn in ways that are not typical. This is a major, though potentially unacknowledged, feature. It is part of the function of the teacher to adapt, differentiate, and implement universal design in order to support the learning process of each child. Thus, when a child has difficulty, it is the job of the team and teachers to problem-solve and try to figure out a more effective method. This does not mean the child has no responsibility in his or her own learning, but there are major implications for the responsibility of teachers. In some settings, isolation may be a factor that needs to be addressed. Community-based programs may not have easy access to special services unless they have established networks with local education agencies (LEAs). Professionals who are working within teams in which there are extremely limited supports for special services may need to become proactive and take initiative to reach out to supports in other agencies.

ACTIVE ENGAGEMENT IN ONGOING PROFESSIONAL DEVELOPMENT

While this text has addressed general methods, trends, and perspectives, its distinctive feature is the active involvement of you, the reader, in a process of reflection.

Personal/Professional Inventory Revisited

It is time now for you to revisit your initial reflections in light of what you have learned during your journey. While engaged in this process you will find it helpful to review your journal, highlighting key insights, observations, and transformations. You will also find it helpful to review your initial goals and objectives, based on your earlier reflections on your own strengths, needs, and style. In considering how you have grown and changed, it is important for you to be specific with yourself about your own professional development. A pat on the back helps, but noticing specific detail and being explicit with your own feedback to yourself also helps. Specific feedback from others can also be integrated. What do you think has been significant? This might involve specific skills you have mastered, or it may relate to changes of attitude or thinking. You may have based your previous worldview on certain unacknowledged assumptions about people and systems, and now you are able to reframe those assumptions and take action in ways you had not formerly considered. You may have previously been intimidated or cautious about your interactions with young children with disabilities, doubting your own ability to address their unique needs. If this was the case, hopefully you have had the opportunity to transform your own perceptions regarding what is possible.

Commitment to Inclusion

The importance of commitment to inclusion has been a theme throughout this book. This must be an ongoing commitment for individuals as well as teams. Given the enormity of changes regarding exceptionality in terms of social justice and advocacy for full accessibility, there is progress in the field though the work is far from done. As with the civil rights movement, there have been changes in laws and significant changes in attitude, but the need remains for each of us as individuals and members of groups, to collectively sustain commitment to change (Copple & Bredekamp, 2008, 2009; LaRocque & Darling, 2008). Early childhood professionals must accept the responsibility of continuing to monitor themselves, being willing to adjust as needed. The DEC/NAEYC joint position statement on inclusion (2009) articulates the priorities during this transformation. Change can be stressful and challenging under the best of circumstances. When change involves reversing deeply embedded patterns of discrimination, it requires a sustained effort and commitment to creating more positive options (Sandall et al., 2005).

Advocacy

Advocates for those with disabilities, including those who have challenging conditions, would surely not wish for pity, condescension, or special favors. Full acceptance and inclusion implies the removal of long-established barriers in systems, laws, practices, and attitudes. It involves a sustained willingness to see and experience situations from others' perspectives, while questioning one's own assumptions. This may at times be difficult, but the rewards are remarkable (LaRocco & Bruns, 2005). The integrity and sureness that perfection is not necessary, but consideration and acceptance are, is a very powerful outcome. Advocacy on many levels has resulted in continued legislative support for early childhood and special education, even during times of significant economic hardship. A commitment to advocacy goes hand-in-hand with a commitment to inclusion because the field is in the process of a major paradigm shift (Copple & Bredekamp, 2008/2009; Robinson & Stark, 2002). The transformation of systems and structures is occurring on many levels globally. While it is clear there is consistent, persistent progress, it is also clear that the process is not finished. There are ongoing needs for continuing to increase inclusive practices, ranging from full physical accessibility to understanding and acceptance of "invisible" disabilities affecting functioning.

Working with Systems

This book has discussed how being able to understand and negotiate the special and general education systems are crucial skills for families and professionals (Anderson, Chitwood, Hayden, & Takemoto, 2008). This must be a dynamic process, as systems are transformed, and often become more integrated. Advocacy is a crucial element to this process, especially if services that are needed are not currently available (LaRocco & Bruns, 2005).

Vicki and her husband John had no way of knowing what the future would bring when their son Max was diagnosed as having autism at age 2. They have served as passionate advocates for him from the time he started receiving birth-to-3 services. When he was in preschool they were instrumental in guiding the local education agency to develop a specialized program for children with autism, and later successfully advocated for the creation of an inclusive option within the community-based elementary school.

Creating Support Networks

Full inclusion is not something that one person ever does alone. It always requires a collective commitment. This implies systemic support for the transformation of programs. Collaboration is one of the areas identified in standards for early childhood personnel working in inclusive settings (Hyson, 2003). As teachers sustain their commitment to inclusive programs, it is important that they are working with a support network. The contexts of work settings may vary. In some settings, there are support networks built in to the structure of the program. In others those responsible for implementing inclusive methods may be more isolated. Support networks provide optimal conditions to effectively and professionally enhance inclusive services.

Reducing Isolation

When professionals create healthy support systems, they model best practices in teams that are inherently conducive to family involvement. Isolation is a well-documented phenomenon when families are getting used to having children with disabilities. This does not mean that every family will isolate themselves, but it is a possibility. Professionals can be isolated, as well. While privacy is certainly valuable, significant isolation can be a risk factor. Social support, in contrast, is recognized as a protective factor. As teachers create or connect with a support network, they may choose to plan and structure, identifying five people, for instance, who may form the support team. On the other hand, teachers may already have strong, supportive connections with others. If this is so, perhaps they just need to reaffirm these connections, and check with them to see if they are willing to be part of the informal support team. Given many possible configurations, the important point to remember is that teachers do not need to do this alone. In fact, working collaboratively with others is part of professionalism. Being explicit and conscious of available support networks will make it possible to use them effectively and explicitly when they are needed most.

Working with a Mentor

Some programs require new staff and emerging professionals to work with mentors. Whether or not this is a requirement for you, this book strongly recommends that you find someone who can be an effective mentor and build a strong working relationship of trust and support. In the field of early childhood special education, a mentor may or may not have extensive background in the field, because it is a rapidly changing area of expertise, and the degree to which fully inclusive practices are being implemented is unprecedented. A mentor does not need to have all the answers. In fact, in the rapidly changing field of early childhood inclusion, experienced professionals may have an easier time admitting that they are constantly learning new skills and gathering more information about various conditions as well as methods.

KaraLee is a seasoned professional with comprehensive certification in early childhood and special education. She has served as a mentor for numerous candidates in a teacher preparation program during their practicum experiences. A wonderful mentor, KaraLee is honest about her own need for ongoing professional development. Recently she has especially focused on children with characteristics associated with disorders on the autism spectrum, as well as children with sensory differences. Her honesty about ongoing professional development is part of what contributes to the excellence of her mentoring others.

The paradoxical wisdom of being able to acknowledge what one does not know appears to increase with longevity. Often, this confidence to know what one does not know is at the heart of how mentors may be valuable, creating a safe zone together for ongoing professional development and experiential education. A mentor may be resourceful and have valuable perspectives, while also providing sustaining support during potentially difficult times. Sometimes having someone who will listen without judging, and who will engage in fruitful reflection regarding options contributes to highly productive problem solving toward constructive solutions to unique, individual situations (Hanft, Rush, & Sheldon, 2004). While professional relationships vary in style, effective mentorship includes what Vygotsky (1978) referred to as "apprenticeship."

Ongoing teamwork is a vital element to effective inclusion.

The degree and type of support received naturally varies from person to person, depending on individual differences, but the valuable support is there, as needed, in the form of what Vygotsky called "scaffolding." This book has discussed scaffolding in relation to the role of adults working with young children. It is also relevant in other contexts. The shift from more to less support as the emerging professional develops, allows each new professional to become more autonomous, at his or her own pace.

BUILDING CONFIDENCE THROUGH CONSTRUCTIVE REFLECTION

Reasonable Expectations for Yourself

With a major paradigm shift, it is natural for professionals as well as family members to wonder if they will be able to effectively address the needs of young children with disabilities. This questioning may not occur with everyone, but if it does, it is helpful and important to know you are not alone. People may have many reasons for doubting their ability in this realm. One frequent reason, especially among those who may be very accomplished, is difficulty shifting from a mode of "perfection" as outcome. When children have disabilities, teachers should focus on their areas of strength as well as areas of need, but the overall goal of "perfection," by definition, is not realistic. Instead, when implementing inclusion teachers should aim to be accepting, which is not the same as acquiescing or lowering the standards. Teachers want the best possible performance for children and themselves. It means professionals must have realistic expectations of children and ourselves (Sandall et al., 2005; Stayton, Miller, & Dinnebeil, 2003).

Realistic Goals and Objectives for Ourselves

Setting realistic goals and objectives during the planning and placement process, within Individualized Education Programs (IEPs) and Individualized Family Service Plans (IFSPs), greatly increases the likelihood that children will be able to attain those goals and objectives (Turnbull, Turnbull, Shank, & Smith, 2004). Likewise, if teachers have realistic expectations for themselves and do not expect that they will be able to save the world or solve all the world's problems single-handedly, they are much more likely to be able to engage constructively in self-evaluation and determine what they are doing that is effective rather than being critical over what has not yet been accomplished.

RESOURCEFULNESS

Resourcefulness: The Importance of Organizing and Using Community Resources

It is necessary to be resourceful and skilled at accessing the most recent information. As changes occur in laws and practices, there is a need to adjust accordingly. The practical implications for working within a profession that is constantly changing include the need for ready access to community resources to ensure that perspectives on service provision are current. In early childhood, there is a range of available community resources, with some variation from state to state but with many common threads nationally. In early childhood special education, unlike programs for older children, many inclusive services may be provided within community-based early childhood programs. In addition, many school systems are beginning to offer their own inclusive early childhood programs. Technically, services do not have to be provided within the school to fulfill the legal requirements of the Individuals with Disabilities Education Improvement Act (IDEIA) (2004). The school is required, however, to make sure programs are provided. A local education agency may provide mandated services based on the IDEIA, within the context of a community nursery school if this is acceptable to the planning and placement team. With the recent options specified in IDEIA, there is a seamless integration of birth-to-3 services, and families may choose to continue services within the same administrative structure that they used for birth-to-3 services (Walsh, 2005). It is not unusual, however, for a transition to occur between birth-to-3 services and those provided for 3- to 5-year-olds (Rous & Hallan, 2007).

Different Types of Agencies

This book has mentioned the local education agency (LEA), community-based inclusive preschool programs, and programs provided by national organizations serving individuals with disabilities of all ages. There are also many other types of agencies, some providing specialized related services such as occupational, physical, and speech and language therapy. Some agencies specialize in advocacy efforts. Some agencies are primarily operated through federal, state, or local governments. These may include "clearinghouses," such as the National Dissemination Center for Children and Youth with Disabilities (NICHCY; http://www.nichcy.org). Some are not-for-profit, private, independent organizations, and some are for-profit businesses.

Web-Based Resources

Most established agencies and organizations in the United States currently have web-based resources, which greatly enhance the availability of information to families and professionals. One of the advantages of using web-based resources is that the information is usually current, with frequent updates. Web-based resources are cost-effective, once an agency or individual is set up to use them. While there is an initial financial investment in this medium, the long-term benefits appear unlimited. Web-based resources are easily accessible and make it possible to be rich in resources and "green" at the same time, using less paper to disseminate information. Another major benefit of using Internet-based resources is that they are time-efficient. Access to technology and knowledge of navigating Internet-based resources yields an enormous amount of information very quickly. Finally, because this is based in the World Wide Web, there is the potential for international networking of resources, without the boundaries experienced on ground (Catlett, 2009).

Cautions Regarding Use of Internet in Early Childhood Special Education

Teachers should be cautious when using the Internet for resources because it might increase the "digital divide" between those who do and do not have ready access to computers. When families do not have access to technology and/or computer literacy, it is important that resources are not provided exclusively using technology. To address this, many organizations have posted brochures and information online in a form that can be easily printed and shared with families. Often, such resources are available in more than one language. When cultural and linguistic diversity are included, it is very important that a person who is fluent in the second language and understands the nuances of linguistic meaning be involved with checking translations of materials. Some resources, such as the Center for Culturally and Linguistically Appropriate Services (CLAS) at the University of Illinois in Urbana–Champagne address these issues extensively (http://CLAS@uiuc.edu/).

Quality of Resources

A second major caution in using Internet resources involves the distinction between types of resources. These could be conceptualized as credible versus less credible, but that presumes a judgment against firsthand accounts of situations, which is not the intent. It is important that families and professionals who are using the Internet for ready access to resources clearly understand the criteria used to identify the many credible resources that have carefully substantiated information. Changes based on legislation and/or research are integrated into websites which are being managed by organizations that actively monitor the content of the information and update it routinely, as needed. This book has referred to the National Dissemination Center for Children with Disabilities, NICHCY, which is a federally supported information clearinghouse, providing web- and paper-based resources. The Division of Early Childhood, Council for Exceptional Children, has a website with useful links to other resources.

Opportunities for Informal Networking Through the Internet

Many opportunities exist in the context of Internet-based communication for families and professionals to network informally with others worldwide. Teachers should recognize the potential value of such communication and support, but they also should distinguish it from resources that include a system of accountability and responsibility for accuracy of information, as distinct from opinion. This distinction may be particularly important regarding subjects that are highly controversial, about which even experts often disagree. It is also true when results of important research are pending, and the Internet provides a vast opportunity for speculation. Thus, while it is evident that Internet resources are exceptionally valuable in keeping up with a rapidly changing field, there are still factors to carefully consider.

Organizing Resources: Sharing with Families

Having a clear sense of resources that are available is useful in a multitude of ways. When teachers create an organized, accessible system to coordinate resources, it is much easier for families to use them on a regular basis. Families often create their own resource files as a way to support their ongoing daily coping. Having up-to-date access to information, including supportive Internet sites, often greatly increases team effectiveness (Catlett, 2009; McWilliam, 2005). When there is a mutual commitment to access and share resources, everyone benefits. Some websites and organizations are dedicated to providing a clearinghouse or collection of relevant materials and resources on topics, either varied or highly focused. Some examples of specific websites that coordinate resources for families can be found at the end of the chapter. Given the quantity of resources, coping strategies to organize and access resources as needed become very important.

SUGGESTED ACTIVITIES

Create your own resource file, with informational materials such as brochures and DVDs from organizations. Put these in a container that is functional, accessible, and durable, so you can use it as needed, with materials readily available.

Develop a listing of websites and organizations you find especially relevant. Writing annotations and/or printing out helpful information may assist you in being confident about resources that are available.

Professional Organizations

This book has discussed many professional organizations. There are international, national, regional, and local organizations to support professional activity. It is time to review some of the major organizations, and to consider how your involvement with them may provide support for your ongoing professional development. The three major organizations for early childhood education include the National Association for the Education of Young Children (NAEYC), the Council for Exceptional Children, Division of Early Childhood (CEC/DEC), and the National Head Start Association (NHSA). These organizations were discussed in Chapter 2; now you may consider how to play a more active role professionally. All of these organizations address the entire continuum of developmental diversity. Of the three, DEC has historically been more focused on exceptional development but during the past decade, there has been a progressively increasing focus on developmentally appropriate practices. It is not required that all professionals be members of these organizations, but it is helpful to know what resources they offer, and to understand that as not-for-profit organizations, they may provide outstanding resources for families and professionals in early childhood inclusive education. Membership in each of these organizations includes a subscription to excellent journals, as well as discounted registration fees to professional development opportunities, such as conferences. Any membership fee generally pays for itself many times over when members use the valuable resources provided with membership. It is also possible to access journals and other publications through libraries and online.

Leadership Opportunities

You may decide to get involved by playing a leadership role within an organization. There are many ways you can make a difference for families and professionals in your community. You may also become involved with online discussion groups and/or choose to subscribe to useful distribution lists, such as *Natural Resources* (Catlett, 2009). Recognizing your own options and choices about involvement is a good place to start. Once the momentum has picked up, this is an ongoing process.

THE IMPORTANCE OF AUTHENTIC MOTIVATION

As this book concludes, it is important to note that your own motivation and inspiration are essential. It is not enough to just implement adaptations in a mechanical way. A central aspect of effective intervention is attaining and sustaining rapport with children. By focusing on the strengths and interests of each child, you will be positioned well to make positive connections. Identifying rather than denying areas of need ensures that you will be able to adjust curriculum and interactions, as appropriate. The effectiveness of your own intervention, as guided by structured reflection with consideration of options, greatly increases the likelihood of success. We strongly believe the process of developing inclusive practices can be very positive.

While at times there may certainly be challenges, we believe a willingness to advocate for quality programs along with a willingness to work constructively with teams greatly increases the likelihood that you will find the process both rewarding and meaningful.

Reflection and Experiential Learning

You have been participating in an ongoing process of reflection throughout this book. This book has discussed some of the history of reflective practice (Dewey, 1910/1933) and certain benefits and procedures used in effective reflection. Reflection is significant in the commitment to ongoing professional development. Continued growth and development is not just a cumulative process of information and skill acquisition. It is transformative. It involves a commitment to open-mindedness, responsibility, and wholeheartedness that is enhanced by reflective practice. It involves authenticity, and the capacity to reposition (Larivee, 2008). Reflective practice is fully congruent with the concept of educator as change agent and as being willing to consider and construct options that do not currently exist, together with other team members (Goodland, J., Mantle-Bromley & Goodlad, S., 2004; Miller et al., 2003). Given the dramatic social changes involved with the process of becoming fully inclusive, reflective practice provides a process and structure for guiding practitioners as they develop ways of interacting with diverse groups of children, as well as individuals (Goodlad, J., Mantle-Bromley, & Goodland S., 2004; Reagan, Case, & Brubacker, 2000). The use of reflective practice may be considered an essential element in restructuring education and preparing teachers for increasing diversity (Yost, Forlenza-Bailey, & Shaw, 1999).

Reflection on Your Own Experiential Learning

This entire book is based on the belief that experiential learning is essential as well as powerful. It is not, however, enough to simply do something in order to derive meaning and learn from the experience (Jalongo & Isenberg, 2008; Larivee, 2006). The process of synthesizing, integrating, and making meaning, creates the opportunity for you to internalize concepts in dynamic ways, so you will be able to apply them as needed. Because reflection is central to this process (Buysse & Wesley, 2006) this book uses a model of guided reflection. Now, as you are finishing, it is important for each of you to consider all you have learned throughout this journey. You have identified your own personal and professional areas of strength, as well as those areas in which you needed to work. In response to this scan or inventory of your own professional development, you identified goals and objectives. You accessed resources to help you address these areas. You monitored your own progress, and adapted your approaches, as needed (Hemmeter, 2000). You reflected on your own experiences, and considered how you might have adjusted what you did to be more effective. You monitored the children's responses to your initiations, and your responses to their initiations.

INVENTORY OF YOUR OWN PROGRESS

Please take some time to consider how your ability to interact constructively with children, families, and colleagues has increased while you have been engaged in the process presented in this book. As you review your journal, are there key elements that emerge? Significant patterns? Are there specific areas you initially identified as less strong for you, which have changed over time? If so, what specific growth have you noticed? You may find it helpful to reconsider some of the original questions in your personal inventory. Are you responsive to children's initiative? Are you available to children? Are you sensitive to family concerns and culture? These are samples from the original guide to reflection presented in Chapter 1.

It is likely that the process in which you have engaged while using this book in conjunction with active experience with young children will continue to be valuable to you as you continue your professional work. There is a well-developed and well-documented pedagogy about experiential and reflective approaches to education. There is an excellent alignment between experiential learning and the need for ongoing professional development to address the individual characteristics of young children with challenges within inclusive settings. While most of the book has been formative in approach, we are now bringing closure in a more summative way, encouraging you to synthesize and conceptualize the scope of what you have learned with the combination of this text and your own experience.

Meaningful Integration

The meaning one derives from one's own experiences will vary depending on your background, prior knowledge, and scope of work. Whatever those conditions, it is possible for you to have grown and transformed your own understanding. It is often said individuals must start with themselves in order to truly change the approaches to working with others. This is surely true when there are multicultural differences (Wah, 2004), and also when there are developmental challenges. Being willing to continue to reflect on qualitative as well as quantitative aspects is integral to continued professional development. As you monitor your own progress, it may be helpful to organize what you are learning in terms of knowledge, skills, and dispositions to align with some of the criteria used to evaluate programs. The more you know about how you learn and the kinds of experiences that are most conducive to your own growth and understanding, the more you can contribute to the quality of your experiences. You may be able to make some choices about the structure of your experiences, as well as the intensity and pacing. You may be able to sustain a relatively transparent process of reflection, which will benefit all involved.

ONGOING CHANGES IN THE FIELD OF EARLY CHILDHOOD SPECIAL EDUCATION

If the integration of all you have learned while actively participating in an experiential journey during the process of reading this book leaves you with a sense that you still don't have all the answers, you are doing very well. This book will not supply its readers with all the answers. In fact, it is based on the premise that all can benefit from knowing what we don't know, especially if we know how to find needed resources and answers to questions. The field of inclusive early childhood education has changed dramatically over several decades. As inclusion becomes more prevalent, the myriad configurations of program structures and personnel require that professionals be prepared in generic ways that allow them to implement high-quality inclusive practice, depending on program models as well as individual needs (Chandler & Loncola, 2008; DEC/NAEYC, 2009). For all these reasons, this text is process-based and offers support and guidance in a dynamic way during your experiential learning.

How You Can Be Involved to Make a Difference

Identifying your need for ongoing professional development is positive. You can continue to be actively involved in ways that make a difference. By identifying, for instance, what needs to be done in specific situations, you can work with other professionals and

There is intrinsic value in collaborative, evidence-based practices.

families to solve problems. You can identify, access, and share resources. Your identified needs for ongoing professional development may be determined by the conditions manifested by children with whom you are currently working. Even if a professional has had previous experience with children who have autism, it is helpful to continue professional development as research provides more information about evidence-based practices (Buysse & Wesley, 2006; Winton, McCollum, & Catlett, 2008). You can advocate for quality services if they do not currently exist in a given community (DEC/NAEYC, 2009; Robinson & Stark, 2002). You can increase awareness and acceptance of developmental difference, as inclusive programs continue to grow. You can make strong positive connections with children and families, forming alliances as you advocate together. Children and families are wonderful ambassadors for the ongoing development of high-quality programs. We do what we do for and with them.

Questions for Reflection:

1. As you consider the many factors related to high quality inclusion, how have you made these a priority in the work that you do? These could include allocating time, using resources and adjusting curriculum.
2. Identify three colleagues or sources of support you know you could rely on if needed.
3. While reflecting on your own professional growth, are there areas you continue to identify as needing extra focus? If so, how will you get the support you need and deserve?

Summary

It is our hope that reading and using this book as a working model has been an integrative experience for you, one that will continue to support you as a lifelong learner. Your resourcefulness, willingness, and ability to reflect, as well as network with other professionals in the field will serve you well as you continue to work with young children and families within inclusive settings. During the past 25 years, there has been an enormous paradigm shift and transformation about beliefs and practices regarding young children with exceptionalities.

We have shifted from a discussion about whether or not to "mainstream" individual children, to the presumption of inclusion of all children. You are part of the process as you learn how to implement effective inclusive practices. Your participation in the reflection and experiential learning accompanied by this book has increased your ability to solve problems and view yourself as a professional with the ability to address diverse needs within inclusive classrooms. As you finish one cycle, you commence another. In your new beginnings, we hope you believe in your own capabilities regarding young children with disabilities and their families, during this exciting and changing time.

Websites

The Center for Culturally and Linguistically Appropriate Services (CLAS) at the University of Illinois in Urbana–Champagne
http://CLAS.uiuc.edu/

Exceptional Parent
http://www.exceptionalparent.org

The National Dissemination Center for Children with Disabilities
http://www.nichcy.org

The National Early Childhood Technical Assistance Center
http://NECTAC.org/

The National Head Start Association
http://www.NHSA.org/

The Pacer Center in Minneapolis, Minnesota
http://www.pacercenter.org

The Waisman Center at the University of Wisconsin
http://www.waisman.wisc.edu/

References

Anderson, W., Chitwood, S., Hayden, D., & Takemoto, C. (2008). *Negotiating the special education maze* (4th ed.). Bethesda, MD: Woodbine House.

Buysse, V., & Wesley, P. (Eds.). (2006). *Evidence-based practice in the early childhood field.* Washington, DC: Zero to Three.

Caruso, J., & Fawcett, T. (1999). *Supervision in early childhood: A developmental perspective.* New York: Teacher's College Press.

Catlett, C. (2009). Natural resources. Message posted to online resources/listserv, archived at gtto://www.fpg.unc.edu/~scpp/nat_allies/na_archive.cfm

Catlett, C. (2009). Resources within reason. *Young Exceptional Children, 12*(4), 40–41.

Chandler, L., & Loncola, J. (2008). Rationale for a blended education. In M. LaRocque & S. Darling (Eds.), *Blended curriculum in the inclusive K–3 classroom* (pp. 1–31). Boston: Allyn & Bacon/Pearson Education.

Copple, C., & Bredekamp, S. (2008). Getting clear about developmentally appropriate practice. *Young Children, 63*(1), 54–55.

Copple, C., & Bredekamp, S. (2009). *Developmentally appropriate practices* (3rd ed.). Washington, DC: National Association for the Education of Young Children.

DEC & NAEYC. (2009). *Early childhood inclusion: A joint position statement of the Division for Early Childhood (DEC) and the National Association for the Education of Young Children (NAEYC).* Chapel Hill, NC: The University of North Carolina, FPG Child Development Institute.

Derman-Sparks, L. (1989). *Anti-bias curriculum: Tools for empowering young children.* Washington, DC: The National Association for the Education of Young Children.

Derman-Sparks, L. & Edwards Olsen, J. (2010). *Anti-bias Education.* Washington, DC: The National Association for the Education of Young Children.

Dewey, J. (1919/1933). *How we think: A restatement of the relation of reflective thinking to the educative process.* Lexington, MA: Heath.

Eggbeer, L., Mann, T., & Seibel, N. (2007). Reflective supervision: Past, present, and future. *Zero to Three, 28*(2), 5–9.

Goodlad, J. I., Mantle-Bromley, C., & Goodlad, S. J. (2004). *Education for everyone.* San Francisco: Jossey-Bass/John Wiley.

Guralnick, M. (Ed.). (2001). *Preschool inclusion.* Baltimore: Paul H. Brookes.

Hanft, B. E., Rush, D. D., & Shelden, M. (2004). *Coaching families and colleagues in early childhood.* Baltimore: Paul H. Brookes.

Hemmeter, M. L. (2000). Self-Assessment: Child-focused interventions. In S. Sandall, M. McLean, & B. Smith (Eds.), *DEC recommended practices* (pp. 121–124). Longmont, CO: Sopris West.

Hyson, M. (Ed.). (2003). *Preparing early childhood professionals: NAEYC's Standards for Programs.* Washington, DC: National Association for the Education of Young Children.

Jalongo, M. R., & Isenberg, J. P. (2008). *Exploring your role: An introduction to early childhood education* (3rd ed.). Upper Saddle River, NJ: Merrill/Pearson Education.

Larrivee, B. (2008). *Authentic classroom management.* Boston: Pearson Education.

LaRocco, D., & Bruns, D. (2005). Advocacy. *Young exceptional children 8*(4) 11–18.

LaRocque, M., & Darling, S. (Eds.). (2008). *Blended curriculum in the inclusive K–3 classroom.* Boston: Allyn & Bacon/Pearson Education.

McWilliam, R. (2005). Assessing the resource needs of families in the context of early intervention. In M. Guralnick (Ed.), *The developmental systems approach to early intervention* (pp. 215–234). Baltimore: Paul H. Brookes.

McWilliam, R., & Casey, A. (2008). *Engagement of every child in the preschool classroom.* Baltimore: Paul H. Brookes.

Miller, P., Ostrosky, M., Laumann, B., Thorpe, E., Sanchez, S., & Fader-Dunne, L. (2003). Quality field experiences underlying performance mastery. In V. Stayton, P. Miller, & L. Dinnebeil (Eds.), *Personnel preparation in early childhood special education; Implementing the DEC recommended practice* (pp. 113–138). Longmont, CO: Sopris West.

Pianta, R., La Paro, K., & Hamre, B. (2007). *Classroom assessment scoring system*. Baltimore: Paul H. Brookes.

Reagan, T. G., Case, C. W., & Brubacker, J. W. (2000). *Becoming a reflective educator: How to build a culture of inquiry in the schools*. Thousand Oaks, CA: Corwin Press.

Robinson, A., & Stark, D. (2002). *Advocates in action*. Washington, DC: National Association for the Education of Young Children.

Rous, B., & Hallam, R. (2007). *Tools for transition in early childhood*. Baltimore: Paul H. Brookes.

Sandall, S., Hemmeter, M. L., Smith, B., & McLean, M. (2005). *Recommended practices: A comprehensive guide*. Longmont, CO: Sopris West.

Shonkoff, J., & Phillips, D. (2001). *From neurons to neighborhoods*. Washington, DC: National Academy Press.

Stayton, V., Miller, P., & Dinnebeil, L. (2003). *Personnel preparation in early childhood special education: Implementing the DEC recommended practices*. Longmont, CO: Sopris West.

Trawick-Smith, J. (2008). *Child development: A multicultural perspective*. Upper Saddle River, NJ: Merrill/Pearson Education.

Turnbull, R., Turnbull, A., Shank, M., & Smith, S. (2004). *Exceptional lives* (4th ed.). Upper Saddle River, NJ: Merrill, Prentice Hall.

Turnbull, R., Turnbull, A., & Wehmeyer, M. (2007). *Exceptional lives* (5th ed.). Upper Saddle River, NJ: Merrill/Pearson Education.

Vygotsky, L. (1978). *Mind in society: The development of higher psychological processes*. Cambridge, MA: Harvard University Press.

Wah, L. M. (2004). *The art of mindful facilitation*. Oakland, CA: Stir Fry Seminars and Consulting Useful Resources.

Walsh, S., & Taylor, R. (2006). *Understanding IDEA: What it means for preschool children with disabilities and their families*. Reston, VA: Division of Early Childhood, Council for Exceptional Children.

Winton, P., McCollum, J. A., & Catlett, C. (Eds.). (2008). *Practical approaches to early childhood professional development*. Washington, DC: Zero to Three.

Yost, D. S., Forlenza-Bailey, A., & Shaw, S. F. (1999). The teachers who embrace diversity: The role of reflection, discourse, and field experience in education. *The Professional Educator, 21*(2), 14.

NAME INDEX

SUBJECT INDEX